W9-BFW-198

THE COMPASSIONATE-MIND GUIDE TO

RECOVERING FROM TRAUMA AND PTSD

using compassion-focused therapy to overcome flashbacks, shame, guilt, and fear

DEBORAH LEE, DCLINPSY
SOPHIE JAMES

New Harbinger Publications, Inc.

Publisher's Note

This publication is designed to provide accurate and authoritative information in regard to the subject matter covered. It is sold with the understanding that the publisher is not engaged in rendering psychological, financial, legal, or other professional services. If expert assistance or counseling is needed, the services of a competent professional should be sought.

Copyright © 2011 by Deborah Lee
New Harbinger Publications, Inc.
5674 Shattuck Avenue
Oakland, CA 94609
www.newharbinger.com

Cover design by Amy Shoup; Acquired by Tesilya Hanauer

All Rights Reserved

Distributed in Canada by Raincoast Books

Library of Congress Cataloging-in-Publication Data

Lee, Deborah A., 1955-
   The compassionate-mind guide to recovering from trauma and PTSD : using compassion-focused therapy to overcome flashbacks, shame, guilt, and fear / Deborah A. Lee and Sophie James.
      p. cm. -- (The New Harbinger compassion-focused therapy series)
   Includes bibliographical references.
   ISBN 978-1-57224-975-2 (alk. paper)
   1. Post-traumatic stress disorder--Treatment. 2. Emotion-focused therapy. 3. Compassion. I. James, Sophie. II. Title.
   RC552.P67L393 2013
   616.85'210651--dc23

                              2012029440

Printed in the United States of America

19   18   17

10   9   8   7   6   5   4

PART I
Understanding Your Reactions to Trauma

PART II
Developing Your Compassionate Mind Skills

PART III
Using Your Compassionate Mind to Soothe Your Traumatized Mind

Acknowledgments

It is, quite frankly, a privilege to thank many people for their inspiration, support, and contribution to this book. But I want to start with my patients because without them I would not have been able to develop these ideas and others would not have benefited from them. So I offer a huge thank-you to you all for your courageous commitment to your recovery and for working with me and offering me insights into your struggles. Over my twenty years of working in trauma as a clinical psychologist, you have helped me develop my clinical ideas about how to use compassion-focused therapy to help people accept and move on from their traumatic experiences. I sincerely hope you are all well and using your compassionate minds!

Some of you have given up extra time to contribute to research projects that look at the effectiveness of using compassion with traumatized people, and I am most grateful to you for taking part. Being able to demonstrate that this approach actually makes a difference to how people feel helps me to continue to develop my ideas.

Undoubtedly my clinical and professional career would have developed in a different way had I not had the pleasure of working with Professor Paul Gilbert, Series Editor, over the last twelve years and I certainly would not have had the opportunity to write this book. So I am indebted to Paul for his inspiration, encouragement, and abundant generosity on both a professional and a personal level, and for introducing me to compassion-focused therapy and offering me the opportunity to contribute to its development. My clinical work has been immeasurably enhanced by his theoretical ideas and clinical practice, and I am extremely grateful for that.

I have also known my colleagues in the Compassionate Mind Foundation for many years, and they too have contributed to many fun and inspiring times as I have developed my clinical practice of compassion-focused therapy. Warm thanks to you all.

I have had many professional colleagues over the years who also work in the field of trauma and they have encouraged me to develop these ideas. I am most grateful to Carmen Chan, who has diligently helped me develop the compassion-focused group that we run in our service and on which this book is based, and to Laura Bowyer for her contribution to some of the exercises.

On a personal note, I want to thank and offer my love to my family for allowing me the space and time to complete this book. My husband, Andrew, and my children, Iona and Dulcie, have graciously put up with 5:00 a.m. writing fests and hijacked weekends and holidays to allow me to complete this project. May love and compassion always fill your lives.

Finally I want to thank Sophie, my sister-in-law, who agreed to embark on this project with me, keep me on task, help me translate my ideas into lay language, and correct my appalling grammar. You deserve a big thank-you, as I am sure you had no idea what you were getting yourself into when you said yes.

—Deborah

Thank you, Deborah, for inviting me to help you with this project. It has been a great opportunity for me and I have relished and enjoyed both the writing and our working together. Thanks also to Paul Gilbert for his helpful comments. Finally to Nick, Mum, and Gay, I want to offer love and thanks to you all; I couldn't have finished this book without your help, love, and support.

—Sophie

And to everyone who reads it, we hope you find the book helpful and we dedicate it to you.

May your compassion always be with you.

Foreword

We have always understood that compassion is very important for our well-being. If we are stressed or upset, it is always better to have kind, helpful, and supportive people around rather than critical, rejecting, or uninterested folk. However, it is not only this common sense that tells us about the value of kindness and compassion; recent advances in scientific studies of compassion and kindness have greatly advanced our understanding of how compassionate qualities of the mind really do influence our brains, bodies, and social relationships, as well as affect our health and well-being. Compassion can be especially important when we are faced with major stresses and traumas. At these times we can find ourselves going numb, having flashbacks and intrusions, and experiencing a change in our normal sense of self and in our emotions.

Our susceptibility to these difficult reactions to traumatic events is due in part to the way the brain processes them. In this landmark book, Dr. Deborah Lee explores many of the common symptoms that are associated with trauma, such as flashbacks and intrusions and at times a changed sense of reality and feeling—sometimes linked to what's called "dissociation"—and how these symptoms are related to the way our brains may be working. Not uncommonly we can ruminate on the trauma and wonder why it happened to us. We can become sensitive to small triggers from sights, smells, or sounds, which can reactivate very unpleasant trauma memories and feelings. Because we struggle at times to fathom what's going on in our minds, or to deal with the intrusions or change of feelings, we can become self-critical, which compounds our sense of threat and difficulties in healing our traumatic experiences. Not only might we feel self-critical about how we are trying to cope with the trauma, we might feel critical and ashamed about the events surrounding the trauma. We can get locked into self-accusatory spirals, feeling that our sense of self has been changed by the trauma.

So why are we so susceptible to having these very disturbing experiences that can last long after the trauma has passed? Dr. Lee uses her wealth of knowledge and experience in working with traumatized people to guide our understanding and help us recognize that actually many of our emotions and the ways we react to frightening events are the result of a very long evolutionary history. We share with other animals capacities for certain emotions such as fear, anxiety, terror, anger, and frustration. Where we differ from other animals is that we have brains that are capable of extraordinary feats of memory and of analyzing ourselves and our environment. Whereas, for example, if a zebra or an antelope is chased by a lion, after it has made its escape it will usually settle down and go back to eating. It is unlikely to ruminate on the event, to wonder why it happened to it or if it could have avoided it by behaving better, or to ponder the implications for its future. The animal probably won't dwell on what could have happened if it had been caught and entertain horrible fantasies of being eaten. If it suffers from flashbacks of the lion attack, then again it's unlikely to ruminate about these, what they mean, and how it can stop them. Of course, we know that animals can be traumatized too and become very anxious or aggressive; people who give homes to these rescued animals will understand this reality very well. Equally, we know that a supportive, kind, and calming environment is what is needed for animals to heal from trauma. If this is true for animals, then it is certainly true for us as well.

So, we have brains that can think, imagine, anticipate, and give meaning to things and events, including our own emotions and experiences. The problem is that the way we think about and ruminate on the stresses in our lives can at times really "do our heads in." Understanding this reality, and being able to stand back from our emotions and what's going on in our minds, allows us to see that our vulnerability to these experiences is not our fault at all. After all, we didn't design our brains with their capacity for emotions like anxiety, fear, and anger. Nor did we design our capacity for complex thinking that can actually make our experience of traumatic events all the more intense and long-lasting. And nor did we choose our backgrounds, which can make us more susceptible to how we deal with trauma. This is a very important message in compassionate mind training and compassion-focused therapy because compassion begins by developing a deep understanding of just how tricky our brains are and a recognition that they are not that well put together! That is quite a strange message, isn't it? However, once we recognize how difficult our emotions can be, we can stand back from them and feel compassion for the difficulties we experience.

Given that our brains have been designed by evolution and shaped by the environments we grew up in and now live in—none of which we choose—what can we do to help ourselves when trying to recover from traumatic events? First, we can learn to pay attention to how our minds work and function, and become mindful and observant of the feelings that arise in us. Dr. Lee shows how we can learn to be very sensitive to the situations that can trigger certain trauma-related feelings, and in this way become more aware of how our minds and bodies are working. She then offers guidance on how to breathe and slow down and reframe some of our thoughts, and use different types of images to generate more compassionate feelings inside ourselves—all of which can have important effects on traumatic symptoms.

If we learn to approach these triggers of inner experiences compassionately, we are more likely to be able to understand and cope with them than if we are critical of and hard on ourselves. If we are unkind to ourselves, then our inner worlds will not be comfortable places to inhabit. Feeling ashamed and being self-critical, self-condemning, or even self-loathing can undermine our confidence, increase pressure on our threat systems, and make us feel worse. Research shows that the more compassionate we are toward ourselves, the happier we are and the more resilient we become when faced with difficult events in our lives. In addition, we are better able to reach out to others for help, seek and accept help when we need it, and feel more compassionate toward other people. One of the tragedies of trauma is that it can rob us of our own good feelings about people because the world can feel as if it's become a dangerous or malevolent place. This change in our feelings for our lives and the people in it can be a great loss.

Despite the value of compassion, it can sometimes be viewed as being a bit "soft" or "weak," "letting your guard down" and "not trying hard enough," or even "letting yourself off the hook." It is a major mistake to think of it in this way because, on the contrary, compassion requires us to learn how to be open to, and tolerate, our painful feelings; be more accepting of things as they arise in us; and yet at the same time develop wisdom about how we deal with these experiences. Compassion does not mean turning away from emotional difficulties or discomfort, or trying to get rid of them. It is *not* a soft option. Rather, compassion provides us with the courage, honesty, and commitment to learn to cope with the difficulties we face and guides us in our efforts to heal and alleviate them. It enables us to do things to and for ourselves that help us to flourish—not as a demand or a requirement but to help us live our lives more fully and contentedly.

In this book, Dr. Lee brings together her many years of experience as a clinical psychologist and therapist working with all levels of trauma in specialized trauma clinics. She has been at the forefront of developing compassion-focused therapy approaches with, and for, people who have experienced trauma and suffer from post-traumatic stress disorder (PTSD). In this book, she explains how compassion can be linked to our understanding of how our brains work, what soothes and calms them, and what builds our courage and confidence so that we can engage with some of the difficulties we face that are linked to trauma. We learn more about the nature of trauma and how it can affect us, why this is not our fault, and how to develop a supportive friendship with ourselves that helps us when times are difficult. Dr. Lee guides us to develop compassionate motivation, compassionate attention, compassionate feelings, compassionate thinking, and compassionate behavior. We learn about the potential power of developing compassionate imagery that focuses on creating a compassionate sense of ourselves and which draws on our own inner wisdom and benevolent qualities—qualities we are most likely to feel when we're feeling calm and/or are showing concern for others. Learning how to breathe to slow down and to engage with these compassionate qualities can be very helpful when anxiety, fear, or anger wash through us. Using different compassionate images, we discover that our compassion focus can be visual or aural (e.g., by imagining a compassionate voice is speaking to you when you need it) and can be especially useful in enabling us to get in touch with our internal compassionate feelings and desires at times of distress.

The approach that Dr. Lee takes is called a compassionate *mind* approach because when we engage compassion it can influence our attention, thoughts, feelings, and behaviors—in other words, how our minds operate *as a whole*. The compassionate mind approach outlined by Dr. Lee draws on many other well-developed approaches, including those of Eastern traditions such as Buddhism. In addition, compassionate mind approaches, especially those that form part of compassion-focused therapy, are rooted in a scientific understanding of how our minds work and evidence-based psychological therapies. Undoubtedly over the years our understanding of the science of the mind will change and improve, as will the therapies we employ. However, one thing that is unlikely to change is the fact that kindness, warmth, and understanding go a long way toward helping us when times are tough. In these pages you will find these qualities in abundance, so you too can learn to be understanding, supportive, and kind, but also engaging and courageous when working with your trauma experience.

Many people suffer silently and secretly with a whole range of difficulties that have arisen because of really unpleasant traumatic events that have happened to them. However, rather than seeking help some people feel ashamed or frightened of what happened to them, how they coped at the time, or how they are coping now. Some may feel that because the trauma happened some years ago they should be well over it by now and so for all these reasons they can keep their feelings and suffering hidden. Sadly, shame stops many of us from reaching out for help. We can take the first steps toward dealing with our difficulties in new ways by recognizing that if we have these experiences we are far from alone, that they are absolutely not our fault, and that we need to open our hearts to compassion. For those of us who are struggling, one of the benefits of this book might be to help us realize how and why some real difficulties can arise and, equally as important, to trust that there are many people who are working to help those of us who have suffered traumatic events. Certainly, over the last twenty years, there have been substantial advances in how people who have been traumatized can be treated. So do be open to the possibility of seeking professional help and if necessary to see your personal physician. I hope that for many people this book will be a source of inspiration and guidance. My compassionate wishes go with you on your journey.

—Professor Paul Gilbert, PhD, FBPsS, OBE

Preface

This book has been written to help those of you who are struggling to come to terms with a traumatic experience and are still suffering from painful flashbacks, memories, and emotions. Up to 90 percent of us will be exposed at some stage to a traumatic event during the course of our lives. Some of us will go on to have difficulties dealing with these experiences in a way that haunts us, disturbs our well-being, and makes it difficult for us to find a way to move on with our lives. This is a self-help book, but some of you may make the decision to seek help from a therapist to aid your recovery. You may consider you need professional help if your symptoms have been persisting for many months and are interfering with your quality of life or stopping you from doing the things that you enjoy. If you feel your friendships or family life is being affected by your symptoms, then again you may want to consider talking to a professional.

Some of the case studies in this book are severe. I mention them because some of you who are reading this book will also have suffered from serious traumas and I want you to know that you are not alone. The people mentioned in the case studies have benefited from these approaches but they did so with support from me in therapy. (Note: the case studies are an amalgamation of my clinical work and do not relate directly to any individual visitor to the clinic.) So if you find that the exercises in this book are too much for you or you feel overwhelmed, then you may want to consider working through them with a qualified and experienced therapist.

This book is based on my twenty years of experience working as a clinical psychologist with traumatized individuals. Hundreds of people who attend my trauma clinic each year are affected by serious traumatic events and are struggling to deal with the aftermath of these experiences. The hundreds of people I have seen and treated over the years come from all walks of life and include men, women, and children whose lives have been touched by all imaginable and sometimes unimaginable horrors. They all took the courageous and difficult step to walk through the doors of the clinic and seek help. Some of them have been diagnosed as suffering from PTSD, a condition that is being increasingly recognized by health-care professionals as a common aftereffect of trauma. (I will explain PTSD in more detail later on.) It is from the experience of working with these inspirational people and helping them overcome, at times, seemingly insurmountable hurdles and move on with their lives that I write this book.

I know that many of you will have difficulties dealing with the troublesome, painful, and traumatic events in your lives, and I hope that you will find many ideas in this book helpful if you are struggling with repeated images and unpleasant emotions associated with those events. This path is well trodden and others have successfully traveled down it, but there are likely to be low times and high times.

This book has been written to help you deal with your traumatic experiences with compassion, particularly if you blame yourself for what happened and are very self-critical. *You are not alone.* Many people with trauma believe that horrific events that happened to them were somehow their fault or that they deserved it, and they suffer greatly as a result. This is not the case.

The emotional shock of the trauma means that some of us may feel overwhelmed with distressing feelings of shame, anxiety, and fear. We may be frightened that other people will judge us, think poorly of us, or turn against us if they find out what happened to us. This sense that other people don't understand what it's like can leave us feeling lonely and isolated. These are often the experiences of the people who come to the trauma clinic. If you recognize yourself in these stories, you will find much in this book that could be useful to you.

I would, however, also strongly advise you that no self-help book is a substitute for professional help: one of the things this book might do is to help you become aware that seeing a therapist might be useful to you. If you find that you are struggling with some of the ideas here because they seem overwhelming, you may want to talk to your general practitioner (GP) and discuss the nature of your difficulties with him or her.

In reading this book, you will come to understand more about the symptoms of post-traumatic stress and perhaps recognize that you don't have to continue to suffer; there are treatments available to you, but you may need therapeutic assistance. Others of you may find that this book sets you on the way to becoming more compassionate with yourself and therefore helps build your capacity to work with your trauma memories.

Compassion-focused therapy rests on the principle that developing acceptance and compassion for ourselves and others is deeply healing, strengthening, and soothing, and can help us to face the many challenges of life. The essence of the concept of compassion is kindness with an awareness of the suffering of oneself and of other living things, coupled with the wish and effort to relieve that suffering.

In developing this therapy, it is important for us to recognize that sometimes being compassionate toward ourselves can be tricky and that it is not always easy to follow a compassionate path. This book provides a series of guided exercises for developing compassion and kindness, but it requires courage and discipline to use the exercises and apply them to our lives. For instance, we are looking to train ourselves to direct our attention to the things in life that stimulate positive emotions and to build on our strengths and talents so that we can experience compassion toward ourselves and others. This means developing lots of sometimes new but really important qualities such as compassionate motivation. *Compassionate motivation* means developing a genuine desire to be helpful, to seek healing and recovery, in contrast to trying to avoid it or just push it away. This helps us become more open to our own distress—and to that of others—and also teaches us how to tolerate and understand it in a way that will enable us to help ourselves and others. We will also learn not to judge ourselves, which means helping us to stop our *instinct* to self-attack. Practicing nonjudgment simply means being aware that we can sometimes automatically condemn, and that this automatic response encourages us to feel anger and contempt toward ourselves and others.

The most important skill we will be developing is the ability to use a compassionate, wise, and kind mind to understand our own trauma histories and the difficulties that have come with them. Bringing compassion, care, strength, warmth, and understanding to our distressing, hurtful, and shameful life experiences will help us to tolerate and accept our distress and suffering and also help us find a way to move on from these difficult experiences.

As we explore these concepts, we will learn that the difficulties connected with our traumatic life experiences are not our fault, but arise from how our brains are designed (by nature) to function and protect us from harm. We will explore what helps us to tolerate and work through our painful and traumatic memories. Finally, we will look at some practical ways to help us to move on with our lives so that we can live the life we want and deserve.

PART I

Understanding Your Reactions to Trauma

ABOUT PART I

This book is designed to provide a compassionate framework in which to think about our experiences of trauma and to help us to understand the range of traumatic things that may have happened in our lives. Some of the very serious traumatic events will be very obvious, but milder events can still be described as "traumatic." Chapter 1 will explore some of the more common and less common symptoms that arise following exposure to a trauma, as well as whether these might be termed post-traumatic stress disorder (PTSD). There may be things we do that actually keep these symptoms going, even though some of this behavior might not appear to be related to the trauma.

Chapter 2 will look at how the brain processes traumatic events and gives rise to the symptoms we have discussed in chapter 1. Because trauma memories and flashbacks can cause us such upset, I've devoted the whole of chapter 3 to understanding them. In chapter 4 we will explain how having a strong sense of shame affects us and can be linked with our self-criticism. This process can shape the way we think and how we act. This is also an aspect of our personalities that feeds into how we react and respond to traumatic events. Sometimes our shame and self-criticism keep us locked into the symptoms that arise following trauma. In chapter 5 we will look at why we need compassion in our lives and how our childhood experiences can affect our ability to be compassionate to ourselves when life gets tough for us.

Understanding these processes of how our minds work will be very helpful for the second half of the book, which builds on that knowledge and offers a range of exercises and practical tasks to help us on our road to recovery.

This book is designed for you to work through either on your own or with a therapist. It will require some time and commitment on your part; I recommend that you go one step at a time, only as far as you feel able each time. Try not to overwhelm yourself. Focus on developing your motivation for taking a compassionate approach to your distress and trauma processes. In this way you may ease your way to recovery and come to terms with your traumatic experience and the trauma you have lived with ever since.

1

Understanding your reactions to traumatic life events

IS THIS BOOK FOR YOU?

At some time during our lives, all of us will experience upsetting and distressing life events. Sadly, we all lose people we love through death, divorce, or the ending of relationships. Some of us may lose our jobs or have to deal with serious ill health in our loved ones or ourselves. In the world of psychology these are known as *major life events*.

Others of us will find our lives touched by traumatic life events. *Trauma* is the emotional shock we feel following an extremely stressful or traumatic event. Events such as traffic accidents and other accidents or acts of violence are known as *traumatic life events*. They are often unexpected, unpredictable, overwhelming, and highly life threatening (to us or other people), and they can be extremely difficult to come to terms with. One of the things that makes these traumatic events different from other, often anticipated, major life events (such as divorce or job loss) is the magnitude and unexpectedness of the emotional shock that we experience—feelings of intense fear, helplessness, and even horror. The intensity of our feelings can often overwhelm us and can seriously disrupt our lives, as these feelings can continue long after the trauma actually happened. Added to this, we are often plagued with thoughts that we did something to deserve the bad things that happened to us and that our suffering is our own fault and of our own doing, and these thoughts can lead to additional feelings of shame. Some examples of traumatic events are listed in the box below. As you will see, some traumas are very personal and are caused by the unpleasant and malevolent behavior of other people, while other traumas are caused by more impersonal events such as train crashes and work accidents.

Traffic accidents	Childhood sexual, physical, or emotional abuse
Train accidents, other transportation accidents, and work accidents	Attempted murder
	Torture
Natural disasters such as tsunamis and earthquakes	Kidnapping
Mass disasters such as terrorist attacks	Physical assault such as stabbing or mugging
Combat and the stress reactions arising from it	Sexual assaults
Diagnosis of life-threatening illness	Rape
	Domestic violence
	Bullying

This is by no means an exhaustive list, but it gives you an idea of the sorts of events that we are talking about in this book. These are the more severe types of trauma, of course, but the fact is that we can all experience smaller events that can really have an impact on us and we can struggle to come to terms with them. For example, going through an acrimonious divorce can be experienced as traumatic. Even major nightmares for some people leave a residue of trauma-like anxiety and flashbacks.

Therefore, learning some of the skills we will outline in this book can be helpful for many types of life-event difficulty that you may be struggling with. If what you have suffered is not on this list, this does not mean that you have not suffered a trauma, or that the event was not traumatic for you. What all these things have in common is that they are physically, mentally, and emotionally shocking and threaten our survival, well-being, sense of self, or hopes for the future. Those of us who have been seriously hurt by others or had our lives threatened may also have had our ability to trust or be intimate with people damaged. We may have experienced some of these things firsthand, or they may have happened to someone we know and love and we are having difficulty coping with the aftermath.

WHAT IS A COMPASSIONATE-MIND APPROACH?

This book is all about how we can develop and use self-compassion to explore the effects of traumatic experiences on our lives in terms of our thoughts, emotions, motives, and behaviors; it also explores some helpful ways to cope. Now, before you think this is soft or easy or that you don't deserve compassion (not as uncommon as you might think), the truth is that being compassionate can be a tough approach to adopt because you have to be willing to face the things that are upsetting and distressing you. Compassion helps to do this and may feel challenging, but not overwhelming.

The basic approach we will be taking here is from a therapy called compassion-focused therapy (CFT), which was developed by Professor Paul Gilbert. My traumatic stress clinic in Berkshire, UK, is at the forefront of using compassion-focused therapy for people who have been traumatized. Through this work I have received enormous insights and feedback, which has helped me to develop this approach as a self-help guide.

THE IMPACT OF TRAUMATIC EVENTS

We know traumatic events have the ability to affect us profoundly because they make us feel that our lives are unpredictable and that we are not in control of our own world; we may find it difficult to feel safe or to trust others, and we can also lose trust in ourselves and our judgments. This issue of safeness is something we will explore throughout this book because it is essential that we find a way to trust in human nature again and reclaim our lives after a trauma. Often we are deeply disturbed by traumatic events because they feel unfair, unjust, inhumane, and cruel. "Why me?" we ask. "Why now?" They can make us question our views and feelings about ourselves, the world that we live in, and the people who may have caused us such harm and emotional pain. We can even lose the comfort of our spiritual belief system in the face of what we perceive as cruelty. This is additional loss, as it results in a feeling of disconnection. It is not just in the face of great human atrocities that people can lose their faith; it can also be when we feel the world is cruel to us and the people we love.

Traumatic events have the ability to shatter our lives, leaving us with the seemingly enormous task of picking up the pieces, putting our lives back together, and finding a way to live and trust in life again. Most of the people we have worked with who have experienced trauma describe being overwhelmed by a toxic cocktail of intense emotions. Some of them also feel bad about themselves; indeed, it is common for people to describe themselves as feeling grief stricken, frightened, alone, ashamed, angry, and guilty.

Blaming yourself

These distressing emotions, described above, are often accompanied by thoughts of self-blame and self-loathing, and feeling responsible for causing the events. Traumatized people can talk as if they were responsible for the events and will say things like "It's all my fault," "I deserved this," or "I should have behaved differently." Self-blame is often at the heart of people's distress. Some of you may know what it's like to blame yourself for what has happened to you; there are countless reasons many people blame themselves for their traumas. Sometimes it's because they desperately want to hang on to a view that they did have, or could have had, control; sometimes it's because they want to make sense of and find meaning in the event amidst what is sometimes simply arbitrary chaos; sometimes they come from backgrounds where parents impressed on them that when bad things happened it was the child's own fault; and sometimes it's because it's easier to blame oneself than to deal with rage at the world or God. Our explanation for negative events happening to us can be crucial to how we deal with them, as we can see in Sally's and Tom's stories below:

• *Sally's story*

Sally had a spontaneous miscarriage at 14 weeks and thought that this was God's punishment for a teenage abortion. She was very depressed as a result of her loss and was fearful of God's further punishment. This is a situation where, because Sally felt bad about the earlier abortion, she assumed others (including God) would want to punish her.

So you can see how sometimes we jump to very harsh conclusions about what others (including God) might think of us and begin to blame ourselves for the sad things that happen in our lives.

• *Tom's story*

Tom was walking home from the train station after work one evening when his briefcase was stolen from him. Tom wanted to blame himself for being mugged. Although this was a swift attack, in which a youth grabbed Tom's briefcase out of his hand unexpectedly as he walked, it had a major impact on Tom's well-being. He could not stop thinking about how stupid he had been to let go of his briefcase. He reproached himself for not fighting off the youth. He just could not let it go in his mind and he would spend hours thinking about the event and what he should or could have done differently. He felt humiliated and angry and was embarrassed to tell people about the mugging in case they also thought he was a wimp. As I got to know Tom, it turned out that blaming and criticizing himself was a long-standing habit. Through therapy we discovered that during his childhood he had developed the habit of blaming himself for things that went wrong rather than looking for other explanations. Essentially he always looked to himself to explain why bad things happened.

I have found in my clinical practice and research that people who are very critical of themselves and blame themselves for things that happen in their lives not only seem to suffer from intensely painful feelings of shame, but also tend to struggle more with the aftereffects of their traumatic experience. Their self-criticism and self-blame keep them in a state of shame, which makes it difficult for them to cope with their trauma in a way that might help them to work through it. People who are very self-critical tend to want to avoid their shame-filled memories—for good reason—because these memories cause them so much pain and distress. Sadly, the unintended consequence of this avoidance is that the trauma is not dealt with and the shame is not resolved.

Are you naturally inclined to blame yourself?

There are some important reasons we *self-blame*, or blame ourselves. In compassion-focused therapy, we look at our natural tendency to blame ourselves when we are confronted by powerful "others" whom we fear or upon whom we may be dependent. For example, over a thousand years ago, ancient cultures would have been subjected to a range of life-threatening events such as famines, diseases, and war. It was widely believed at that time that various powerful gods controlled these occurrences and that the people needed the gods on their side to protect them and to avoid being punished. This allowed people to gain some feeling of control over the life-threatening events in their lives. In a number of cultures, this feeling of control was often achieved by making human sacrifices to a named god, such as the Egyptian sun god Ra, in the belief that this demonstrated loyalty, obedience, and love toward the higher being. They saw their gods as potential helpers and saviors, but also as potential punishers who could cause horrible things to happen.

We know from history that despite such sacrifices being made, life-threatening events continued to happen. How do you think the people explained why the diseases still came and why their children still died of malnutrition? Typically, *people blamed themselves* and thought that they had done something wrong to upset their gods. So the solution was that the following year they made even more sacrifices to appease the angry gods. We can therefore see a process of *self-monitoring* taking place in which we question ourselves (What did we do wrong?) and then blame ourselves (We didn't get our sacrifice right). This example demonstrates our innate and natural human tendency to self-blame when confronted by those we both fear and/or upon whom we are dependent.

Once we understand how this can occur, we can appreciate how easily it happens in child/parent relationships. Children need the love and attention of their parents but can also be frightened of them. Children can learn to monitor their own behavior so as not to anger or upset the parent and to blame themselves if their parents become angry—"Mommy is only upset because I made her cross. I shouldn't have acted that way. It is my fault that she is angry." You see, just like the people who worshipped the sun god, the fear of blaming those who are more powerful than us is bigger than the fear of blaming ourselves. And so over the years we learn to monitor ourselves and our behavior, and when things go wrong, particularly in relationships, we blame ourselves rather than another person because that is one way to try to retain some sort of control.

Just as the ancient cultures would not find it easy to blame their gods or even consider that such gods didn't exist, so it is with us. We can find it extremely difficult to find fault with our parents or to blame them for their behavior even if it has caused us harm, such was their position of power in our early lives. To think in such a way can make us feel that we are betraying those who we believe could have acted only in our best interests. It can therefore often be easier to blame ourselves rather than blame other people. We may not be consciously aware that we are doing this or be aware that there are people in our lives who have such power over us. We may say about the trauma we've experienced at the hands of others, "Well, even if I think I'm not to blame, when I start to blame other people it makes me feel very bad." And, of course, when we shift from blaming ourselves to blaming someone else, additional and very powerful emotions can be ignited, for example, rage, which in itself can feel terrifying. Even if we are able not to blame ourselves it does not necessarily mean we feel any better because we still have to face and cope with the fact that others have caused us such pain. This is why it may feel easier to continue to blame ourselves rather than someone else, even if we recognize the event was not our fault. We will explore this situation in more detail in chapter 4.

Another reason we blame ourselves is because we want to see the world as meaningful and to believe that *there must be a reason* for the bad things that happen in life. For instance, it is difficult for us to look at the recent tsunami in Japan—a tragic natural disaster—and comprehend that it was the result of a shift of tectonic plates on the seabed, which is a process that's been going on for millions of years. How can so much suffering have so little meaning? Difficult to accept, isn't it? Yet this act of nature is the only reason for this tragic natural disaster, and it's hard to cope with its meaninglessness. The way we engage compassionately with this level of suffering is very important in how we cope with it, both when it affects our lives and when it affects the lives of others.

HOW DO YOU COPE WITH TRAUMA?

You may have noticed that we often compare ourselves to others. It is a way in which we take a measure of our lives, and such comparisons don't stop if we become traumatized. Many of us are concerned that our trauma is not as bad when compared to other peoples' trauma, or it is not serious enough, or that others have suffered "greater, more serious" traumatic events, or that they are coping with things better. Of course, this can make us feel that we must be weak and flawed in character, which is not the case.

comparisons are not helpful to our recovery. There are very good and understandable reasons we are struggling in our lives, regardless of the extent of our traumatic experiences.

Our previous life experiences and how we coped before we were traumatized help us to understand how we are managing our current distress. There are many things that influence how we are able to work through and deal with traumatic experiences. While some of us may be able to come to terms with our traumatic experience in time without any help, others of us will struggle with our reactions and may even develop symptoms of what is called post-traumatic stress disorder (PTSD). These symptoms may present immediately or may develop over the weeks and months after the event and can then last for further months or even years.

If you are struggling to come to terms with the aftermath of a traumatic experience, it is not a sign of weakness or of an inability to cope with your life. It is just the way it is for you, and there may be a host of other important influences in your life that will help you to understand yourself and the difficulties that you are currently struggling with.

Our personal histories are a key part in understanding how we feel about, react to, and respond to what is happening in our lives. Our childhood experiences are one such important influence. For example, consider what it would be like if we had been bullied at school. The experience may have undermined our self-confidence, affected our ability to trust in other people, and left us with a legacy of feeling bad about ourselves or believing that we are not as good as other people. This is a hard and painful set of beliefs to carry around in our minds throughout our lives, and you can perhaps imagine how easy it then becomes to blame ourselves for other things that "go wrong" later in our lives.

We also know that having loving and supportive friendships can help us deal with difficult life events. There is lots of evidence from research to suggest that good-quality social support can buffer us from stress because friendships provide emotional support, encourage caregiving, and create a sense of being connected to others. A good social support network (in other words, close friends and family) can protect us from developing, or reduce the extent of, problems we incur from traumatic experiences. However, the very experience of trauma can itself lead us to feel disconnected from our loved ones and emotionally numb, and leave us with a sense that no one understands what we are going through. This makes us feel more alone and stops our talking to our friends and family, which is the very thing that could help us through our difficulties.

Other factors that are important to take into account when thinking about our reactions to traumatic events are things like our age and life stage when we were traumatized. For instance, children who experience traumatic events such as abuse tend to blame themselves. This is often because they are told by the adults involved that they are bad and deserve to be punished. The adults will often say things like "You made me do this to you, so you only have yourself to blame." If the child does not tell anybody about what is happening, and perhaps does not have a caring adult to reassure him or her that he or she was not to blame, then it is easy to see how such a child grows up into an adult who believes that the bad things that happened in his or her childhood were his or her own fault. Of course, adults who abuse children also create a web of secrets and lies and will emotionally manipulate and blackmail children into not telling other people about the abuse. Consequently, these children are often denied access to the adults who are most able to protect them and who could tell them that what is being done to them is wrong. Where the trauma is caused by a parent or other caregiver, this will be such a breach of the child's trust that it can badly affect how the child is able to develop relationships throughout his or her subsequent adult life.

DO YOU HAVE PTSD?

Sometimes after traumatic events people develop PTSD. You may have already heard about this condition and wondered whether you have it. PTSD is a recognized diagnosis, which, put simply, means that you are suffering from known symptoms from which it can be deduced that you are suffering from PTSD. (This is just the same as saying that there are known symptoms such as an aching body and a sore head from which you can be diagnosed as suffering from flu.) The symptoms associated with PTSD fall into three categories, which are outlined below:

- Reexperiencing the traumatic event again and again by having flashbacks. Flashbacks are reoccurring and intrusive images of the event that you find painful and upsetting. You can find images popping up in your mind when you don't want them to.

- Avoiding your traumatic memories. You may find it too upsetting to relive your experience over and over so you find ways to distract yourself or avoid people and places that remind you of the trauma. You may find yourself withdrawing from family and friends. Most likely you will also have developed lots of ways to avoid thinking or talking about the event to help you steer clear of the negative and painful feelings caused by it.

- You may experience hyperarousal or the feeling that you are "on guard" at all times. You may also suffer from poor concentration, irritability, and poor sleep. You may experience mood swings and high levels of anxiety because you are on guard and constantly looking out for danger.

Those of us working in the compassion-focused therapy field have observed that there are varying degrees and dimensions of responses to experiences of trauma. People experience some, most, or all of the symptoms, most or all of the time. On the other hand, difficulties may ebb and flow over time.

The purpose of this book is to help you if you are having difficulties. When reading this you may try to diagnose yourself, but rather than trying to figure out whether you have PTSD or not, it may be more helpful to focus on the difficulties you are having and think about ways this book can help you overcome them. If, as you read through this book, you are concerned that you are having serious difficulties arising from your trauma, then visit your GP, or seek out a counselor with experience with trauma.

Below are outlined the main symptoms or signs that can point to the existence of PTSD or trauma.

What are the main symptoms of PTSD?

Flashbacks

- Upsetting memories come into your mind when you don't want them (images, feelings, sensations, and sounds)

- Nightmares

- Feeling as if it is happening to you again

- Feeling physically and emotionally upset

Avoidance

- Trying not to think or talk about what happened

- Staying away from reminders

- Feeling as if you have no feelings

Being "on guard"

- Problems sleeping

- Problems concentrating

- Feeling angry and frightened

- Constantly looking out for danger

Other common emotional reactions to trauma

- Feeling depressed or anxious

- Mood swings or feeling irritable

- Withdrawing from family and friends

- Feeling disconnected or numb

- Feelings of guilt or self-blame

Now let's look at Alex's experience of trauma and what symptoms she developed in the aftermath of the event. This is an example of someone who suffered from a serious sexual attack and who attended the trauma clinic to be helped with recovering from her trauma.

• *Alex's story*

Alex was walking down the street one evening after having dinner with some friends when she was attacked by a couple of men at knifepoint. Earlier that evening a friend had tried to persuade Alex to take a taxi home but she had insisted that it would be fine to walk. As the men approached, Alex tried to run away but they caught up with her, sexually assaulted her, and then robbed her. During this attack, Alex was convinced that the men would kill her.

After the attack, Alex was troubled by feelings of shame and self-blame and did not want to tell anyone what had happened to her. She was very concerned that people would think she was stupid to have walked home alone at night and then blame her for the attack. Alex started to feel panicky and very jumpy whenever she was walking alone on the streets when it was dark. Memories of the attack haunted her several times a day, during which time she felt as if she were reliving the events. This made her feel scared and full of dread. She kept playing the attack over and over in her mind, in a desperate attempt to work out why this had happened to her. Over time Alex started to avoid going out at all because she felt safe only in her own house. Whenever something reminded her of the attack, like seeing a knife, she felt her heart pounding, as if the attack were happening all over again.

When Alex came to the clinic for help, it was apparent that she was suffering from feelings of shame and self-blame as well as the symptoms of PTSD. Her symptoms included:

- Seeing horrible, painful images in her mind of what happened; these left her feeling frightened and awful.

- Feeling that she was reliving the event time and again.

- Imagining that she could smell the aftershave and hear the voices of her attackers.

- Difficulty getting to sleep and staying asleep, and being plagued with distressing nightmares about being assaulted again.

- Overwhelming feelings of shame, disgust, and guilt. These were accompanied by self-blaming and self-critical thoughts such as "You brought this on yourself; you're stupid; you deserved this to happen."

- Fear that others would find out what had happened to her and think that she was dirty and disgusting.

- Problems feeling close to people or trusting others.

- Problems establishing intimate relationships with men.

The symptoms that Alex suffered in the aftermath of this distressing and life-threatening traumatic event are characteristic of someone who is not only suffering from PTSD but is also struggling with overwhelming feelings of shame and self-blame. You may have noticed that her feelings were self-focused rather than externally focused on her attackers; there was no sense of vengeance or rage. Try to consider why she was self-blaming.

When something traumatic happens in our lives we may experience some or all of the symptoms set out in the exercise earlier in this chapter. Not all of us who experience a trauma will have PTSD, though, or be diagnosed with PTSD. If you think you have these symptoms, please be reassured that you are not alone, and consider visiting your physician to discuss your current difficulties and ways of accessing more formal support if you feel you would benefit.

A special word on flashbacks and nightmares

Flashbacks and nightmares deserve a special mention in this chapter, not only because they are a key symptom of trauma but also because they can be frightening and make us feel as if we are losing our minds. Flashbacks are often referred to as the hallmark symptom of PTSD: most of us who have been traumatized will experience them. They are the most common and most distressing symptom for those of us who have lived with trauma, making us feel that we are reliving the traumatic event over and over. To help learn to deal with flashbacks it may be helpful to first explain what a flashback is and why it occurs so that we can understand what is happening in our minds. Understanding what flashbacks are may help us to begin to feel in control of them, and it is for this reason that I have devoted the whole of the next chapter to helping you understand your trauma memories and flashbacks.

OTHER WAYS TRAUMA CAN AFFECT YOU

Traumatic experiences affect our lives in many ways other than the symptoms described above. This can be particularly true if we have had to endure repeated experiences of being traumatized or harmed by other people over long periods of time. These sorts of experiences may have happened in our childhood (sexual, physical, or emotional abuse) or in adulthood (domestic violence, torture).

That said, keep in mind that a key to trauma can be the degree to which a sense of intense fear is activated in our minds. So, for example, parents may create feelings of intense fear in their child even if they are not physically abusive. Enduring intense, repeated, and prolonged periods of fear (without any physical or sexual harm) can also have a profound impact on the way we think about ourselves and other people. This might help some of you understand why you feel a certain way about yourself even though you don't have a big "skeleton in the closet."

Some ways trauma can leave a legacy on your life follow:

- You may have difficulty controlling your emotions and/or you may have an overwhelming strong emotional response to things.

- You may find yourself having suicidal thoughts.

- You may feel angry and irritable all the time.

- You may find yourself doing impulsive or reckless things such as driving too fast, gambling, shoplifting, or having casual, unprotected sex.

- You may find that you hurt yourself on purpose.

- You may feel cut off or numb from what is going on around you and maybe even have periods when you can't remember what you did. This is sometimes called dissociation.

- You may find yourself reliving your traumatic experience and being very preoccupied with trying to work out why this happened to you.

- You may feel helpless or struggle to make plans for your life.

- You may have overwhelming feelings of shame and guilt and may blame yourself for what happened to you.

- You may feel that you are different from everyone else and think that you are somehow damaged and are not able to live a normal life like other people.

- You may feel separated from friends and family, which can lead you to feel lonely an

- You may sometimes feel confused—perhaps because you don't hate the person w perhaps because you still have a relationship with him or her.

- Your relationships with friends and family may no longer feel the same, or you may   ..e any relationships any more.

- You may feel disillusioned and have given up your faith or religious beliefs.

- You may feel life has become meaningless and that it makes no sense, resulting in hopelessness and despair.

DISSOCIATING, DAYDREAMING, AND DISCONNECTING

Have you ever had the experience of driving home and finding yourself outside your house before suddenly realizing you can't really remember the journey because your mind was thinking about other things? This is a mild form of what we call dissociation, where our bodies are acting automatically and our minds are distracted. The ability of the mind to do this is well known: it is a type of daydreaming. Dissociation literally means "difficulties integrating information" from the different parts of the mind. Generally, dissociation is a defense mechanism that everyone uses every day. There are varying degrees of this state and it can certainly occur when the mind is traumatized. Strange as it may seem, our minds and brains will try to protect us from trauma and its effects as best they can.

Sometimes the way our brains do this is to try to switch off certain systems to avoid things becoming overwhelming. When this happens we can have all kinds of experiences of disconnection, such as going numb at certain points, zoning out, or feeling that our emotions aren't real or even that we aren't real. Some people who have been traumatized describe themselves as being on automatic pilot, as if they are on the outside looking in (an out-of-body experience) and things around them feel surreal.

Dissociation occurs when our minds can't integrate information and so they shut down instead. It is a crucial survival mechanism that protects us during a crisis and afterward. The first person to recognize and note how dissociation works was the French therapist Pierre Janet (1859–1947). Later, Sigmund Freud (1856–1939) argued that dissociation could be a way of defending against painful memories or emotions.

Although dissociation can be very troublesome and unhelpful, it is best thought of as a natural protection mechanism, not some sort of terrible illness or something wrong or bad about us. However, sometimes we do need to learn to override this protective system in order to start to integrate and heal some of our traumatic experiences.

If you experience an event as unreal or dreamlike, or things seem to go in slow motion, or it feels as though you are watching life unfold as if it were part of a film without your actually being there, then you may be experiencing dissociation. This can occur because things have become so scary or stressful that the mind automatically cuts out in order to protect us. It means we are still able to function without fully experiencing the emotional impact of an event. In this way, dissociation is an understandable thing to have happen. Flashbacks, nightmares, and highly stressful situations can trigger bouts of dissociation. You may also experience these feelings if you have been taking drugs.

When dissociation happens frequently or is very intense, it can be a distressing problem.

Signs of dissociation

- Periods of time when we feel spaced out

- Finding time passing without our noticing

- Having periods of time that feel unreal or dreamlike

- Talking to someone and not being able to remember what he or she just said

- Feeling as if we are leaving our bodies

- Feelings of numbness

- Finding ourselves in places and being uncertain how we got there

- Finding we have belongings that we can't remember buying

There are varying levels of dissociation. Everyday dissociation, which we all experience, encompasses daydreaming and spacing out. Traumatic dissociation can also include feeling numb, having deadened emotions, and experiencing the sensation that you are leaving your body. If these symptoms continue after the traumatic event, they can cause problems. For example, difficulties can arise in relationships because there may be times when you are just "not there." It can also be a safety risk if you are unaware of what you are doing or where you are going when you are driving or operating dangerous machinery. These feelings may be frightening in themselves, although this is not always the case. There is no reason to panic and they are not an indication that you are going mad.

Do you recognize yourself in this list of difficulties mentioned above? Very often if you are experiencing these sorts of fears and problems you will feel unable to overcome them, which is understandable given the enormity of what you have endured, but this book should be able to help.

SUMMARY

We began this chapter by highlighting the idea that coming to terms with painful and traumatic life events is a common difficulty. Indeed, it seems that many of us can have difficulties with certain traumatic events that involve flashbacks, intrusive images, and painful memories that are hard to deal with. When this situation becomes severe and when the emotional shock and trauma are also major, people are sometimes diagnosed with PTSD. Studies of how we process emotional shock and trauma have revealed some very important information about how our brains actually work and why we suffer from the symptoms that we do. We will look at this issue in more depth in chapter 2.

The traumatic events we experience range from being mild in nature to very serious, as does the emotional shock or trauma that results from them. We may experience some of the milder symptoms described earlier in this chapter, or we may experience most or all of the serious symptoms of PTSD. The thing we have in common is that we have all been affected in some way and we all want to improve our well-being and get on with our lives.

Those of us suffering as the result of a traumatic or life-threatening event will know what a powerful effect it can have on our quality of life. Very often the spectrum of negative emotions can make us feel miserable and as if our lives have been ruined. The most powerful and affecting experience of PTSD is the occurrence of flashbacks. These nightmarish relivings of the traumatic event are triggered without conscious control and can often feel entirely unmanageable. That said, please bear in mind that you don't have to have PTSD to suffer from flashbacks. Most people who are traumatized to a greater or lesser degree will suffer from flashbacks and intrusive memories.

Most of the people who attend the trauma clinic blame themselves for what happened to themselves. They talk to and about themselves in a critical and derogatory way and are desperately trying to cope with overwhelming feelings of shame and self-loathing.

Some of us may be struggling to trust people and form relationships, especially if we've been hurt by others. It naturally feels too risky. There are those of us who may have been struggling with these difficulties since childhood who think that this is just the way our lives are, and that we will never be able to have trusting and safe relationships.

For some, our efforts to deal with painful memories and emotions will lead us to dark places in our minds, and we may engage in all sorts of unhelpful behaviors aimed at ending our pain. We may cut ourselves, drink too much, take drugs, starve ourselves, push people away before they hurt us, or even have suicidal thoughts. It is important that we compassionately remind ourselves that the ways we have found to cope with our feelings, memories, and fears are our best efforts to deal with things. However, in the end, they may serve to become part of our problems, as they have all sorts of unintended consequences in our lives.

Whatever we are going through and however bad the extent of our suffering, it is important to appreciate the reality that our difficulties are natural and understandable reactions to what we have experienced. It's no wonder that we may struggle, especially if we have not been taught how to cope with either the trauma or the traumatic memories. We need to remind ourselves that dealing with traumatic events is not part of our everyday lives. The skills that equip us to cope with "normal life" are not always sufficient to help us manage trauma, which is why the memories of the event are so troublesome and distressing.

2

Understanding your responses to traumatic events: Your brain, your motives, and your emotions

One of the most powerful ways to help us understand how we are affected by trauma is to understand how our brains work, and particularly how our brains detect and respond to traumatic events and threats. In this chapter we explore how our brains have evolved and how they process information, particularly in relation to traumatic experiences. This will help us to understand that many of the difficulties that we have with our trauma, such as flashbacks, intrusive thoughts, nightmares, and even feelings of shame or self-criticism are natural responses—and are our brains' best efforts to deal with overwhelming threatening events. So let's look more closely at how the brain has evolved.

"OLD BRAIN" DESIRES VS. "NEW BRAIN" DILEMMAS

The process of evolution has developed our brains to enable us to survive and thrive as a species. In doing this we must also cope with the threats of everyday life. If we can understand how our minds and bodies have evolved over eons of time, we can begin to understand and appreciate our connection to nature, animals, other human beings, and our planet. This understanding will also reveal to us the extent to which the response mechanisms of our brains are actually automatic and can be very primitive (basic).

Our brains (like all other human brains on the planet) have evolved to function so that we can survive and reproduce. We are part of what is sometimes called the flow of life, and understanding how all living things in this flow of life are designed to work gives us very important insights into how we experience our own lives.

Our brains have been designed to function in a way that ensures a number of things. In common with all living beings, we must gain sufficient nutrients from the environment to sustain life and flourish; we must avoid threats and injuries as best we can; and we must form relationships with others for reproduction. This means that the brains of all species have evolved to perform these kinds of functions; different species do this in slightly different ways.

Human beings have basic desires, feelings, and needs (such as food, warmth, sex, and shelter), and these desires have successfully contributed to our survival as a species. Many of these basic motives are not new to humans; they are part of what we call the "old brain," and we have these in common with other animals. Like all animals, we seek food and warmth, and we like living in groups rather than in isolated caves, having sexual relationships, looking after children, and even forming friendships. Fulfilling these motives and goals has ensured our survival.

Our brains are made up of different systems and parts that have evolved at different times in our evolutionary history. This means that we share basic desires and motivations with other animals as well as have some abilities that are unique to human brains.

For instance, in common with all animals, we are capable of hunting for food, avoiding becoming food, finding shelter, mating, and fighting with each other.

About 120 million years ago, mammals evolved and with these changes came warm-bloodedness and a new set of motives for forming alliances/friendships and caring for offspring. These motives supplemented the basic ones, which govern our desires and needs such as food, warmth, sex, and shelter from predators. Importantly, therefore, with the advent of mammals came a new set of emotions. We evolved to become attached to, and to look after, our children and protect them from threats, feed them, and interact with them.

What's special about humans, however, is that about two million years ago there began a further evolution of the brain that gave rise to our ability to think, to be aware that we are thinking, to see ourselves in the mirror and to recognize who we are, to plan for a future, to mull over things, and to fantasize. This can be thought of as the "new brain," which works alongside the old brain. The new brain is particularly linked to an area of the brain called the frontal cortex (which we will discuss in more detail later in this chapter). The new brain has given rise to our sense of self, our identities, being able to think about the future as well as the past, and being aware of all kinds of possibilities and opportunities, but also threats. These capacities have resulted in art, science, and culture, which are part of the human experience.

The problem with this sophisticated thinking brain is that it has to work with motives and emotions that are governed by the older, more primitive, part of the brain. Our sophisticated thinking brain stirs up our emotions in all kinds of ways that other mammals don't suffer from. For example, zebras will all be on the alert for lions when they are awake and feeding but they probably don't stay awake at night thinking about where the lions are going to be in the morning. Neither do chimpanzees sit under a banana tree worrying that they have put on too much weight and risk heart disease! These are very human characteristics brought about by our new brain.

Our sophisticated-thinking human brain has given us a whole range of ways of *thinking* about threats in the world, but the problem is that how we *deal* with threats to our well-being is still quite basic and governed by the older part of our brain. There is a real conflict between our old brain desires and the dilemmas resulting from our new brain. We don't just act and experience like animals and reptiles do; we are able to think about our experiences and our desires, how they make us feel, and what they make us think about ourselves. We are also able to torture ourselves with our thoughts and feelings and memories.

So we have a brain that has taken us from living day-to-day in the jungles and savannas to living in modern cities. For the most part, our capacity to think in the way that we do—to be able to reflect, plan, and turn things over in our minds; to worry; and to have a sense of ourselves—can be useful to us, but not always. Sometimes thinking in this way is a real liability and we get trapped in a vicious circle. The more anxious we become about something, the more our thoughts focus on that anxiety and so we become ever more anxious.

There is probably no other species than humans that, if traumatized, will *think* about what that means to them, or have a negative view of themselves as a result of the trauma. Our human brains can cause us all sorts of problems and mental distress. For example, an animal that lives on a see-food-and-eat-it diet will do exactly that, see the food and eat it, whereas we humans will see the food, eat it, and then beat ourselves up for our lack of self-control! An animal will have a basic desire to reproduce and have sex, whereas we humans share the basic desire to have sex but afterward we might worry about the act or its timing in some way: "Did I really want to do that?," "Do I want to see that person again?," "Was that too soon in the relationship?," "Will he still love and respect me?" It is this mental chewing over that gives rise to our distress and is at the heart of the conflict between our old brain and our new brain. Our old brain gives us our basic desires but our new brain gives us the ability to think about and examine our actions and emotions.

We have a range of emotional drivers and desires that have been around for millions of years but are now linked to a sophisticated thinking brain. This can be a source of fantastic human creativity but can also cause us trouble. To understand more clearly how our emotions work we need to think about how our emotions have been designed and how they function.

UNDERSTANDING YOUR EMOTIONS

Our emotions indicate how we are doing in our lives. It is our emotional responses to things that help us to find meaning in our lives by directing us toward events, achievements, and relationships. For example, if we are passionate about soccer, then if our nation gets into the World Cup we feel excited, whereas if our team fails to qualify we might feel downhearted or maybe even annoyed. Our emotions reflect the things that we are interested in.

Our emotions also indicate to us our *state of need*, which means that our emotions motivate us to get our needs fulfilled. For instance, if we are depressed we may recognize that we want to be able to enjoy life more and therefore may accept an invitation to a party even when we are aware that we may not get any enjoyment or good feelings from attending. Our desire to take pleasure in the party indicates the "need" to try to alleviate our depression and create good feelings for ourself.

Whether we are succeeding or failing in the basic tasks of life can also be signaled to us by our emotions. Imagine that you want to buy a new house; during the process you will experience lots of different emotions. If you succeed you might feel happy, excited, and relieved. If you are unsuccessful you might feel unhappy or disappointed. So our emotions such as feeling good or feeling anxious are linked to, and guide us toward, achieving our goals, and they tell us whether we are succeeding or failing in our pursuits.

The point about these ideas is to understand that our emotions are key to indicating our needs and that once we understand how our emotions work and that they are linked to certain motives and outcomes, we are better placed to deal with them. We have several different types of emotion systems, and understanding this can be critical to understanding our trauma and how to deal with it.

YOUR EMOTIONAL REGULATION SYSTEMS

There are many different emotional systems within our brains that interact together to regulate our emotional world and ensure that our basic needs for survival (such as food, reproduction, and so on) are met. There are three particularly important emotional regulating systems that work with each other to help us to manage the ups and downs of life's challenges by helping us to calm our emotional experiences. Each system is designed to do different things and also to work with the other systems so they remain in balance with each other. Professor Paul Gilbert outlines the importance of these three types of emotional systems in his book *The Compassionate Mind* (see the resources section in the back of this book), and they can be summarized as follows:

- The first system is a threat protection system, which detects and deals with threats and involves emotions like anger, anxiety, and disgust. This is the system designed to protect and defend us. It is also referred to as the threat emotion regulation system.

- The second system is an achieving and activating system, which stimulates and directs our desires so we achieve good things like food, sex, and friendship, and it also helps us to pursue goals. It is linked with feelings of pleasure. This is the system designed to help us prosper. It is also referred to here as the achieving acquisition system.

- The third system is an affiliative and soothing system and is linked with feelings of being soothed and feelings of "safeness" and peacefulness. It is linked with being relaxed and experiencing compassion and connection with others. This is the system that is designed to help us regulate the other two and experience states of contentedness (so we are not always out rushing around seeking things or running away from threats). For ease of reference we will refer to this as the contentment and soothing system.

The interesting thing about these systems is that they help orient or adjust our mind-set or mentality. They enable us to manage our emotions and state of mind and help us to change and adjust our outlook.

So, for example, if our threat system has identified a potential threat, we begin to feel anxious, our hearts race, and we adopt a threat-focused mentality. By *mentality* we mean the way in which our minds are organized. When we are threatened, what we pay attention to, the way we think (how we work out our escape routes), what happens in our bodies and to our feelings, and what we actually do is all more or less focused on the issues of threat. Our minds are organized in a certain way—a threat-based mentality. Consider how your mind would be organized if you were going on vacation or enjoying Christmas with your loved family. The emotional systems orchestrate a mentality by triggering a specific type of emotion that focuses our attention in a certain way and causes us to act in a corresponding manner.

Below is a diagram that shows how our three major emotional systems interact. When in balance the *achieving and activating* system, the *threat protection* system, and the *contentment and soothing* system can be very helpful in guiding us to meet the challenges of life.

Figure 1: Three emotional regulation systems

Source: Reprinted with permission from P. Gilbert, *The Compassionate Mind* (London: Constable & Robinson, 2009).

The threat emotion regulation system

The threat emotion regulation system (threat protection system) and the processes associated with threats are key to understanding trauma, and for this reason I am going to focus on them in detail here. The threat system is designed to protect us and keep us safe from physical and psychological harm. We are far faster and better at detecting and responding to unpleasant emotions than to pleasant ones. This makes a lot of evolutionary sense since we humans, like all animals, often need to detect threats from other animals, from people, or from our environment (for example, poisonous foods). The threat system is set up to deal with many situations on the basis of "better safe than sorry" thinking.

The threat system has a range of particular emotions it is able to activate; the most common ones are anger, anxiety, and disgust. These emotions are associated with different bodily feelings, ways of thinking, and behaviors. For example, when we feel anger we may experience our bodies tensing, or our jaws clenching, or maybe a rush of energy through the body. When we feel aggrieved or have a sense of frustration we may experience wanting to hit out or speak out. Anxiety shares the same high arousal state as feelings of anger but we think and behave differently: we want to run away or find a way to get to safety. If we feel disgust we may have a sense of slight nausea or distaste, and our thoughts are focused on unpleasantness and we want to get rid of, expel, or remove the cause of our disgust.

The different bodily feelings, ways of thinking, and behaviors associated with each emotion tend to form patterns in the brain, which are partly determined by the way the brain has evolved. This means that when any human feels anger or anxiety or disgust, his or her bodily feelings, ways of thinking, and desires for behavior will be similar.

DEFENSIVE OPTIONS FOR THE THREAT SYSTEM

As I have already explained the threat system has a number of fast-acting emotions and behaviors at its disposal. These include:

- fight—which gives rise to feelings of frustration and irritation or even rage where we want to shout, hit out, or be aggressive;

- flight—which gives rise to feelings of anxiety and fear, which means we want to escape;

- submission—which gives rise to wanting to appease or close down, hide, not say anything, make oneself as small as possible;

- freeze—which gives rise to a state of near-paralysis because of the overwhelming nature of the threat (this reaction is common in certain types of trauma); and

- dissociate—which gives rise to feelings of wanting to turn away/inward and zone out. You may remember that this is a symptom of trauma we explored in chapter 1.

When we are under severe threat we can have more than one defensive response triggered. For example, we can want to both fight and run away at the same time. This can make processing our response much more complicated and difficult. If we consider a person who is being assaulted, he or she may cower and curl up to protect him- or herself, while at the same time thinking "get up and hit them." This can be terribly confusing if we assume that we can feel only one threat emotion at any one time. In fact we can feel a variety of threat emotions at the same time and this can disorganize our minds.

HOW YOUR BRAIN WORKS TO PROCESS THREATS

The key areas in processing threat and trauma are the *thalamus, amygdala, hippocampus,* and *frontal cortex.* They might sound like complicated names, but don't be put off. When I am describing these parts of the brain to the people who visit the clinic, I often use analogies. An analogy that people find particularly helpful is to think of the different parts of the brain as characters. Outlined below are the different parts of the brain explained as four characters that have different jobs to do.

The thalamus, or "gatekeeper"

First, there is the thalamus, whose job it is to be a gatekeeper and to direct any visito[r] the right part of the brain. In this analogy, the visitors to the brain are sources of informati[on] in five different ways through our five senses. Information from our external world is receive[d] via sight, sound, smell, touch, and taste (the five senses). The thalamus, or gatekeeper, is diligent and hard-working and not only registers the visitor (the information) but makes sure it is sent correctly to the next part of the brain to be dealt with.

The amygdala, or "customs'"

Our second character is the amygdala. We have two amygdalas that sit on each side of the brain just behind the ear. The amygdala acts as the "customs service" of a country (in this case, the country is the brain), checking incoming information for potential threats. The amygdala is the brain's "alarm system," and its main job is to react to the emotional signal sent by the gatekeeping thalamus and notify us that there is a potential source of threat in our outside world—or as we will learn, sometimes inside our own minds, such as our memories, images, and thoughts. The amygdala gives us bursts of feelings such as anxiety or anger to alert us to take action and to help us to protect ourselves from the incoming threat identified by the gatekeeper thalamus. Our bodies have a variety of defensive actions to threat as we have described earlier, namely, fight, flight, submit, freeze, and dissociate.

Better safe than sorry

For a number of reasons our brains have evolved to be very sensitive to threats and can even make mistakes by overestimating threat and overfocusing on it. If you watch birds eating on your lawn or in the park you will see that for much of the time they check the environment around them for threats when they could be eating. This shows how threat conscious they are, even at the risk of attaining a smaller amount of food. We too can have sudden flashes of anxiety from unexpected noises or movement, because these are alerting our threat system.

The problem with the amygdala is that it can be very sensitive and overreact, so it will categorize things as being a threat even if the risk is only slight. It's designed to do this to ensure our safety. It operates on the principle that it is better to be safe than sorry. The amygdala can therefore be a bit trigger-happy, in part because we must be ready to respond to threats at a moment's notice. The amygdala works in concert with another threat-focused system called the hypothalamic-pituitary-adrenal axis. This is a bit of a mouthful, but essentially it's the part of the brain that mobilizes the body by sending a variety of chemical messages to various organs such as our adrenal glands (where we produce cortisol—a stress hormone). It also activates the sympathetic nervous system to increase our heart rate and push oxygen into our muscles to prepare us for action.

Emotional body memory

The amygdala is also responsible for emotional and body-focused memory. It is where we store our emotional memories, including our trauma memories. Our body-focused memory is a memory that is very much in the body. For example, imagine you go to a party and have a can of beer that within a few minutes makes you ill and then you're very sick. The next time you have a can of beer and you smell that hoppy aroma, what happens in your body? There is an immediate trigger of nausea. The smell triggers what we call a *body memory*. This is your body remembering how it felt (nauseous) the last time you drank beer—thanks to the amygdala—and you may therefore actually feel sick. If your amygdala wasn't working, then you would still remember that the last time you drank beer it made you ill, but you wouldn't have the actual bodily sensation of feeling sick.

Conditioning

The amygdala is also responsible for *conditioning*. This means that the brain can *learn* to become frightened of the things that we associate with the threats that have created body memories for us.

• John's story

John was bitten by a dog when he was a child, and for many years the sound of a dog barking or the sight of a dog would stimulate an immediate anxiety reaction. He would feel his heart hammer and experience anxiety and feel the need to run away. Thanks to the amygdala, these are the same emotional and body memories he experienced as a child when he was bitten by the dog.

Body memories

It is important to remember that the amygdala can reactivate bodily feelings and memories. So when we experience a traumatic event (which our brains interpret as a threat) the trauma memories such as flashbacks, nightmares, and intrusive thoughts will all be stored in the amygdala. Anything that reminds the amygdala of these traumatic memories will be treated as threats and re-create the bodily feelings and memories from whatever happened to us that was traumatic. This means our brains have conditioned us to treat as threatening anything that we associate with our trauma memories. We will explore flashbacks and trauma memories in more detail in chapter 3.

Hippocampus and event memory, or "the busy administrator"

Our third character is the hippocampus. Imagine that the hippocampus is like a very busy administrator who is trying to verify the customs service's, or amygdala's, threat assessment. The hippocampus is like a filing clerk, noting the times and places of events. To do this the hippocampus cross-refers the threat (which has been identified by the gatekeeper thalamus and sent to the customs amygdala) to other memories held in the brain. If the hippocampus unearths a vital piece of information that determines that there is not a threat, it sends a signal to the amygdala to let it know it can begin to calm down because the perceived threat is not an actual danger. Similarly, if the hippocampus discovers a piece of information that confirms that there is indeed a threat, then the whole brain orchestrates a response designed to get us out of danger and keep us safe. The ultimate goal, of course, is to keep us alive and to avoid injury. Later we will explore how the frontal cortex also orchestrates our reactions to threats.

Context

The hippocampus, or administrator, also puts our memories into context by allocating them a place and time. This helps us to distinguish whether something is happening in the present or in the past. People who have damaged the hippocampus can't form time–event memories. If you meet them on Monday they will have forgotten that you met them by Tuesday. People with hippocampal damage can still acquire those bodily reactions to threatening events called body memories, but they will forget how or when they acquired them. So the hippocampus when sizing up a threat is the part of the brain that assesses whether the threat is current (i.e., is actually happening now) or whether the threat has passed (i.e., it happened in the past).

The frontal cortex, or "conductor"

The fourth character is the frontal cortex, which is a part of the new brain that can be thought of as a conductor of the brain's emotional "orchestra" (in this case the orchestra comprises the *threat protection*, the *achieving and activating,* and the *contentment and soothing* systems). This part of the brain orchestrates the three emotional regulation systems; we will explore it in more detail later in this chapter once we have looked at the *achieving and activating* and the *contentment and soothing* systems, which are the two types of systems governing our positive emotions. It is especially important to understand how these two positive emotion systems can regulate the threat system.

The achieving acquisition emotion regulation system

Clearly in leading our lives we have to do more than just avoid threats or respond to them when they arise. We also need to achieve and acquire things. The *achieving acquisition* (achieving and activating) system gives us positive feelings that guide and motivate us to seek out and find things that we need to help us survive and flourish as human beings. This includes what we are motivated by and find pleasure in like food, sex, status, power, and relationships. It is this system that provides our motivation, energy, and desires. Imagine what it feels like when we win or achieve something in our lives, for example, pass our driving test, or do very well on an exam, or perhaps win a sporting event. We experience feelings of excitement, pleasure, and high energy. And when we are on our way to success we get small buzzes that keep us on our chosen path. These feelings are generated by the *achieving acquisition* system, one of whose important functions is to guide us toward things in our lives that will help us thrive and achieve our goals. These can be, for instance, finding a life partner, making a friend, getting a new job, or taking up a new hobby. Because we find all of these things pleasurable, we will seek them out.

It is useful to understand how our desires or motives to pursue the goals such as food, sex, friendship, and the like are regulated within the *achieving and activating system* because this is done by our emotions. It doesn't really matter what our goal is: if things are going well we will tend to have pleasant feelings. This pleasant emotional response is designed to keep us on track. If, on the other hand, our goals are not being satisfied, then our emotional response will be less pleasant and we will experience the threat-related emotions of anxiety and frustration. It is these feelings that will inspire us to either change tack and alter our goal or give up. So, for example, whether we want to pass an important exam, go out on a date, or get a new job, we will feel good or bad according to whether we are successfully achieving that goal or whether we are being thwarted in some way. And it is whether we are feeling good or bad that makes us carry on or give up.

THREAT AND POSITIVE EMOTIONS

One of the difficulties with the threat system is that it is designed to overrule positive emotions. For example, imagine you are having a good time with a friend and then your cell phone rings and you find out that another friend or your child has had an accident. Or imagine that you are having a nice picnic in the park and you suddenly notice an escaped lion. In both of these situations the positive emotions are quickly turned off as you direct your attention to dealing with the threat that has produced feelings of high anxiety in you. Sometimes when we are feeling stressed it is difficult to engage our positive feelings because the *threat* system is activated and our positive emotions are toned down or turned off. There are, of course, occasions where even in the presence of certain threats we still feel sufficiently in control that other positive feelings are triggered, say excitement, for example, in the case of parachute jumping. Indeed some people like to engage in activities that activate the threat system, such as extreme sports, because they enjoy the buzz. These examples highlight some of the complexities of the relationship between the *threat* system and the *achieving* system.

When the *achieving acquisition* system is in balance with the *threat* and the *soothing* systems, it can guide us toward important life goals. Overstimulation of this system can lead us either to wanting "more and more" or feeling so overenergized that our minds race and we find it impossible to sleep. When the *achieving acquisition* system is understimulated, we experience a lack of motivation and a loss of energy and desires.

The contentment and soothing emotion regulation system

Now you can imagine that when animals are not under any threat and are satisfied (i.e., not seeking out resources such as food) they can relax; they have time for play and exploration. Sometimes this is called a state of contentment, of nonstriving and nonthreat. The *contentment and soothing* system (affiliative and soothing system) releases chemicals in our brains called endorphins and these are associated with creating a sense of peaceful well-being. They are also produced when a distressed baby is comforted by its parent and its threat-based emotions are soothed. If we meditate or go on retreat and learn to slow down our minds, we often feel calmer inside with a stronger sense of well-being, and more content. So what we learn from this is that it is possible to have positive feelings that are not about excitement and being all geared up, but are quiet and positive feelings that help us to soothe our threat-based emotions or ones we associate with a sense of peacefulness. Compassion and kindness come from the *contentment and soothing* system.

What is interesting about the *contentment and soothing* system is that it is very important in the evolution of compassionate and caring behavior. If a baby is distressed and crying (the threat system), the parent is able to calm and soothe the child by holding it, stroking it, and talking to it in a gentle tone of voice. All these actions are registered by the baby's brain, causing the release of hormones called *endorphins* and *oxytocin*, which make the baby feel safe again. Endorphins are linked to our peaceful and calm sense of well-being, and oxytocin plays a key role in how we feel safe and at ease in our social environments.

This demonstrates a really important point, which is that the *soothing* system can regulate the *threat* system and help to calm the emotions we experience when we are in danger, such as anxiety, anger, and disgust.

Supposing something has upset us, what are the things we might do to help ourselves feel better? As we already discussed we might undertake a task and activate the *achieving acquisition* system. But often we find talking to other people can make us feel better because we feel supported, understood, and validated and this really does help us to feel better when we are upset. This is because the *soothing* system is calming down our threat-based emotions.

As mentioned above, if a baby is distressed and is with a loving parent who is affectionate, the parent hugs the child until it calms down. This tells us that we humans, like other animals, can tone down emotions that are activated by our threat system (e.g., feelings of distress and anxiety) by receiving kindness, affection, and compassion. Indeed affection and kindness are so important to us that they actually affect how our brains develop. There are also special areas of our brains that produce particular hormones and that respond to the kindness of others, and self-compassion and self-kindness. So there is no doubt that kindness does help us to settle or calm our sense of being threatened.

These positive emotions—feeling content, safe, and affectionately connected to others—are very different from the ones gained by achievement. The soothing positive emotions can be beneficial to us in two ways. They can help calm our threat detection and protection emotions (such as fear, anxiety, and anger) when our threat system is activated. They can also help us to manage the unpleasant feelings we experience if our positive feelings associated with achievement are interrupted, for example, because we don't pass an important exam or our much desired driving test.

Returning to the example of the distressed baby, perhaps you can begin to imagine what happens in the baby's brain when it's crying and the parent does not soothe and comfort it or perhaps even hurts or shouts at it. The baby's brain will register the neglect and/or negative behavior as highly threatening and the threat-focused system will remain activated and the baby will continue to experience distress. This, in turn, means that the *contentment and soothing* system is not being activated, and therefore the baby is not developing the experience of receiving positive feelings of care and warmth in response to its upset. Of course, all parents have times when they become irritable with their children and don't provide the care that they would like to; after all we are all only human. This can, however, become problematic if this manner of treatment continues consistently throughout childhood, as the child's brain is not learning how to activate the *contentment and soothing* system. If a person doesn't experience compassion as a child, he or she may struggle as an adult to have compassionate feelings of love, kindness, and warmth toward him- or herself. The essential childhood development steps toward creating these feeling are absent. Instead, the child (and then the adult) remains threat focused.

The frontal cortex, or "conductor"

As we described earlier our fourth character is the part of the brain called the frontal cortex that acts as a conductor to the brain's "emotional orchestra," which comprises our emotional regulation systems: threat protection, contentment and soothing, and achieving and activating. Just as a real conductor guides the musicians to play their instruments at certain times, in a certain tempo, and at a certain volume in order to create a recital, so your brain's conductor plays a vital role in integrating the three emotional regulation systems.

REGULATES EMOTIONS

The frontal cortex matures quite slowly as we pass through infancy, enter childhood and gradually into adolescence, and slowly it connects with our more emotional brain areas. Eventually it acts as a regulator of our emotions, partly through learning and partly through modeling our parents. One of the key things that helps this part of the brain to mature is the degree to which we experience caring, "safeness," and helpfulness from those people around us as we are growing up. There is an excellent book that describes this by Sue Gerhardt, called *Why Love Matters: How Affection Shapes a Baby's Brain* (see the references section at the back of this book).

EXECUTIVE FUNCTIONS

The frontal cortex also gives rise to our abilities to think, anticipate, plan, calculate consequences, and have empathy for other people. It is very much the part of our brain that we engage when we consciously "think." It also plays an important role in our experience of trauma and how we can learn to deal with it because it is responsible for reactivating past emotional associations and events that form part of our experience of our traumas in terms of flashbacks, nightmares, and the like.

RECOGNIZES EMOTIONS

This area of the brain provides us with the ability to recognize our emotions and to make decisions about whether to act on them or not. It also enables us to assess how to respond to the feelings in our bodies generated by our threat-conscious amygdalas. For example, if you have to take an exam or a driving test, your amygdala recognizes this as potentially threatening to your well-being and will go full throttle generating all the responses to threat with which you are now familiar. Your stomach is tight, your heart is racing, you're feeling really anxious, and part of you would really like to go home. But it is our frontal cortex that calculates the consequences by assessing the current situation over the longer term, by recognizing our emotions, and working out whether to act upon them. It recognizes that if we remain in the situation (rather than fleeing from it) and stay with our anxiety, then we will master our feelings of anxiety and be able to perform the task (take the exam or driving test) and then reap the benefits. And so our frontal cortex enables us to override the messages of the amygdala (which triggers our urges to fight, take flight, freeze, or submit)—because it has the ability to recognize the future consequences resulting from our current actions.

EMPATHY

The frontal cortex also helps us to have empathy and to think about what is going on in the minds of other people. Moreover, it helps us work out what is going on in our own minds. The frontal cortex enables us to stand back and reflect.

The frontal cortex is very sensitive to signals of feeling content, safe, and happy, and being caring and cared for. It plays a key role with a number of other brain areas in activating the *contentment and soothing* system. Indeed, as mentioned above, one of the main factors in helping this part of the brain to mature is the experience of affiliation from others (i.e., if we received love and were cared for by other people). It turns out that if we learn to be kind and supportive of ourselves by practicing ways in which we can adopt a caring, supportive, validating, and encouraging approach to ourselves, we can trigger our own emotional systems associated with feelings of contentment, safeness, and self-soothing. In sharp contrast, if we are self-critical and prone to experience shame, this tends to activate our *threat* system. We will explore our experiences of shame in more detail in chapter 4.

SUMMARY

This chapter has shown us some of the ways our brains process trauma and in particular has explored how the design of the brain can cause us difficulties. This is absolutely not our fault.

We have seen that the amygdala is a part of the brain that stores trauma and body memories and can flash us with powerful feelings. It is the hippocampus that helps us to locate our memories by placing them in context as having a time and a place. The frontal cortex also plays a key role because it allows us to have an overview of what's going on both inside us and outside us. The problem is that trauma can create such a massive surge in the threat system (and trigger bursts of cortisol) that it temporarily knocks out the hippocampus and frontal cortex, causing us to reexperience our trauma through our body's threat reactions.

One of the key points about understanding how our brains work is to recognize that it's not our fault that we are designed in such a way that we run into these problems. Understanding that our reactions to trauma reflect how our memories are coded in our brains because of how our brains have evolved can be the first steps to helping us. We have evolved brains that function in a way that is beyond our conscious control. The brain is very concerned with keeping us physically and mentally safe to prolong our survival on this planet. In order to help us achieve this goal, the brain has a highly developed threat-focused system. If we are threatened, our feelings of anxiety, anger, disgust, and sadness are not only normal but are important in helping with the brain's foremost mission to keep us safe. We will feel these threat-focused emotions in all sorts of situations throughout our lives, and what is important is that we can regulate them by experiencing the emotions governed by the *contentment and soothing* system, where we feel peaceful and calm. This is one reason compassion can be so helpful because it calms our threat-sensitive brains.

freeze mode "bad" occurs if something leaving body temp until threat is over

3

Understanding your trauma memories: Flashbacks, nightmares, and intrusive thoughts

A key insight in helping us to understand, with compassion, our reactions to our traumatic experiences and our trauma itself is to appreciate that our brains process everyday memories differently from the memories of our traumatic experiences (our trauma memories).

Put simply, our brains store traumatic memories in a different way from the manner in which they store everyday memories. This may be because the overwhelming emotions we experience during a traumatic event stop the brain from processing the event in the same way as an everyday event. When, later in the chapter, we explore how these memories are stored differently, it can help us to understand some of the upsetting and disturbing aspects of our trauma memories such as why we have flashbacks.

We can also experience our memories as being very much *in the body*, where our bodies are able to re-create the bodily sensations associated with a specific memory. In chapter 2 we used the example of going to a party and having a glass of beer that makes us sick. The next time we smell beer, we experience an immediate trigger of nausea. The smell triggers a *body memory*, remembering the sensations of a previous occurrence. This memory is automatic, rapid, and ripples through the body.

So when we have strong emotions about things that affect our bodies, these bodily experiences can be triggered again automatically and quickly with just small signals or cues. Therefore, when we experience a trauma-associated signal we can also experience a rapid change in how our bodies are feeling.

In order to understand in more detail the problems arising from trauma, how they affect us, and how we make sense of our experiences, we need to look more closely at how our brains actually process traumatic events.

THE DIFFERENCE BETWEEN EVERYDAY MEMORIES AND TRAUMA MEMORIES

The first thing we need to understand is that we have everyday memories and trauma memories. These different types of memory are stored in different parts of the brain. Experiencing traumatic events can disrupt the way we experience our memories working. Our trauma memory is a highly emotional recollection of the traumatic experience. It is stored—together with all our other emotional memories—in a primitive part of our brains called the amygdala. It is the trauma memory that makes us feel that we are reexperiencing feelings, emotions, and body sensations that happened at the time of the trauma and why nightmares and flashbacks feel so real and frightening. During flashbacks our brains "trick" us into thinking that we are reliving the traumatic event. Our memories feel "real" as if we are going through the same things again. Even if we logically know that the events happened in the past, our flashbacks make us feel as if we are back there again. Why does this happen when with our everyday memories we are able to recognize that what we are remembering is simply a memory?

With our everyday memories we are aware that we are thinking about an event from the past. For instance, can you remember your first day at primary or secondary school? If you can, and you are recalling it now, you will also be aware that the memory is related to a past time in your life. Though we are able to remember the emotions and physical sensations connected with the memory and we are able to describe them in words, we don't actually reexperience those emotions or sensations in our bodies at the actual time of recollection. Although we might remember feeling nervous or shy, we don't actually have a feeling of nervousness when we think back to that first day. You may not have thought about this before, but it has important implications for understanding trauma memories.

The two different types of memory, and how they are stored and processed, are discussed in more detail below.

Everyday memory

The everyday memory that most people use day-to-day is stored in an area of the brain called the hippocampus. Whatever our traumatic experience, we will be able to recount part of it as an everyday autobiographical experience that is stored in the memory with a time and a place. For example, John was able to recount his memories of being mugged, when asked by his therapist, as follows:

- ## John's story

I was mugged on Friday, June 27. I was twenty years old at the time. I was on my way from the train station to my house and I recall it was about 5:00 p.m. It was a light and balmy late afternoon and I was in a total world of my own as I walked home. The next thing I remember was a feeling of being held from behind. I didn't hear anything because I was listening to my iPod, so I didn't have any warning. But I vividly remember the feeling of being restrained and of someone pulling at my bag. I thought that I was being attacked and it did occur to me that I could be seriously injured or even stabbed. I do remember feeling quite terrified yet I was totally unable to fight back. The guy eventually got hold of my bag after a lot of jostling with me and made a run for it. The whole thing probably lasted for only a few minutes but when I think about it, it is as if time stood still and everything happened in slow motion.

John's account of his trauma as an everyday memory has a number of important features that are outlined below:

- *It is organized and continuous.* The memory has a beginning, a middle, and an end. For example, the memories are remembered as a continuous set of linked events, like an episode on television. The order in which things happened is generally remembered, with no major pieces missing.

- *It can be recalled when you want to think about it.* You can decide when to think about the memory. The memory doesn't just pop into your mind at random and unpredictable times. When you have finished with it, you put it back into your long-term memory store and it's safely tucked away until you want to remember it next.

- *It can be triggered by words and situations.* Everyday memory is readily available through talking with other people or being in similar situations. Your own words can directly access particular memories.

- *It is time tagged.* When you remember an everyday memory, you know that it feels as though it happened in the past. You don't get the sense that it is happening now.

- *It is updated.* The everyday memory changes according to any new information you may acquire afterward. For example, you may feel that a friend who has stood you up has let you down and that she is no longer a good friend. If you later learn, however, that she tried to contact you and you did not get the message, then you may feel differently toward her and your memory and understanding of that event will be "updated" according to your new information.

Now that you have read about these features, see if you can identify them in John's account above.

Trauma memory

The following is John's account of the events as a trauma memory:

"I can feel him pushing at my back, an intense pain in my side, God I've been stabbed. Is this it? I'm dying, I can't breathe, my heart is pounding, I can't move. Fight, fight, just get him off you. Whack to my face."

John reported his heart pounding, feeling terrified and trapped in his body, and experiencing an intense pain in his side as he revisited his trauma memory. This was understandably a very distressing and confusing experience for John because the feelings were so intense and yet the mugging had happened over two years ago.

You can see that this description is quite different from John's previous autobiographical account because, when we experience a traumatic event, the memory gets stored in a different way and in a different part of the brain from the everyday memory. When something traumatic happens, it is very overwhelming for our brains, and because we are not relaxed and in a calm state, we do not process the information in such an efficient and effective way. During a trauma, our memory is stored in a part of the brain called the amygdala.

The important features of this kind of trauma memory are:

- *It is fragmented and not organized.* It is very uncommon for this type of memory to have the same organization as an everyday memory. It isn't coherent; it doesn't have the beginning, the middle, and the end of one continuous memory. Events within the memory are recalled in a haphazard way and do not make up an organized "story" of the event being recalled. The result of its not being organized is that the memory is not a "whole and complete" memory, but is fragmented. That means that you remember only isolated parts rather than the whole thing as a continuous event.

- *It is recalled involuntarily.* In your trauma memory, bits and pieces are recalled and pop into your thoughts even though you don't want to remember them and don't consciously decide to remember them—they just spew out. Flashbacks and nightmares are examples of this; they come into your head even though you don't ask them to. This can be very distressing as it feels as though you have no control over them.

- *It is triggered by situations.* Trauma memories are triggered by particular situations that remind you of the trauma. Quite often particular smells, noises, places, or sights can trigger a traumatic memory (e.g., loud noises, buses, screaming, the smell of smoke). For some people, even similar feelings can trigger traumatic memories. This can be very upsetting because you can't always control what you smell or what you hear, and you find your memories triggered when you don't want them to be recalled.

- *It is not time tagged.* This means that when you remember it, it does not feel as though it happened in the past but as though it is happening now. Even though you know it happened months or years ago, it feels as if it is happening in the present and your body actually experiences the emotions you experienced at the time of the event. Consequently this can make you feel as though you're still in danger.

- *It is frozen in time.* The memory remains exactly as it was when you first formed it. This means that unlike everyday memory (which is constantly updated as new information comes in), your trauma memory does not change as you learn new information about the event. This also means that the feelings you had during the trauma are also "frozen" in time. You can feel exactly the same emotions that you experienced during the traumatic event. For example, if at the time of an attack you thought you were going to die, when you recall the traumatic event you still experience the feeling that you are going to die, even though you know you survived the attack.

See if you recognize the important features of trauma memory in John's account above.

FLASHBACKS ARE NORMAL

Now that we can see the difference between everyday and trauma memories, let's look at our threat-focused brains to help us understand more about our flashbacks.

Flashbacks are in fact a normal experience and a by-product of the way our brains process intense emotional experiences. That means that we all experience flashbacks. A good example of this flashing back can arise if we've been to a particularly emotional film, which was either sad or frightening. It's very common to have scenes flashing back into your mind after a film has finished. When the film *The Exorcist* first came out in 1973, large numbers of people were very distressed by it, in part because they were having flashbacks to some of the horror scenes. People can even have nightmares from seeing particularly unpleasant films. Similarly, if we've had a very major argument with somebody, it's not uncommon to have flashbacks to the disagreement and find ourselves getting angry again. Over time, however, we come to terms with the flashback and eventually the memory settles down. We can also have flashbacks to positive events, for example, falling in love. We can find our minds constantly being intruded upon by thoughts of the person involved. These are not usually feared in the same way that unpleasant or threat-based flashbacks are though.

So we usually experience flashbacks to intensely emotional experiences (both positive and negative), but the flashbacks should fade over time. Now if this does not happen and the flashbacks are negative and distressing, then they can become problematic and greatly affect our well-being. They can leave us feeling as terrified as we were at the time when the original traumatic event took place. It may feel as if the painful memories that belong to the past continually haunt us in the present. People who have attended the trauma clinic describe being unable to move on from their traumas caused by a traumatic event because these experiences are constantly on their minds, or when they think everything is normal and safe suddenly out of the blue they have a flashback.

TRAUMA MEMORIES AS WARNING SIGNALS

When we experience something in life that is traumatic, our brains treat even a memory of this experience as a threat. This means that when we remember something relating to the traumatic event—a trauma memory (that is, a flashback)—our brains also treat that *memory* as a threat. One way to think about trauma memories is that they act as warning signals to our brains, alerting us that something threatening is about to occur. When we recall a trauma memory, our brains think that we are still in danger, even though, in fact, the original traumatic event is long over. Therefore the function of our trauma memories, as in flashbacks and intrusions, is to alert us (often as a false alarm) to the fact that we're still not safe.

WHY DO FLASHBACKS HAPPEN?

Earlier in this chapter we learned that our trauma memories are stored in the amygdala and that trauma memories can include flashbacks, nightmares, and intrusive thoughts. *Flashbacks* are fragmented memories of our trauma, which can relate to any of our five senses (sight, sound, smell, touch, and taste) and are emotionally charged so that they make us feel as if we are reliving the event. Flashbacks can be triggered by a whole host of reminders of the traumatic event. When this happens (even long after the traumatic event is over) the thalamus, or "gatekeeper," will send the potentially threatening information to the amygdala, or "customs service," to assess whether we are in danger. Information of a similar nature to anything that happened at the time of the traumatic event causes our amygdala to react to it as a threat. We then have an emotional reaction like the one we felt at the time of our traumatic event, and so our bodies begin their preparations to respond to the threat. This means that we release the stress transmitters and hormones adrenaline and cortisol to help us fight, take flight, freeze, or submit. In summary, once a flashback has been triggered, our brains treat that flashback as a repetition of the original traumatic event, and we experience a whole reaction to that threat: our hearts race, our bodies surge with adrenaline, we may experience body memories, and we feel the urge to either fight, run away, freeze, or submit.

The hippocampus will send out the signals to calm our threat reactions if it considers that the information (in this case, a flashback) is nonthreatening or occurred in the past. However, the stress hormones we generate when we are under threat (cortisol and adrenaline) anesthetize the hippocampus, whose job it is to tell us that the threat occurred in the past and is no longer a current danger. So the brain treats the trauma memory as a current threat and orchestrates an entire threat-based reaction. This means that our brains' basic threat-detecting system is unable to distinguish between past and present threats and therefore keeps us living as if we are in constant danger, which, as we explored in chapter 1, can result in many of the symptoms associated with trauma and PTSD.

The threat system is put into overdrive when it can't deal with the quantity or quality of threats that result from repeated trauma memories. Each time these threats are assessed, pulses of the stress hormone cortisol are released, suppressing the brain's ability to recognize a memory as having occurred in the past. In addition, release of these stress hormones can have a negative effect on our well-being. Indeed, those who suffer from depression have high levels of cortisol in their system.

All of this tells us that the brain can experience threats that remain unresolved. Normally to resolve a threat we take action to eliminate the danger, so we fight, run away, freeze, or submit. Where the brain functions optimally and a threat is identified (for example, we see a lion), the brain is able to identify that this is a current and live threat and that there is an appropriate action to be taken (that is, we run away). When the brain has become flooded with stress hormones because of repeated threatening events or memories and is no longer able to distinguish whether a threat—in this case a traumatic memory—is current and live or in the past, then the threat remains unresolved. As far as the brain is concerned, it has identified a threat against which no action is being taken.

Where threats remain unresolved the brain uses a technique to remind us that we may need to take action against these threats. These are things that pop into our minds unexpectedly and are known as *intrusions*. You may recognize times when you have been in what you thought was a relaxed state of mind, and apparently out of nowhere an image pops into your mind. These intrusions are commonly experienced as niggling worries. For example, you are on your way to the airport for a vacation, and you suddenly think you may not have locked the front door. This is our brain's way of checking out and verifying memories that may also be potentially threatening. When we experience trauma our brains continue to try to protect us. That is why images that may be traumatic in nature pop into our minds unbidden. Our brains are effectively trying to say to us, "We know you are relaxing now but do keep in mind that you have experienced something traumatic that is unresolved, and keep checking that you are safe because you appear to be ignoring the threat." These thoughts and memories, which appear when we least expect them and which may feel really hard to live with, are our brains' best efforts to protect us. When we experience flashbacks we are experiencing a type of intrusion that has a sensory element (smells, noises, tastes, etc.) and body memories (physical sensations in our bodies), causing us to feel like we are reliving the traumatic experience.

TRAUMA, THE FRONTAL CORTEX, AND COMPASSION

As helpful as the frontal cortex can be in dealing with trauma, one of the problems with how our brains work is that the high levels of stress hormones produced as a consequence of the threat system being activated knock out some of the frontal cortex's functions. We find it very difficult to think logically or sometimes even to think at all when our threat system is activated. This is because some of the key areas of the brain that process information simply get turned off because all attention is turned to the immediacy of the threat. In extreme cases people can experience *dissociation,* where they become almost paralyzed and are temporarily unable to think or process information clearly.

This is one of the major reasons we focus on compassion when we are dealing with trauma, because compassion stimulates our contentment and soothing system, and that helps regulate the threat system and also keeps our frontal cortex working.

The frontal cortex and thinking again

We can see that having the "new" thinking brain—which gives us a sense of ourselves—can also result in major additional problems when confronted with traumas, *but* there is an upside to this as well because we can also stand back and begin to think about how our brains are working. We can develop a more mindful, aware, and compassionate approach to our minds. This enables us to be much less likely to get caught up in negative ways of thinking and dwelling on things that make us feel worse.

As we begin to understand how our brains and our minds work, we can learn to actually change the way we think, something no other animal can do.

Studies have shown, for example, that if people meditate in particular ways they can change the structures in the frontal cortex. Indeed, new research has shown that the brain is much more plastic than was previously thought, and because it is malleable it can change its wiring with specific kinds of exercises. So when it comes to learning to deal with trauma, we are going to be getting the frontal cortex (and other brain areas) to do some work by learning how to recognize, stand back, and compassionately orient ourselves to our trauma. We are going to be using our brains' *natural systems* to help us to deal with, and move on from, the painful emotions associated with our traumatic experiences.

We can therefore learn to deal with trauma in such a way that we regulate and settle the threat system, rather than keep activating it by our self-critical thoughts or by going over and over the event in our minds, or trying to avoid painful things by pushing them out of our heads. As we explored in chapter 1, there are many ways in which we naturally deal with trauma that can make it much worse for us.

WHAT DO FLASHBACKS FEEL LIKE?

Some of the things we find particularly distressing and difficult to deal with as a result of traumatic experiences are intrusive thoughts, flashbacks, and nightmares. These types of memories are very common in people who are traumatized, and they can make us feel that we are unable to move on from a distressing experience and our brains will not let go of the trauma and memories. Not only can these memories be upsetting and troublesome, they sometimes make us feel as if we are losing our minds.

People can be reluctant to talk about flashbacks and nightmares simply because of the stress they cause, but also because they feel shame about the experience and do not want to admit how disturbed they are by their memories. If a trauma memory also conjures up feelings of shame and self-criticism, the memory becomes even more difficult to bear in our own minds, let alone to talk about with other people. In chapter 4 we will look at shame as a threat-based emotion and explore why we experience this feeling as a response to our traumatic reactions.

We all probably know what it feels like to wake up from a bad nightmare and, for a few minutes, to be confused about whether we dreamed it or whether it really happened. Sometimes the feelings of the nightmare stay with us for a few minutes or a few hours and disturb our peace of mind.

A similar thing happens to us when we have flashbacks or intrusive thoughts. Our memories make us *feel* the same way as we felt during the traumatic event. So it sometimes becomes difficult to work out whether we are just remembering or whether it is really happening all over again. The confusion may not last long, but it happens because the memory feels so real and as if it is in the present.

Most normal memories take the form of pictures in our minds—for example, think about your most recent meal and see whether you can "see it in your mind." Yet when we remember traumatic events, we often see pictures, hear sounds, smell things, and feel in our bodies in the way we did at the time of the event. These memories are not therefore limited to being in picture form. We can experience both everyday and traumatic memories with each of our five senses (sight, sound, smell, touch, and taste).

We can have *hearing*, or auditory, flashbacks, when we can literally hear things that other people cannot hear. This is very common in combat veterans, who often hear helicopter engines, or commands being shouted to them, or gunshot fire months and even years after they have left the armed forces. It is also quite a common experience for people who have been bullied. They hear the voices of their bullies in their heads, usually saying mean and critical things about them. These are the things that were said to them when they were actually being bullied, and it may continue years after the event.

We can also have *smell* memories. Have you ever thought a day smells like a day from your past? Some of us will be able to smell powerful fragrances or odors that we smelled at the time of the traumatic event, even though the smell is not actually present in real life. For example, combat veterans will often describe being able to smell the scents of diesel fuel or artillery fire long after their combat experiences are over.

We can also have body memories, which make our bodies *feel* the same way they did in the past. One visitor to the trauma clinic described having a body flashback in which she described the sensation of a wave of energy passing over her whole body. She found living with this experience quite alarming, until we were able to work out that this was the physical experience she had had when she was involved in a gas explosion. She had been blown a few feet away by the power of the blast, and it was this sensation that she was reliving over and over. Interestingly, she could not remember the explosion, but it appears her body remembered it very well.

Sometimes we can have *taste* memories, which can leave us feeling disgusted. For example, Martin, a traffic police officer, used to have a taste memory of burning flesh as he thought a piece of human remains was in his mouth. He could still remember the taste of it in his mouth as he tried to rescue some people from the wreckage of a road accident, and it made him feel disgusted.

You may be reassured to know that it is quite common following a trauma to have all sorts of intrusive thoughts and flashbacks. These are not limited to images but include all the sensory aspects of our trauma experiences, as outlined above. This is not a sign that you are losing your mind, but rather that your mind is playing tricks on you.

PAST MEMORIES THAT HAUNT YOU

A flashback is a particularly vivid and fragmented memory and is associated with a feeling of reliving all or part of a previous emotionally distressing experience. For some of us this experience can be very intense, intrusive, and frightening, as we can see from Anna's description of her flashback of being raped:

• *Anna's story*

It is as if I am back there again. I can smell him, I can hear him, and I feel so powerless. I can feel it in my whole body and it makes me really scared. I think I am losing my mind as I know on one level that this is not happening again to me—but it just feels so real.

As we mentioned earlier, flashbacks are not a sign that we are going mad or losing our minds. They are a particular type of memory. In our minds we may see something that related to our traumatic experience, such as flashes of a face or a body or a building from the scene of our trauma. The flashback can therefore call upon any of our five senses to re-create all or part of our traumatic experience. This of course can make the experience feel very real, alarming, and distressing. So a flashback is not necessarily a complete memory of everything that we went through. It can be a single aspect of the past event such as the physical sensation of the incident, the sound of a voice, a particular smell, or a powerful feeling of danger.

Yet it is not so much the *images* we see in our minds that cause us angst and distress; it is how the images make us feel emotionally and what they mean to us. We can see this point illustrated in the case of George below:

• *George's story*

George was in a head-on collision with another car. Sadly, the driver of the other car died on impact. When George described what happened to him, he recalled a troublesome flashback during which he could see himself trapped in his car, being helped by the emergency services, and he was looking over at the dead man in the other car. Understandably, George found this memory very distressing. When I explored with him how this memory made him feel, he said it made him feel humiliated.

His sense of humiliation was related to feeling trapped and helpless in his own car while being helped by the emergency services. So we were able to understand why George felt not only the distress but also humiliation by helping him work out what the memory meant to him. This is an important process in recovering from trauma, as you will see later in this book, because experiences will have different effects upon different people. For example, another person trapped in a car accident may well have felt different emotions in this situation, rather than humiliation.

We can understand our experiences of flashbacks and nightmares when we begin to appreciate that, as human beings, we have a *threat-focused brain,* which has evolved to keep us safe. In fact, keeping us safe is the primary job of our brains. Nothing else matters if we are not safe. We have therefore evolved a brain that is very good at detecting threat. As we have already mentioned, our flashbacks act as a warning signal to alert our brains that we are in danger. The trouble is that we are not often in danger any more, as the original traumatic event is long over. So the question remains, why do we continue to have flashbacks after traumatic events?

WHAT TRIGGERS FLASHBACKS?

Flashbacks are usually triggered by something that brings the frightening and traumatic memories back. Working out what the trigger is for us can be extremely valuable in helping us begin to feel in control of our minds again. Triggers can include smelling a fragrance or odor, hearing a noise, seeing something, reading something, having a physical sensation, or just being in a situation where we have an uncomfortable feeling in our bodies. Almost any everyday happening can act as a trigger and this is why flashbacks can feel so uncontrollable.

• *José's story*

Take, for example, José, who used to come to the clinic for help relating to his experiences of being tortured.

José started off well with his treatment but soon began to dread his appointments, as they always triggered a major flashback to his torture experiences. After some close observations and diary keeping we realized that his flashbacks were triggered by a strong smell of baking wafting from the bakery next door to the clinic. The significance of this was that the room where José was tortured was also close to a bakery and he vividly remembered the smell of baking bread as he was being hurt and threatened. Working out that the bakery smells were a trigger helped José enormously because he felt more in control of his flashbacks.

Smells are very powerful triggers of emotional memory, and they very readily result in flashbacks. You may have already noticed this in your own life.

NIGHTMARES

Flashbacks can be particularly distressing if they occur at nighttime, as the memories can be especially vivid and difficult to manage. They can disrupt our sleep, either making getting to sleep difficult or disturbing the duration and extent of our sleep. Nightmares are very much like flashbacks in that they are often triggered either while we are sleeping or from events during the previous day. So, for example, nightmares may contain scenes from a film we have recently watched merged with some of our own memories. Sometimes people find that their nightmares are not necessarily a repeat of what happened to them, although they can be. Often people describe a theme to their nightmares, perhaps relating to a loss, fear of dying, or of being chased and not being able to escape from others. Our nightmares often have a theme related to our fears but are not actually a rerun of what happened to us.

In some cases of reoccurring nightmares we can experience serious difficulties and may stay up at night to avoid our memories and dreams, only letting ourselves fall asleep in the early hours of the morning. Turning night into day is a pattern that we often see in seriously traumatized people at the clinic. In fact, some even begin to dread going to sleep, as they know that they will have nightmares and wake up feeling anxious and scared. Regardless of the extent of our disturbed sleep, not getting enough sleep leaves us feeling exhausted and with little respite from our active and troubled minds.

Below is a summary of the characteristics associated with flashbacks:

- A powerful sense of something familiar and upsetting, or danger.

- Reexperiencing physical sensations that you felt.

- Other sensory memories such as smells, noises, and tastes.

- It may be like watching a film of what you went through.

- The sense that you are reliving the experience all over again.

- A vivid and recurring nightmare.

There may be many triggers in our daily lives that set off our trauma memories. So it's not really surprisingly that this can make us feel very out of control and at the mercy of the seemingly random whim of our memories. Beginning to understand what triggers our flashbacks and understanding what flashbacks are can really help us start to gain control of our minds and realize that we are not in fact losing our minds or going mad.

WHAT KEEPS A SENSE OF CONSTANT DANGER GOING?

Feeling as if we are in constant danger or as if danger is just around the corner is one of the hallmark features of PTSD. We have already described above how everyday happenings can trigger our trauma memories. Psychologists refer to this as experiencing *a sense of current threat*. Much of the time, this feeling of constant threat is fueled by the frequent flashbacks and nightmares. This is because we are being constantly reminded through the flashbacks of what happened to us and how it made us feel. Consequently it can seem as though there is no respite from our painful life experiences and that we are trapped or caught in minds that are living in the past.

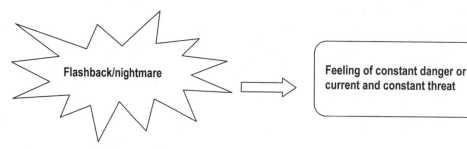

Figure 3: Flashbacks

In addition to the feelings of constant danger, experiencing a traumatic event and what happens afterward can also cause us to think negative thoughts or to think badly about ourselves, about others, or about the world. For example, we might start to think that we are horrible, worthless, or powerless people as a result of our traumatic experiences or because of what other people have done to us. Some of us might develop the belief that other people cannot be trusted or that the world is a dangerous place. If these thoughts and beliefs become stronger and stronger, possibly through the frequent reexperiencing of the traumatic event through flashbacks, then the feeling of constant danger will also strengthen.

Figure 4: Flashbacks are linked to our thoughts

As the feelings of constant danger increase we may become increasingly scared. It is natural and normal to want to avoid the things that frighten us. We might do this physically by avoiding certain places or certain people; or we might mentally try to avoid the scary memory by distracting ourselves, sometimes in harmful ways such as by self-harming, self-medicating, taking drugs, or drinking alcohol. We do this because avoiding whatever scares us is often our best way of coping with something that is extremely stressful or distressing and can help give us a sense of control. However, these methods can lead to unintended consequences, as we may discover that we have, for example, become addicted to drinking or drugs. Or we may find that we have lost all our friends, as we have stopped going out to meet them, or that we are depressed because we can no longer leave the house.

Another really important unintended consequence of avoiding the painful memories is that we never get the chance to work through them, come to terms with them, and resolve them. So the consequence of this is that we live in a mind that is tortured by the past and we feel unable to heal ourselves.

MEMORY BANKS

How memory works often contributes to our difficulties in dealing with flashbacks and traumatic events. Imagine that memory is like a memory bank and that every new experience we have goes into it, and every time we remember something that also goes back into the memory bank. With a normal memory, when we remember and go back into our memory banks the original memories get updated by what happens after the events occurred. For example, if we had a memory of being in an airplane and being scared about crashing in midair, we might choose never to fly again to avoid those unpleasant feelings. However, because our normal memories are updated (provided the airplane landed safely), we also know and remember that the plane did not crash, and therefore the feelings of being scared about dying are updated by the knowledge that we landed without a problem.

For those of us who have had a traumatic experience, the trauma memory has gone into the memory bank, creating feelings of fear and distress. Whenever we avoid reminders of the trauma (say, by not leaving the house), we are actually failing to create new memories to go into the bank to update the memory that we are now safe and that the traumatic event is over. The same thing happens when we try to distract or mentally avoid thoughts of the trauma. We fail to update the trauma memory in the memory bank, so we never get to remind ourselves that we are now safe. This means that the things that we do to try to cope with the feelings of constant fear and threat may unintentionally actually result in keeping these fearful and threatening feelings going.

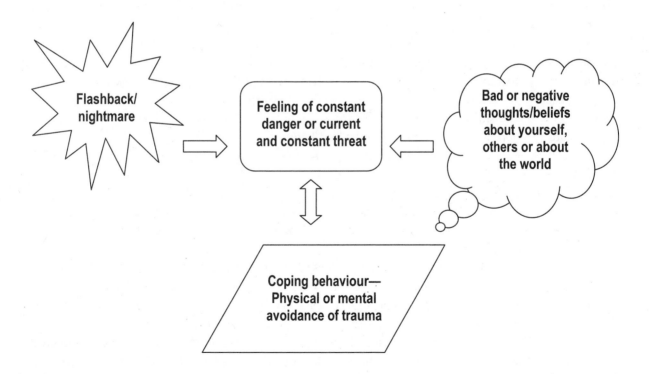

Figure 5: What keeps our flashbacks going?

iderstandable that we seek to avoid these painful memories, but if we don't deal with
they will not go away on their own. This means that we will be caught in a cycle of
iented memories and of using a range of coping strategies that may be self-destructive
vhich actually prevents us from moving on with our lives.

SUMMARY

The reason we have flashbacks is because our original trauma experiences were so frightening and distressing that anything that triggers a reminder of them mobilizes our brains as if they were again in grave and current danger, but they don't establish that the threat they have identified is in the past. Consequently, our brains are unable to process the emotional memories related to our traumatic experiences. Normally, it is when our memories are processed that the memories begin to lose their emotional charge. As a result, the emotional trauma memories remain fragmented and not integrated so they continue to play out in our mind time and time again in a terrifyingly real way.

Perhaps one of the most important things to remember when thinking about how our brains work is how little conscious control we have over our rapidly responding amygdalas. Our brains essentially respond automatically to certain stimuli, which means that we are left to deal with the consequences. These consequences might not be very pleasant, as they are frequently associated with high levels of stress hormones, which make us feel agitated, anxious, and hyperaroused. How we then seek to understand our experiences can lead us to dark places in our minds, places that are filled with self-criticism, self-blame, and strong feelings of shame.

I hope you will be reassured to learn that many of the difficulties you experience are the result of how our brains are designed to deal with threats. Flashbacks that can occur across the whole range of mild to very serious trauma are often the most distressing symptom of trauma and PTSD. Our brains treat flashbacks as a threat, and this means that in addition to the unpleasant and sometimes distressing reexperiencing of the trauma through the flashback, our brains also release adrenalin, which produces fight-or-flight reactions such as a thumping heart and hammering in our ears.

Frequent exposure to the flashbacks and our brains' reactions to this threat such as dissociation may have led us inadvertently into other patterns of behavior that are either negative or destructive to our sense of well-being. As it can be too upsetting to have to relive our traumatic experiences over and over, we may be using avoidance strategies to limit our exposure to the flashbacks. We may avoid the people who love us, hurt ourselves, misuse alcohol or drugs, or feel as if we are always on our guard and looking out for potential danger.

We may not originally have been aware that these behaviors even related to the original traumatic event or that they can contribute to feelings of shame and low self-esteem. I hope now that you will see that some of the behavior that may cause us to feel shame can be viewed as the unintended consequences of our traumatic experiences.

As we learn to respond to ourselves in a compassionate way by following the guided exercises in chapters 6, 7, and 8, we will find ways to calm ourselves down when we experience frightening and upsetting flashbacks. This will also help us to moderate and stop some of the negative behaviors we have adopted to help ourselves avoid the distressing effects of the flashbacks.

4

Understanding shame and self-criticism in relation to traumatic events

We human beings have lots of potential hazards in our world, many of which involve physical threats to us. Lots of traumatic experiences are associated with physical danger—the threat of death or physical harm, such as traffic accidents or physical assaults. The depths of fear we can feel when faced with the possible moment of our death is a truly terrifying prospect that can induce panic and feelings of helplessness. Our brains also detect threats that relate to danger that is not just to do with our physical safety.

The other major threat that we humans are concerned with is what psychologists call *social* threat. This type of threat relates to what we believe other people think of us and what we think of ourselves. Therefore, when we are traumatized, it might not just be our physical safety that has been jeopardized—it may also be that our views of ourselves or other people's views of us have been damaged. Threats can therefore also be a psychological danger to us, that is, a danger to our mental or emotional well-being. This psychological or social threat is highly linked to the experiences of shame, disgust, and humiliation. This means that we may believe that who we are has been contaminated or damaged by our traumatic experiences, or we may fear that other people will think less of us if they were to know what happened to us. Helping us to deal constructively with these types of responses to our trauma and traumatic experiences is very much the focus of this book.

SHAME AND SOCIAL THREAT

To understand how our sense of shame relates to our experiences of social threat, we need to understand how important it is to us as humans that we experience ourselves as being accepted by other people and that we have a sense of belonging. We also need to understand what in our life experiences can contribute to our experiencing a strong sense of shame. Human beings have evolved over millions of years to function best in social groups. Our survival as a prehistoric species was dependent upon our being part of a group; the earth's territory was too harsh for an individual to survive alone. We are a deeply social species, we have an evolved social brain, and we can't survive well as single individuals. Even in modern life our brains are dependent on the relationships that we have with others. For example, our ability to learn to speak is dependent upon speaking with and being spoken to by other people; we would never learn to speak if others never spoke to us. Other people and our relationships with other people touch each and every aspect of our lives. As young babies we learn through our interactions with others, both adults and children. Children are educated in schools where they are grouped together in classes. We work with other people, socialize with other people, and pursue sport and hobbies with other people. Indeed, from the day we are born until the day we die, the support and kindness of other people will have a huge impact on our lives.

Social threat means the sense of being rejected by people who matter to us; this could be family, friends, or even any group of people who matter to us, such as work colleagues, teammates, and the like. The people in our lives who make up various groups become like protective bubbles around us. If we fall outside this protection we can experience the loss of being part of any particular group as a major social threat to our well-being. If we think that other people don't like us or think badly of us, we fear that they may reject us and stop providing care and support or even maltreat us. So the point is that we are biologically set up with a need to feel valued and to be accepted by others, and to feel part of a group with a sense of belonging. It is very often the important relationships within any given group that provides us with our support and helps us to maintain our sense of well-being. If you think about the people in your life, you will recognize many groups such as family, friends, schoolmates, church members, teammates, work colleagues, and so on. When we refer to the group we are referring to the network of people around you who are the significant or the important people in your life. You may also be aware that some groups of people in your life make you feel safer and more secure than others. If we think about what it actually means to feel safe with other people, in part what we're talking about is feeling free of the fear of being judged by them and rejected by them for who we are or for what we may have done.

When we are feeling ashamed, in part, some of our reaction is related to our fear that the group will reject us (be it either some or all of the different groups). A consequence of this fear of criticism or rejection is that we are denied the support and help of the group. The fear of rejection means that we can become scared to talk about the very things that are the cause of our struggles in life because we believe the group will judge that we have done something unacceptable to them. Our fear is that the group may judge and reject us. This is a serious problem for human beings because the group is our support and social network. Rejection by the group (in whatever guise it comes) is probably our greatest social threat because it has the potential to affect both our physical and our psychological well-being.

We can't really escape this evolutionary legacy. Sometimes we may try to convince ourselves that we don't care about what other people think of us. But we do care, and our brains are designed to care because that is what keeps us safe. So there are several important steps of self-discovery we need to be able to take to help us move on from our trauma. We need to discover what our traumatic experiences mean to us, how they challenge our "safe" world and our fears about what other people might really think of us, as well as our fears about how the group will respond to us and our judgments about ourselves.

Beginning to understand and appreciate our social brains is an important step in developing our compassionate minds. Compassion comes from learning to experience the giving and receiving of care which, for many of us, happens initially within our nuclear families growing up and later as part of the various groups of people in our lives.

When we are experiencing shame-based flashbacks, our recovery will be greatly enhanced if we are able to access our compassion. Yet compassion, although a naturally occurring emotional response, does not come naturally to all of us. This is why so many of us will benefit from developing a compassionate mind, where we literally train our minds to think and feel kindly toward ourselves and our traumatic life experiences. This enables us to deal constructively with our fears relating to social threats and our feelings of shame, which may be linked to our traumatic experiences. We will look at some of the ways we can begin to train our minds to be compassionate in chapters 6, 7, and 8. But first, let's explore what we mean when we refer to feelings of shame.

UNDERSTANDING YOUR SHAME

Shame is a blend of lots of different emotions that can be like a toxic cocktail made up of a range of feelings such as anger, anxiety, humiliation, embarrassment, and disgust mixed with all sorts of thoughts and behaviors.

Shame is an emotion about our sense of self (about who we think we are) and how we think that we exist in the minds of other people (i.e., what we believe other people think of us). In other words, shame is about how we *see ourselves* and how we think other people see us. Shame is a normal emotion, experienced by all of us. After all, we all do things that we later regret and think reflect badly on us. Sometimes we can feel socially stigmatized if something has happened in our lives that we think sets us apart from other people—for example, if we have a sexually transmitted disease such as HIV, suffer from depression, or have been sexually abused or raped.

The experience of feeling shame is very much a part of the human condition: all of us experience it to some degree at some point in our lives. However, it can become troublesome when we feel shame but we do not know how to deal with it. We may feel as if we are caught up in an endless cycle of shame that we are unable to turn off. This can often lead us to feel intense emotional stress. Learning to live and deal with our feelings of shame follows the same principles as learning how to deal with our anger, our anxiety, our disgust, or our sadness. These emotional states are part of our human emotional world, and most importantly we feel them for a reason, not because we are "bad" or "flawed" human beings. Difficulties emerge when we don't know what to do with these often intense emotions, and so they can cause psychological mayhem and emotional stress.

Shame related to external threats

We can experience shame when we assume other people think badly of us. How we think other people view us is called *external shame* because it relates to an external threat, something that is happening outside of us and our own minds. When we experience a traumatic event it is very common for us to also experience shame as part of our trauma. Sometimes the focus of our attention and thoughts is on what we believe other people might think and feel about us if they knew about the traumatic things that have happened in our lives. We feel self-conscious and worry about how we exist in the minds of other people.

External shame can arise from being criticized, or feeling looked down upon or negatively judged in some way. For example, when a victim has to talk about an experience of rape, she can have an overwhelming sense of fear about how she will be perceived by other people. In some cultures women who are raped are shunned; and indeed this extreme social stigma can be so terrifying and distressing that some are driven to suicide because of their overwhelming sense of shame. So this fear of how *we exist in the minds of others* and what other people think of us is what we call external shame. This experience of external shame, and the fear of being shamed, is one reason we don't talk about things we feel ashamed about. We have a terror of others looking down on us or wanting to distance themselves from us, perhaps treating us with a sense of disgust, ridicule, or even horror. We are vulnerable to this kind of shame because as a species we depend upon having good relationships with others. To feel valued and supported by others is essential to our sense of "safeness," so to feel devalued or diminished in some way in the minds of others is a major *social threat* to us.

Earlier we talked about social threat meaning being rejected by the group. The people in our lives who make up various groups become like protective bubbles around our lives. If we fall outside this protection, we may experience the loss as a major social threat to our well-being. When we are also prone to feelings of shame, this can feel really threatening.

Shame related to internal threats

The focus of our shame can also be linked to our own personal judgments about how we think and feel about ourselves. We call this *internal shame* because our attention, thoughts, and feelings are coming from our own internal self-judgments. We can tell ourselves that we are useless, inadequate, worthless, inferior, disgusting, bad, and so on. Recent research has even suggested that we can have different types of feelings toward ourselves, which have different effects on us. We can feel angry, irritated, and frustrated with ourselves or we can have feelings of disgust or contempt and self-hatred. Both types of feelings can be detrimental, but feeling that we hate ourselves or that we hold ourselves in contempt is especially damaging to us. This is very important for us to reflect upon because if we are very self-critical and self-hating, then we will be continually stimulating our threat system, which gives rise to our symptoms of trauma such as flashbacks.

So we can see then that shame is a complex experience in many ways. We can have thoughts about ourselves as part of a wider social group and about how other people see us; we can experience ourselves in certain kinds of ways as inadequate, worthless, or bad; and we can have a range of emotions such as anger, anxiety, disgust, and humiliation. We can develop all sorts of behaviors to manage our feelings of shame, and some of them can be quite extreme and even damaging to us, for example, aggressiveness or submissiveness, withdrawal, self-cutting, or drinking.

Let's see if you can get a feel for an experience of shame without going too deeply into it—just to touch the surface and identify personally with the emotions and feelings conjured in us when we feel shame.

Exercise 4.1: Personal exercise—shame

Spend a moment thinking about the kinds of things you feel ashamed about, and when you are ready, take note of:

- Why you feel ashamed about those things

- What you think other people think of you

- How you think about yourself and the kinds of things you say to yourself when you feel ashamed

- The emotions this exercise has generated

- The kinds of behaviors and ways you cope with these thoughts and feelings, which are related to your behaviors

The idea of this exercise is only to touch upon these feelings, not to get too deeply into them or to upset you. This is to help you gain insight into how complex our shame and the feelings and reactions it generates in us can be. It is quite natural for it to be so—this is what shame is.

I have listed below some of the common fears and concerns we have when we have been traumatized and are also feeling ashamed. You may recognize some of your own answers from the exercise above:

Worrying that other people think badly of us or perceive us in a negative light.

Being very self-critical and disapproving of ourselves and thinking that we are not good enough or somehow inadequate.

Feeling different from other people; feeling that there is something fundamentally wrong with us.

Believing that we do not deserve love, kindness, and care, or for good things to happen to us.

Feeling intense anxiety when we think that other people might find out about what happened to us.

Thinking that we are to blame and deserve the traumatic and distressing events that happen to us.

Believing that if people knew what happened to us they would judge us and think us weak, disgusting, damaged, or soiled in some way.

Believing that we should have behaved differently during traumatic events.

Believing that we are weak and pathetic for not being able to "get over" the events and get on with our lives.

HOW DO YOU TRY TO PROTECT YOURSELF FROM YOUR FEAR OF OTHER PEOPLE?

We know from research that there are three main ways we might behave when we have fears about other people. These are outlined below.

Attack

We might decide that "attack is the best form of defense" and therefore engage in behavior that attacks other people (before they attack us). This may involve making ourselves unlikeable by being rude, aggressive, or unfriendly toward people who make attempts to befriend us.

• *James's story*

James, a veteran from the Gulf War, used this strategy a lot to cope with his feelings of shame relating to his combat experiences. His strategy was becoming very problematic for him, as he had been caught up in a number of fights with members of the unsuspecting public, and his relationships with his wife and children were in tatters due to his aggressive and violent outbursts.

Submit

Within our relationships we may adopt a role in which we always submit to the demands of others and ensure that we appease them. This can very often happen even where other people's demands are unreasonable. We find ourselves doing anything to ensure that we don't upset anyone or aggravate them in any way.

• *Amanda's story*

Amanda came to the clinic several years ago, and at the time she was struggling to come to terms with a violent rape. This was to avoid having people get upset or aggravated with her, which she found triggered her feelings of shame. She was terrified of upsetting or being confrontational with people. She found it easier to submit to people's demands of her. Over time this made her feel cross with herself for being what she thought of as "weak."

Hide

We may hide from other people. We may simply refuse to form friendships and decline and rebut any attempts by other people to engage with us. We may remain aloof and always unavailable if invitations are extended to us. This enables us to avoid entering any sort of relationship and risk being harmed. We become a "loner."

•   *Anna's story*

Anna, an intensive care nurse, used this strategy to manage her feelings of threat and shame. In spite of the fact that she was terribly lonely, depressed, and sad, she just felt too scared of what others would think of her for having been sexually abused as a child to be able to extend her hand of friendship and step into the social world.

So you can see that the types of behavior described above are designed to keep us safe either from the attack of or rejection by other people.

TRAUMA AND YOUR SELF-IDENTITY

The ways in which we come to think about ourselves can be very strongly linked to the existence of any powerful or traumatic events in our lives. For example, children who have been called stupid, useless, or worthless can incorporate these views and believe this of themselves as adults, even where there is evidence to the contrary. It's not uncommon for people who have been physically and/or sexually abused to believe there is something wrong or inadequate about themselves. But even isolated events can have a profound effect on our sense of self.

•   *Jane's story*

Jane was a good runner. One day when she was about eleven and feeling very good that she had won a race at the annual sports day, she heard a new teacher comment to her gym teacher, "It's no surprise she's a good runner with that big nose of hers." Probably the comment wasn't meant to be overheard, but from that day onward Jane believed her nose made her look ugly. This event deeply affected her sense of self.

This example illustrates how powerfully our sense of self can be affected by our life experiences.
How we behave when we experience a traumatic event can also powerfully affect our sense of self. For instance, we might think of ourselves as able to cope relatively well and to be fearless, and then during a traumatic experience we discover that we become paralyzed with fear and cannot cope as we expected. This can have a profound effect on how we think about ourselves as individuals. So the traumas in our life can affect how we view ourselves when we are in the habit of judging ourselves in a negative way. Sometimes our traumatic experiences confirm our fears about who we think we are: "I am bad, so I deserve bad things to happen to me." Sometimes our traumatic events shatter our beliefs about who we think we are: "I can't believe I was mugged. I thought I was invincible."

SHAME AND YOUR TRAUMATIC EXPERIENCES

Lots of us feel ashamed about our traumatic experiences. We can feel ashamed about who we are, what we have been through, what the experiences make us feel like inside, and what we believe other people would think of us if they knew what had happened. We can also feel ashamed about how we are coping, for example, if we find ourselves becoming irritable and angry with loved ones or anxious or depressed, or if we find ourselves avoiding our friends and family.

I frequently observe at the trauma clinic that many people who have lived through traumatic experiences also experience very difficult and distressing feelings of shame, which seem to relate to their traumatic experiences. They feel very ashamed and somehow "damaged" or "contaminated." They struggle with internal shame and have very self-critical thoughts and often describe having voices inside their heads that says things like "You are worthless, bad, dirty, and disgusting" and "If other people knew what you were really like and what happened to you, they wouldn't want to know you, because they'd think you are disgusting."

Others feel inadequate and inferior because they don't seem to be able to get over their trauma. People involved in a severe car accident or who have had very traumatic operations in the hospital can have repeated flashbacks and nightmares leading to depression, anxiety, and irritation. They can have feelings of being out of control and having been changed as a person, which can in itself be traumatic and distressing. They may compare themselves with others and think that they are coping poorly and this is to do with a weakness or some flaw in themselves. Troops who have been in a combat zone can feel guilty and suffer sorrow and remorse because of the things they have seen or have had to do. Similarly EMTs (emergency medical technicians), police, and firefighters can be traumatized by what they have witnessed in the course of their jobs, either accidents or the violence of others.

You are by no means alone if you recognize these thoughts and feelings in yourself. Yet one of the sad things is that we can become so terrified and scared of telling other people what we have been through for fear of being judged that we don't experience the care, understanding, and compassion that other people can offer us in our suffering.

Our feelings of shame can keep us separate and apart from people who could offer us connection and comfort in our times of need. It's also crucial to recognize that our own self-criticism can keep us separate from the parts of ourselves that can be understanding, supportive, kind, and compassionate. We can renounce or ignore these parts of ourselves because we feel we don't deserve them or because our self-critical voices are so strong. Compassion-focused therapy teaches us to be helpful, supportive, and encouraging toward ourselves, which can actually help us to heal. So, just as understanding, care, and validation by other people can help us with our external shame, so can developing understanding, caring, and validation toward ourselves help us with our internal shame.

Case studies

I describe two people below who feel ashamed of what happened to them to help you begin to understand how our minds react to traumatic events.

• *Martin's story*

The first is Martin (whom we met in chapter 3), who was suffering from PTSD and was troubled by profound feelings of shame.

Martin was a traffic police officer who had been involved in many traumatic incidents throughout his career. He had recently been very affected by a distressing event where he and his female colleague were assaulted. This life-threatening and terrifying incident had left him anxious, depressed, and lacking in confidence. But he was also troubled by other distressing thoughts that made him feel very ashamed of himself. These thoughts seemed to relate to how Martin thought he had behaved during the assault. Martin admitted that he was terrified he was going to die and was worried that he did not do enough to protect his colleague. His colleague was more seriously injured as a result of the attack and spent some months rehabilitating from her physical injuries. Martin was also injured but his physical recovery was quicker.

Following the assault, Martin felt hounded by flashbacks and memories, and every time he thought about the event he began to feel very ashamed of himself. So he needed to recognize how the feelings of the self in the present moment—that is, of shame—have become linked with the memory of the past. He was very concerned about what his colleagues would think of him and how he behaved during the incident. He was ashamed because he was given a leave of absence from work because of his symptoms of depression and PTSD, when his colleague, who was more seriously injured, had returned successfully to work some months previously. Martin just did not seem to be able to turn off the self-critical voices in his head that were constantly telling him, "You're weak and pathetic; look at the state of you" and "Can't you just get a grip and get on with things?"

What seemed to make things worse for Martin was that he never expected to feel like this. He'd always prided himself on his ability to cope with things that his work and personal life threw at him. So he had been caught unaware by this assault, and facing possible death had understandably seriously distressed him. Yet he thought he ought to have been able to cope with this serious threat, and the fact that he was struggling made him feel ashamed and very self-critical.

Where did Martin's shame originate? This was a question he would repeatedly ask himself during sessions. He couldn't understand why he felt the way he did about himself and he would often say, "I had a nice, normal childhood. I had a mom and dad who are still together and a brother who I get along with. Nothing bad ever happened in my childhood. It was really routine."

Of course, Martin is right about his childhood in the sense that nothing "bad" happened. The skills to give children the best opportunity of growing up liking, loving, and accepting who they are and having the ability to make themselves feel better when things in life are not going well need to be demonstrated, taught, and nurtured in us by loving and compassionate adults. One of the key abilities we all need as humans when dealing with threats in our world is an ability to be able to make ourselves feel emotionally and physically safe again. That requires us to be able to draw on what we learned in childhood about how to self-soothe. Here lies the answer to Martin's question about why he felt so bad.

Through no fault of his own, Martin and his brother grew up to believe that it was not good to feel frightened, anxious, upset, and angry, and found that the best way to deal with these feelings was to ignore them and adopt a stiff upper lip. Martin was brought up to believe that men don't cry and can cope with everything. Many of us reading this book will recognize this set of family beliefs and may even have been taught them ourselves.

The problem for Martin was that no one taught him how to feel better about himself when he was tearful, frightened, or angry, which are of course natural, normal human emotions. When Martin felt like this he thought there must be something wrong with him and that it was because of his failings as a human being that he was not strong enough to cope. So we can see why Martin began to feel ashamed of himself and couldn't self-soothe to make himself feel okay about things.

• *Amanda's story*

Amanda's case study is a useful example for those of us who identify with the actual trauma, but it also demonstrates how our backgrounds can set us up for self-blaming, self-loathing, and other shame-related emotions.

Amanda (whom we met earlier in this chapter) described herself as living in a tortured mind. In fact she said her life was "a living hell" and that she often wished that her attacker had killed her on the night of the rape rather than leaving her to suffer such mental torture. There had not been a day or night since the attack when Amanda had been free from flashbacks, images, smells, and sounds that took her right back to the rape. When Amanda revisited memories of the event in her mind, she felt dirty and disgusting. (Remember how we talked in chapter 3 about emotional and body memory?)

For Amanda, the feelings of disgust that would have been there at the time of the rape somehow got caught up with a sense of herself, leaving her unable to distinguish between a memory of disgust and feeling herself to be disgusting. Furthermore, Amanda strongly believed that she had somehow invited the rape and that it was her fault. The consequences of her self-blame were twofold. Not only did Amanda believe that she did not really deserve any help—"How can I ask for help when I brought this on myself and deserved what happened?"—but also that she could not report the rape to the police—"I can't go to the police because it's my fault and I feel too ashamed to tell them what happened, as they will judge me and tell me I've only got myself to blame."

In the sessions, Amanda would say:

What he did to me was so disgusting, it makes me feel that I must be disgusting too. I can't bear to tell anyone what happened to me because I feel so embarrassed and ashamed. I know people say they won't judge me, but I don't believe that, and I think they will think badly of me and not want to know me. They only say they won't judge me to make me feel better, but I know what people are like and what they think. Besides, I don't deserve to be helped because I am a worthless piece of nothing and I've brought this on myself. Sometimes I feel that I was just born this way and that I don't really belong or deserve a place in the world because I'm so toxic and I make people feel horrible. Sometimes I just detest myself and I just want to die. I don't deserve your help either. I know you're just being nice to me because it is your job and you are being paid to do this. In fact, sometimes I feel really irritable and angry when you are nice to me or try to reassure me. It makes me feel worse because you don't know what I'm really like, and if you did, you would probably change your opinion of me and would not want to help me.

Amanda's thoughts are not uncommon in men and women who have been raped. Amanda was in no way to blame for this violent attack. The blame rested 100 percent with the attacker, and yet because of how Amanda was thinking about herself and the attack she couldn't see this, and consequently struggled with overwhelming feelings of shame and self-blame.

So why would Amanda take this self-blaming approach to the rape? Is there something in her background that makes her particularly vulnerable to having difficulties in distinguishing between what other people do and what she experiences as feelings toward herself?

Our histories can make us vulnerable to turning the feelings of disgust we have toward somebody else inward on ourselves so that we end up feeling self-disgust, even when it is not our fault. Amanda was thirty-two years old, and, sadly, as a child she had been sexually abused by a family friend. This experience of inappropriate sexual contact had left her hurt, confused, ashamed, and frightened both as a child and then later as an adult. Even as a child she remembered feeling that somehow she must be responsible for her abuse. That was certainly what the man who abused her would make her feel, as he would say, "You make me do this to you and if you tell anyone they won't believe you." So for years, and until therapy, Amanda didn't tell anyone and carried the secret with her in the belief that she must be an awful person to have wanted this to happen and that what happened to her was deeply shameful. As she grew older, her self-belief and confidence suffered. She always struggled to like herself or to believe that she was deserving of good things. She was also often preoccupied and concerned with what other people thought of her. She would frequently think that other people were being kind to her only because they felt sorry for her. She never told any of her friends or family about what happened to her because she thought that they would blame her and be angry with her.

Amanda developed all sorts of ways to help her cope with her feelings of anxiety and shame. As a teenager, she found relief by cutting herself with a razor blade on her arms and legs. This was a secret and, in Amanda's view, shameful habit that she carried into adulthood. Amanda also used alcohol to help her cope with intense and painful memories from her childhood, and her use of alcohol increased after she was raped. She found that alcohol was a quick and effective way to "anesthetize" her feelings and so lessen the intensity of the distress she felt.

Given all that Amanda went through as a child, it begins to make more sense why she would think she deserved to be raped and that it was her fault. Whenever Amanda had a flashback to the rape, she experienced a very strong sense of shame about the abuse and the rape, despite neither being her fault.

However, that said, it is a sad fact that many women and men blame themselves for being raped and have not suffered childhood abuse. As most rapes are committed by people known to the victim, and whom they might even be close to, it is easy to see why they might question their role in the attack or whether they somehow sent out the wrong message about sexual intercourse. So even though rape is a serious crime, this can lead to their not reporting it to the police for fear that somehow they have brought it upon themselves.

Amanda is by no means alone in her suffering. What we often observe in people at the clinic who really struggle with self-criticism and shame is that the origins of their self-critical thinking styles and emotional states can be traced back to key childhood experiences. Such experiences have often affected them in a profound way and left them with a legacy of self-hatred through no fault of their own.

Yet sometimes, for some of us, it's not obvious why we blame ourselves so much. We may well not have been abused, beaten, or sexually violated as a child, nor do we have a skeleton in the closet that would help us understand why we don't like ourselves and why we blame ourselves so destructively for the things in our lives. In fact, we often say that the fact we have no obvious reason to help us understand the extent of our self-loathing is in itself even more shaming for us. This is because we feel that we shouldn't feel as bad as we do and we ought to be grateful for the childhood experiences we had. People often say things like, "I have no right to feel like this; it's self-indulgent and self-pitying and it just makes me hate myself even more."

We will explore these key issues about childhood and parental experiences further in chapter 5.

HOW YOU AVOID YOUR SHAME

Sometimes we can become very skilled at hiding how ashamed we feel from ourselves and from others. Those of us who know the pain and distress associated with shame will understand all too well the extremes we will go to for relief from this tortured state of mind. Yet some of the behaviors we engage in to help us escape our tortured minds can in themselves become the source of further shame. We then become caught in a vicious cycle of shame and self-attack. We are ashamed of who we are and what we have been through, and ashamed of the strategies that we use to cope with our feelings.

Things we might do to help us cope:

- Avoid people who either remind us of a part of our life we are trying to forget or who ask probing questions that make us have to think about the things we want to forget.

- Be aggressive and irritable with people we care about, perhaps in an attempt to keep them at arm's length and thus protect ourselves from being "found out."

- Deliberately self-harm by perhaps cutting ourselves or making ourselves sick.

- Misuse or abuse alcohol or drugs.

- Engage in casual sex.

This is by no means an exhaustive list, and we may have found other ways to help us deal with these distressing experiences. However, many of the things we do are to help us *avoid* our pain. It is important to understand that when we try to avoid or turn away from our painful experiences and feelings, the very act of avoiding our memories can make it much worse for us.

For example, we may not admit to ourselves that we drink too much to take our minds off our pain. Some types of self-harming behavior—such as cutting ourselves or making ourselves sick—we may do in secret and therefore not even admit to ourselves that the behavior is causing us any harm or is even related to the things in our lives that we are struggling with.

• *Martin's story*

Martin felt so ashamed of how he behaved during his life-threatening event that he could not go back to work. His strategy to cope with his strong feelings of external shame was to avoid them by withdrawing and drinking too much. He was terrified of going back to work because he believed his work colleagues would think he was weak and pathetic. The unintended consequences of this strategy for Martin were that he became more isolated and depressed over time. Martin coped with his internal feelings of shame and self-loathing by using alcohol to numb his feelings.

•   *Amanda's story*

Amanda used to self-harm and drink too much alcohol. She felt desperately ashamed of herself after she was raped. Her mind was full of horrible thoughts about the event, and she would constantly say to herself that she was a terrible and despicable person. She found relief from her internal shame when she cut herself or got drunk, but then afterward she just felt more ashamed for that behavior. She was trapped in a painful circle of despair. Amanda was terrified that people would find out about what had happened to her and the ways she had found to help her cope. She managed her external shame by withdrawing and distancing herself from her friends so that they would not know what was going on.

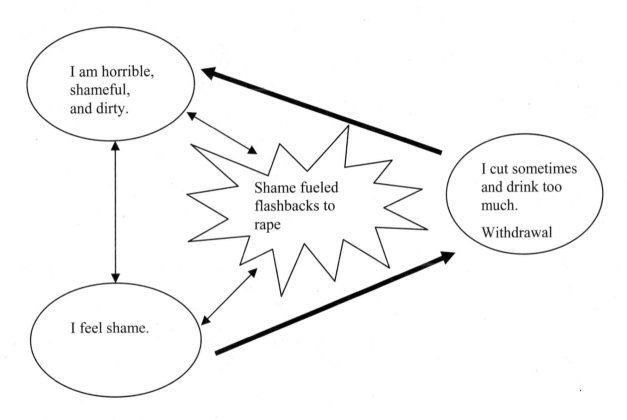

Figure 6: Amanda's maintenance cycle

Some of the things we do to help us cope may lead to a temporary release from our difficulties and feelings of shame. Eventually, however, the very things we did to help us forget become part of the list of things in our lives that we feel ashamed of. We may even feel ashamed of our avoidance tactics, of our drinking and cutting behavior, and become even more self-critical and blaming of ourselves. This in turn can fuel a belief that we deserve to be punished and that we are not worthy of help. So the consequences of our best efforts to make ourselves feel better often make us feel worse and thus increase the likelihood that we will carry on engaging in those same self-destructive behaviors.

Compassion-focused therapy can help us to develop feelings of compassion and empowerment toward ourselves so that we are able to face these feelings of shame and our self-destructive behavior.

SELF-CRITICISM AND SHAME

Why is it that some of us are particularly prone to feelings of shame and self-criticism? Perhaps if we have past experiences (possibly from childhood) of other people treating us in a hostile or rejecting way, it can make us particularly sensitive to feelings of shame. For example, some of us may remember adults in our lives who have criticized us a lot, who put us down, or who repeatedly said unkind things to us. We may have been bullied at school by our peers or even at home by a family member. When we think back to these occasions we may remember that awful sensation of not feeling wanted, loved, or being good enough.

Even as adults we remember the cruel and unkind things people said and did to us as children. We may also believe them to be true and that we deserved to be treated like that. When as adults we are being self-critical we often say the same hostile things to ourselves that other people have said to us previously. It may even sound like a conversation in our own minds, but the conversation is a bullying, horrible one.

• *Amanda's story*

Amanda used to say to herself, "You are horrible. Who do you think you are? You don't deserve good things to happen to you. No one likes you. Why don't you do yourself a favor and disappear?" Over the course of therapy Amanda began to realize that these were the same words that her abuser had said to her as he sexually violated her.

How we learn to deal with our emotions and our feelings of shame and self-criticism is powerfully influenced by our upbringing. Our parents, or those who are responsible for our care in childhood, teach us to react and respond to our childhood experiences. They regulate our exposure to threat when we are children, and this then becomes a template for how we manage threats in our adult lives. If we had poor experiences of being loved and cared for by our parents and were neglected or abused by them (or by the caregivers who were meant to love and protect us), then this key ability to bring negative feelings to an end is going to be underdeveloped so that we struggle to deal with our feelings of shame and being self-critical and find it hard to bring these feelings to an end.

Some of us, through no fault of our own, are unable to deal with shameful feelings in a helpful way despite shame being a normal emotion. We struggle to overcome these feelings, and so we live in a downward spiral of being critical of ourselves and having unending feelings of shame.

It is therefore really important that we are able to regulate our feelings of shame and self-criticism so that we do not live in a cycle of self-criticism and shame. One way to do this is to be able to talk to ourselves in a way that is supportive, caring, kind, and compassionate. Using our compassionate minds will enhance our ability to deal with feelings of shame and self-critical thoughts in a way that will promote our mental and emotional well-being and improve our sense of belonging.

One of the key tasks of this book is to help us face the fear of what we believe others think of us and what we think of ourselves by helping us to develop a new supportive and compassionate way of communicating with, and thinking about, ourselves. We all need to be able to self-soothe when something happens that makes our emotions feel overwhelming. By being compassionate toward ourselves, our brains will release chemicals that actually make us feel positive and safe (such as oxytocin and opiates).

DEALING WITH SHAME-FILLED TRAUMA MEMORIES

One of the challenges of dealing with shame-filled memories is for us to learn to be able to apply feelings of care and warmth toward ourselves—these techniques will help us update the memories so that things that happened in the past to cause us to feel shame can begin to lose their emotional charge. This way we are learning to deal with our memories so that the threatening potency is reduced and we learn to switch off feelings such as shame, anger, and disgust. Sadly, one of the great difficulties for us if we feel lots of shame is that we can really struggle to be kind and caring to ourselves, often because we might feel undeserving of any care and comfort. Being kind to ourselves and/or accepting kindness from others can even make us feel anxious and threatened.

When being kind to yourself makes you feel anxious or threatened

Some of us just don't feel we deserve kindness from ourselves or other people. This belief may stem from our childhood experiences. Our memories of how the people who should have been caregiving treated us may actually make us feel anxious rather than soothed. For example, if a child seeks comfort from his or her parent when he or she is upset, but the parent behaves in a way that rejects the child or hurts him or her, the self-protective brain will associate the child's need for comfort with the rejecting behavior of the parent and categorize the need for comfort as a psychological threat. This means that the next time something happens to upset the child, the brain will remind him or her that when he or she sought comfort he or she was punished or pushed away. And so immediately the feelings of wanting to be soothed will be shut down as the child backs away from pursuing this because of the feelings of anxiety about further rejection or pain. Some of us are literally terrified of being kind to ourselves in case it makes us vulnerable to more hurt. Some people may even have thoughts such as "Don't let your guard down or you'll get hurt" or "You deserve to suffer." In trying to protect ourselves from expressing emotions that could get us into trouble we may actually end up not really understanding our emotions, which again makes it harder for us to deal constructively with them. So being compassionate and caring is not only alien, it can feel very frightening to some of us. None of this, of course, is our fault and we hope that by learning to understand ourselves and our emotions we will also be able to learn to cope with them.

SUMMARY

Shame is a complex mixture of unpleasant emotions that relate to how we view our self and how we think the world views us. Social threat can feel particularly threatening to us when we are living with shame. Shame is also commonly associated with our trauma and the flashbacks we experience.

One of the critical aspects in understanding our life stories is to appreciate the link between our experience of shame and our own self-protection strategies. The brain has evolved so that it ranks self-protection higher than happiness. Anything it interprets as a threat sends our bodies and their systems into high alert. Many of the symptoms associated with traumatic experience are viewed by our brains as threats. In order to help keep our "self" safe, our brains persistently send us into the fight, flight, submit, or freeze response, and we may have been living our lives on a high-alert status because of this.

In addition, if our traumatic flashbacks trigger feelings of shame—either because of the nature of the traumatic event or because of earlier life experiences—the very experience of shame will also be viewed as a threat by our brains, and so this too sends us back into a state of high alert. This can feel like an unending cycle.

Understandably, in trying to cope with all of this we may have formed a habit of acting in a self-harmful way and be engaging in behaviors that serve only to help us forget.

By understanding these aspects of yourself, I hope that you now recognize that these things are not your fault. By learning to feel compassionately about yourself and your life experiences, perhaps you can begin to soothe the negative effects of everything you have been struggling with. Having a compassionate mind and directing it toward yourself is not a magical quick fix, and so it will take time and practice to experience a change in your life. Most importantly, by reading this far in the book, you are already making good progress on your journey of compassion.

5

Understanding your need for compassion in your life

To summarize the journey so far, in chapter 1 we explored the nature of our trauma and some of the traumatic experiences we may have encountered. We also looked at the potential effects these experiences can have on our mental, emotional, and physical well-being. We learned about flashbacks being the key symptom of PTSD and trauma, and we explored how trauma can disrupt our ability to process our traumatic experiences and interfere with how we record our memories.

Chapter 2 explored the different kinds of emotions we have that are designed to do different things. Being able to feel a range of emotions is both natural to us as human beings and important because it gives richness and depth to our life experiences. However, sometimes our emotions become very difficult to tolerate and manage because they are so powerful and fuse with our memories from the past. When that happens, both our internal worlds (our inner experiences of our emotions and how we feel about ourselves) and our external worlds (whether we feel safe or not in the outside world) can become frightening places. Through no fault of our own we can feel overwhelmed and as if our feelings, emotions, and lives are out of our control. However, learning to find a way to end these intense emotional experiences can help us move on with our lives.

In chapter 3 we looked at flashbacks in more detail and how they can feel threatening to us both physically and emotionally. When our memories of threatening events are triggered, it can feel as if they are happening to us all over again. Our threat-detecting brains identify a flashback as being threatening and can result in our living in a state of high alert. In chapter 4, we explored the link between feelings of shame, traumatic experiences, and behaviors that we develop (some of which are self-destructive) to try to cope with our overwhelming traumatic and shameful experiences. Most importantly, we learned that none of this is our fault because this is how the brain operates under these conditions, and the reason it does this is partly linked to the way it's been designed.

As we have explored in previous chapters, although our brains can go into overdrive (when we feel threatened by memories of our traumatic experiences) and our emotions can feel overwhelming, the good news is that we can also learn how to stand back from our unpleasant feelings, understand them, and learn to resolve them and make ourselves feel better. We can actually learn new skills for working with our emotions, which will help us to deal with our traumatic experiences. It is this ability to soothe and calm ourselves (by being compassionate toward ourselves) that is particularly helpful in dealing with our feelings of shame, disgust, fear, and anger. Through no fault of our own, these abilities may be underdeveloped and consequently may be hindering our recovery from trauma (which we explore later in this chapter).

We can turn our minds to compassion, a mind-set that can help us enormously with our trauma.

THE COMPASSIONATE MIND

What is compassion?

Over thousands of years, the fields of philosophy, religion, and psychology have explored the concept of compassion and the need for us to live with compassion. For instance, Aristotle wrote that in order to be compassionate we first need to notice the distress in others and believe their suffering to be justified. So we can't feel compassion if we don't believe in the cause of the distress. Buddhism defines compassion as openness to the suffering of ourselves and others, and being committed to and motivated in trying to reduce and alleviate that suffering. In other words, being compassionate means we want to do something to bring an end to our pain or the pain of others. The meaning of *compassion* as we use it in this book is based on Buddhist teachings; scientific thinking and evidence about how our minds have evolved to work and process suffering; and the work of Professor Paul Gilbert (author of *The Compassionate Mind*; see the resources section at the end of this book).

THREAT-FOCUSED MIND, TRAUMATIZED MIND, AND COMPASSIONATE MIND

We know from previous chapters that when we are traumatized we have a threat-focused mind. One of the reasons that we develop PTSD is because we struggle to regulate or calm our threat-focused minds, so we live in a state of "current threat." The good news is that we are able to alter our states of mind and switch into different frames of mind. Therefore we can also be in a compassion-focused state of mind, where we look at the world with thoughts of compassion, caregiving, kindness, courage, and action.

We have all known what it is like to be in different states of mind—being calm or angry, excited or frustrated. An overall state of mind can be called a mind-set, and the type of mind-set we are in will affect how our minds work and will orchestrate a whole pattern of effects. It will direct our attention; focus how we think and our urges to behave in certain ways; texture our emotions; and influence our motivations and dreams or worries.

Let's take a look at the key characteristics of the two most important mind-sets necessary for understanding and healing our trauma. The first one we will look at we already know very well, the threat-focused mind-set, and the other is one that we are going to get to know very well and that can help us to heal, the compassion-focused mind-set.

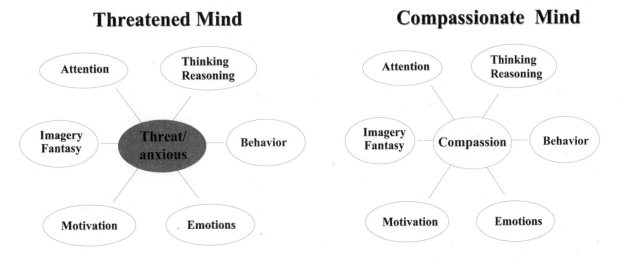

Figure 5.1: Two types of mind

Source: Adapted with permission from P. Gilbert, *The Compassionate Mind* (London: Constable & Robinson, 2009)

We will explore these concepts of different types of mind-sets because they are integral to developing the compassionate mind.

The threat-focused mind

Imagine that we are about to take a driving test. This kind of event is naturally likely to activate our threat systems because we could potentially fail the test. Remember, our threat systems are easy to activate because they are there to help us detect and respond quickly to threats or avoid them. So even before the test we will notice our threatened minds are working for us—and we may notice that we have started to feel anxious and to think anxious thoughts. Let's look at this pattern by working our way around the circle in figure 5.1.

MOTIVATION

What are the basic desires, wants, and wishes of the anxious mind? Perhaps in the moment of intense anxiety, the behavioral urge may be to run away and avoid the situation that is making us nervous and to do so as quickly as possible. We are motivated to reduce that anxiety and any potential threat as soon as possible—that is the way our brains are built. Consequently, how we respond when we are feeling very anxious is not our fault. Afterward, when we feel calmer, we may notice the focus of our attention shifts.

We may feel sad, for instance, because we've missed an opportunity, and then some of us may start to "beat ourselves up" for running away.

ATTENTION

In an anxious pattern, what are the things we attend to and focus on? We may well be focusing on what the driving examiner will be like. Will he or she be kind and forgiving or harsh and strict? We might have intrusive images or thoughts about crashing the car or knocking someone over.

THINKING/REASONING

not helpful is and not being positive

Are we imagining how well we will do? Focusing on how good an impression we will make? How skillful we will be? If we're anxious, that kind of thinking is unlikely, and we will probably be imagining that we might shake as we change gears or be too anxious to drive properly. We might worry that the examiner may think we are not in control. So our thinking and reasoning are focused on the possible threats in the situation.

IMAGERY/FANTASY

The imagined worlds we create in our minds are linked to where we are directing our attention. When we become anxious we can have fleeting images of memories of previous anxiety or premonitions of future threats. For example, if we are anxious about making a speech we might create a picture in our minds of us mumbling, forgetting the words, and going bright red in the face. We might see the audience laughing at us.

BEHAVIOR

How do we behave? Although we may really want to pass the test because of the benefits of freedom and independence, another part of us would rather not have to face the test itself and would prefer to avoid going to it. We could convince ourselves that we are not ready and cancel the test or not show up. When our anxious mind-sets are running the show, they can fill us with strong urges to run away or avoid things.

EMOTIONS

Sometimes we not only feel anxiety (maybe things would be simpler if we did), but we can also have mixed emotions of both wanting to do things and being frightened to do them. This is referred to as "the approach–avoidance" dilemma by psychologists. Our positive desires to fulfill our personal goals are pulling against the protective ones of avoiding the risk of failure. Ironically, sometimes the more we want something, the more anxious we often are because it's meaningful to us and there's more to lose.

Sometimes when we are anxious about things we would like to do, we can get angry with ourselves for feeling this way because we feel it's holding us back, and annoyed or disappointed with ourselves for not acting in the manner we wanted to in certain situations. Exhausting, isn't it? Perhaps you can begin to see how increasing stimulation to the threat system by becoming angry in situations where we are already feeling anxious is not likely to help us feel calm or soothed.

The traumatized mind

The traumatized mind is very much in the threat mind-set, so what would this look like?

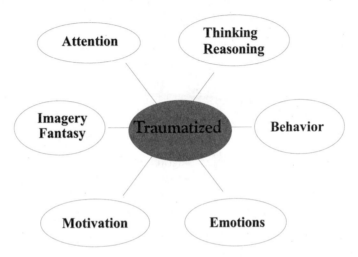

Figure 5.2: The traumatized mind

Source: Adapted with permission from P. Gilbert, *The Compassionate Mind* (London: Constable & Robinson, 2009)

We are able to think about the pattern of the traumatized mind by looking at the following example. It may be helpful to reread chapter 2 to remind yourself what happens in our brains when we are traumatized.

• *Jeff's story*

Jeff was caught up in the London subway bombings—he was a passenger on one of the trains when the bomb was detonated. He felt the force of the bomb, was injured, and was rescued by firefighters. At the time of the blast Jeff's brain became very threat focused because his life was in danger. He felt intense fear. His thinking was rapid and threat focused because he was trying to work out how to survive. This was an overwhelming experience for him and his amygdala. In the days and weeks after the bombing, his brain tried to make sense of the experience, but every time Jeff's mind flashed back to the event, he was overwhelmed with intense feelings of fear again. His brain responded to the images and memories (flashbacks) as if he were in real and present danger and so released lots of the threat-focused hormones such as cortisol and adrenaline. These hormones "anesthetized" Jeff's hippocampus and blocked access to the thinking part of the brain, where there is sense, meaning, context, and self-soothing. Put simply, Jeff's experience of the flashbacks was that he was back at the traumatic event rather than simply remembering it, so he then became trapped in a mind that was reliving the horror of the bombing with all of its intensity and without any of the relief of knowing that the horrors belonged to an event in the past. His mind-set during these terrifying flashbacks was threat based, which meant a whole host of other reactions were orchestrated at the same time, namely, that his attention, thoughts, feelings, behavior, motivation, and images all became threat focused too. (We give examples of how these reactions were effected below.) These reactions all served to fuel, reinforce, and maintain his threatened state because he was being frightened by his own mind.

Let's look at this pattern by working our way around the circle in figure 5.2.

TRAUMATIZED MIND FOCUS

Motivation

At the moment the bomb exploded, Jeff's heightened threat-focused mind was motivated to survive at all costs. Jeff had strong automatic desires to run as far away as he could and escape the danger. This overwhelming urge was not Jeff's fault; it was the automatic reaction of his threat-focused brain, which was beyond his conscious control. The trouble began for Jeff when his mind calmed down. Then he could not understand why he had turned his back on people who still needed his help and run away. This made him feel dreadful about himself (internal threat) and made him think that other people would think badly of him (external threat).

Attention

When we are traumatized our attention becomes extremely threat focused. We can therefore become very vigilant to what we perceive as danger. In Jeff's case, as a result of the bombing and his threat mind-set, he became very focused on young men who appeared to be Muslim, carrying rucksacks. He would also scan his environment looking for signs of bombs (i.e., any suspicious package or bag).

Thinking/Reasoning

Jeff's thinking and reasoning was very focused on how much danger he was in. He would consider all the possible harm he could come to outside his home and would think about how unsafe the London Underground was. Jeff would think about how terrifying it was to face his own death and would mull over the fact that he should have known that something bad was going to happen. He would dwell on how he behaved after the blast and would worry that he did not do enough to help the injured. Jeff thought that he should be stronger and get over this, and he would criticize himself for being "weak" and for "not coping." Jeff would worry about what other people would think of him if they knew how "selfish" he had been in the aftermath of the blast, when he did not help other injured passengers.

Imagery/Fantasy

The imagined worlds we create in our minds are linked to attention. In Jeff's case, his images were linked to intrusions and flashbacks of the bombing. Rather than the focus being on future threats, Jeff's mind was filled with images of a past threat! These powerful memories had the capacity to "trick" Jeff's brain into acting as if he were in actual danger, which is why people who are traumatized get a sense of "current threat" linked to events that are clearly over. The images keep their minds trapped in the past.

Behavior

avoidance

After the blast, Jeff didn't return to using the London subway. He just couldn't face the risk that the bombing could happen again. He even avoided walking in the vicinity of the subway stations because they made him feel too anxious. But that still wasn't enough to stop his remembering his horror, so Jeff stopped watching television or reading the papers in case something reminded him of the events. He became very avoidant of young men who seemed to him to be of Muslim appearance, having learned after the fact that four young men of Pakistani and Jamaican descent had perpetrated the bombings. This was very problematic for him, as he lived and worked in multicultural London. In fact, he soon began not leaving the house at all, as that was the only place he felt safe. His alcohol use increased, and he began to drink several cans of beer a night to help switch his mind off from the stream of thoughts and images.

Emotions

Jeff felt beholden to a whole host of threat-based emotions. He frequently felt intense fear as he relived the memories of that day. His flashbacks made him experience the same emotions he felt at the time of the blast—utter terror and helplessness. Jeff would then start to feel angry with himself for not being able to get over it. He would start to criticize himself for his mental and emotional weakness. This would, in turn, make him very angry with himself, but then he would start to feel angry with the bombers too. So the more anxious and scared Jeff felt, the angrier with himself he would become, which, of course, just fueled his threat system even more. To add to his distress, Jeff also felt guilty and ashamed. He felt guilty that he did not do enough to help the injured and this, in turn, made him feel inadequate and shameful. He feared that others would look at him with disappointment and sadness if they knew how he had reacted during the aftermath of the explosion.

How mind-sets fit together

Our threatened mind-set and our traumatized mind-set both draw on different aspects of our minds to create a pattern, and these different aspects are all interlinked. The images that we create in our minds will affect our attention, our thinking, and our feelings, and how our bodies work. The way we think and reason about this difficulty will affect our attention, our feelings, our motivation, and our behavior. This is why we can call it being in a "state of mind" and in this case an "anxious state of mind," as it captures the whole experience of many aspects of the mind working together with the sole focus of trying to deal with what we perceive to be a threat. Now remember, none of this is our fault because we have very troublesome brains to deal with, thanks to evolution. The type of mind-set we are in will be decided by the problem we are trying to deal with.

An antidote to a threat-focused mind—the compassionate mind

You can see from Jeff's story that there is not a lot of evidence of his being able to soothe his threat system; rather, it is being fueled with more threat-based emotions. Metaphorically speaking, Jeff is fighting fire with fire—all his horrible flashbacks are orchestrating more threat reactions. What Jeff's brain needs is a big dose of compassion to soothe and calm things down so that he can begin to think about his recovery. As the compassionate mind is based on understanding and caring, it is more likely to activate the soothing system, which as we saw in chapter 2 is a natural regulator of threats. The kinder and more understanding we are, the easier it is to tone down threats and to bring us back to a sense of well-being.

This is because a compassionate mind is not a critical mind but rather it's an understanding mind that knows how hard it is at times to be human. Its motivation is to care and to help us, and it has our best interests at heart. There is no right or wrong way in a compassionate mind, just an opportunity for reflection and growth through wisdom and strength.

So what might it feel like if we were able to bring ourselves into the compassionate mind-set? If we look back at the diagram of the threatened mind and the compassionate mind (figure 5.1), we can examine each element in turn and try to find some answers.

LOOKING AT THE COMPASSIONATE MIND

Motivation

Compassionate motives are our desires and intentions to relieve our own suffering and the suffering of other people. These motives guide us to flourish and support our well-being and the well-being of other people. This involves harnessing our desires and intentions to reduce our suffering (as a result of our traumatic experiences) and to act in ways that support our well-being.

Attention

Our compassionate minds will turn their attention to helpful, supportive memories with a positive focus.

Thinking/Reasoning

Our compassionate minds will focus on understanding that our trauma is a more common experience than we might have originally thought and that as human beings we all suffer to a greater or lesser extent because evolution has given us troublesome brains and bodies to deal with, and this is not our fault.

Imagery/Fantasy

Compassionate images are supportive, understanding, kind, and encouraging. When we are anxious it is very easy to generate frightening and self-critical images. The good news is that we can train ourselves and our minds so that we can call compassionate images to mind that stimulate our *contentment and soothing* systems.

Behavior

This is taking actions that are in our best interests and the best interests of others, which might mean developing the courage to deal with things that frighten us or that we find difficult. Compassionate behavior could also involve learning about how we live and react to our traumatic experiences (such as reading this book). We might also learn how to nurture ourselves in practical ways like mastering new forms of behavior that help us to calm down, for example, meditation or guided relaxation. These may all be new things to us, and when learning anything new it's always a good idea to take it gradually, one step at a time, so that we prepare ourselves properly for the next step.

Emotions

These emotions are linked to feelings of warmth, support, kindness, and connection. The guided exercises later in this book are all designed to help us experience the compassionate emotions.

Developing compassion will not necessarily rid us of all our fears and anxieties, but it can help us to cope better and to find a better balance between the emotion regulation systems in our brains.

WHY BEING COMPASSIONATE CAN BE TROUBLESOME FOR US

As evolved beings, our brains and minds have developed the need to be cared for from the day we are born to the day we die. Research shows us that feeling cared for has a huge impact on how our brains, bodies, and minds work; and it impacts our emotions, the quality of our relationships, and our abilities to understand and cope with difficult feelings and desires.

THE POWER OF EMOTIONAL MEMORIES

Our emotional memories of what it feels like to be safe, cared for, and soothed are developed in our early attachment relationships with our parents and others. We can draw on these emotional memories in adulthood when we need to feel safe and cared for, as they can be used to help tone down the threat system and bring our emotions into balance. In other words, when we need to soothe ourselves as adults and make ourselves feel better when we are distressed, we are unconsciously linking back and recalling how we were soothed by our mothers (or other main caregivers) during childhood.

Experiences in childhood that include receipt of emotional and physical affection, kindness, warmth, protection, and understanding can all enhance our ability to develop compassion for ourselves and others.

Caring experiences (talking to and showing interest in children, sharing positive feelings, validating and exploring what children are feeling) are signals to the child's brain that he or she is loved and valued. This means the *soothing* system is regulating the *threat* system. By providing a soothing and an understanding response to a baby or child's distress, the parent is helping the child to learn that his or her own sometimes fierce emotions can be regulated and brought to an end, as outlined in the following scenario:

Jesse, Johnnie, and Billy

Jesse, Johnnie, and Billy, all five years old, were playing together on the playground when suddenly they were caught in a thunder and lightning storm. The boys were very frightened, as it was scary, and they started crying and running to their mothers.

- ### Jesse's story

Jesse runs over to his mom, crying, "Mom, are we going to die? I'm really scared!" Jesse is really upset, and we can imagine his amygdala firing off all sorts of threat responses. Mom responds by holding Jesse tightly to her, stroking his hair, and saying in a calm, soothing voice, "Don't worry, you're safe with me. It's a thunder and lightning storm, and it does sound a bit loud and scary, doesn't it? I can see why you're scared. That's okay. So let's collect our bags and get into the car and go home, and we can have a nice cuddle on the sofa together until the storm passes." Jesse visibly calms down and his sobs become less intense as he relaxes in his mother's arms. You can imagine his threat system literally being calmed down by the validation, care, and comfort it is receiving from the signals of touch and tone of voice from his mother. This is a big lesson in self-soothing for Jesse because although he doesn't know it, he is learning that his emotions are normal, that he is allowed to feel them, and that they are valid and that there is a way to end them.

- ### Johnnie's story

So what happened to Johnnie, who was just as scared as his friend? He ran to his mom, sobbing, but his mom was talking on her cell phone and seemed oblivious to her son's distress.

"Mom, Mom, I want to go home, I'm really scared."

"Sssh, can't you see I'm talking on the phone?" says Mom.

"Please, Mom, please."

"BE QUIET, don't be such a crybaby," says Mom in a stern, irritated voice.

Mom turns her back to carry on talking on the phone. Johnnie is left sobbing and trying to cuddle his mom as she roughly pushes him away. So what do you think is going on in Johnnie's amygdala—feeling soothed or feeling more anxious, angry, unloved, and unsafe? Johnnie will be experiencing all sorts of threat-based emotions such as fear, anger, and sadness in response to his original fear; so rather than calm his threat system down, his efforts to seek care and comfort leave him feeling more distressed, frightened, angry, and ashamed as well as rejected by his mother. You can even imagine, in later years, that "Don't be such a crybaby" could become part of his self-critical repertoire.

- ### Billy's story

And finally, what happened to Billy? Well, he was also just as scared as his two little friends, and he ran, sobbing, over to his mother, who was sobbing with fear herself. "Quick, Billy, run, run, Billy, before you get struck by the lightning," she said in an agitated, high-pitched voice. Little Billy started running for his life into his mother's arms. She scooped him up and started saying with increasing levels *of agitation, "Oh my golly we've got to get home, sssh, there there, calm down, stop crying. Quick, let's get to the car, we might get hit, sssh everything's all right, here my poor baby." She rocked Billy back and forth in a somewhat fretful manner in an attempt to calm her tearful son down. Did it work? Do you think Billy's amygdala got the message that he was safe? Probably not, as Billy would have picked up on his mother's signals of being anxious and become more anxious and clingy as he realized that his mother thought they were in danger too.*

Of the three examples of caregiving in times of distress, Jesse probably has the best chance of developing self-soothing skills and being able to use them successfully as an adult to regulate threat in his world. How we (as children) experience the emotions of other people toward us becomes the foundation for how we feel about ourselves. We will believe ourselves to be lovable if we can call upon childhood memories of being treated in a loving way. This is also true of negative perceptions. We will believe ourselves unlovable if we can call upon childhood memories in which we were treated in unkind and unloving ways.

WHAT HAPPENS IF YOU DIDN'T FEEL CARED FOR?

Perhaps you are already questioning what happens if we do not have any childhood memories of being loved and cared for, but rather emotional memories of being harmed by others and then feeling anxious and angry toward those who were meant to love and protect us as children. Well, we may struggle to find any emotional memories that make us feel loved and soothed. Consequently, we may find it hard to regulate our threat-focused minds because, through no fault of our own, we never learned that we could be comforted out of our distress. This, of course, does not mean we can't learn to do this because that is what this book is all about. The key insight here is that we appreciate that it is not our fault that we struggle to regulate our threat-focused minds.

We may even find ourselves rejecting people who are trying to be kind and caring to us. This is because if we had abusive or harmful experiences at the hands of people throughout our childhoods (who had initially been kind to us and then later abused us), kindness will be registered by our brains as a threat. It's no different in principle to people who have been through a painful divorce and who may be very wary about undertaking new relationships, even with those who are genuinely caring. Our histories influence our experiences of kindness and caring, and at times we can find ourselves actually shunning it. Therefore, having a good start in life by way of a healthy and loving *attachment relationship* can set us up with the belief that we are lovable, and that other people want to be in our company and have our best interests at heart.

WHAT CAN HAPPEN WHEN PARENTS OR CAREGIVERS DON'T MAKE YOU FEEL SAFE?

Feeling disconnected and isolated

If because of how our parents or caregivers treated us, we have not had the experience of being loved and protected and therefore we don't know how to love and protect ourselves (because we have not been taught this), then we may find that we struggle to self-soothe. This can result in our feeling isolated and disconnected from others because we think what we feel and experience of life is different from what everyone else feels and experiences. Some of us feel fundamentally different from other human beings and are without a sense of connection to other people. There are even those of us who have a chronic desire to run away and hide, to not let anyone see who we really are, or the real us. You may recognize yourself in some of these examples and you are certainly not alone.

• *John's story*

John, who was sexually assaulted in his twenties, felt disconnected and isolated. He described himself as a total outsider, and in therapy, he would say things like, "I have no place in this world, I just don't belong"; "I don't know what I'm supposed to feel and I don't feel anything"; "I feel numb and alone."

Feeling unworthy and unlovable

If we have been hurt and unprotected in the early years of our lives then it is entirely understandable that we may grow into adults who feel that they are not worth loving or protecting. This can also lead us to have a very self-critical internal voice. The internal voice is the conversation we have within ourselves. Internal voices can make positive or negative comments on our life and behavior. When we have a very critical internal voice, we will often attack ourselves with self-denigrating statements and say really rude and hurtful things about ourselves in our own minds such as "You're toxic," "You're a liar," "If people knew what you were like, they'd hate you," "I hate you." Not only do we self-attack in this way, we often fail to take care of ourselves, and we engage in all sorts of behavior that demonstrates this—for instance, we may abuse drugs, not eat healthy foods, or not clean ourselves properly. Much of this behavior is because we may feel we are not worth anything.

• *Michelle's story*

Michelle used to speak in a self-critical manner and engage in all sorts of distressing and destructive behaviors to manage her inner turmoil. She had been sexually abused as a child, emotionally neglected by her mother—who was an alcoholic—and later entered into a violent marital relationship. Not only did she not like herself, as evidenced by her self-attacking derogatory thoughts, but she also cut her arms to relieve the intense pressure she felt inside her all the time. She was very overweight, having developed a habit of overeating when she felt overwhelmed by her emotions.

"BUT NOTHING BAD HAPPENED TO ME IN MY CHILDHOOD!"

Sometimes people who visit the trauma clinic who feel very ashamed and highly self-critical will say, "The thing is, I don't know why I hate myself so much; I had a nice childhood and nothing bad happened to me, so I don't understand why I feel so much shame and so much self-loathing." Often, despite not having suffered abuse, they have lots of memories of being emotionally ignored or neglected. Neglect can also be damaging and affect whether we learn to manage our feelings and learn how to calm our intense emotions when we are distressed.

• *Martin's story*

In chapter 4 we met Martin, the police officer who together with his colleague had been assaulted. His parents had given him the impression that it was not good to feel frightened, anxious, upset, and angry, and that it was best to ignore these feelings and adopt a "stiff upper lip" approach to life. His kind and loving parents certainly wouldn't have thought they were causing Martin any difficulties by encouraging him to get on with things and not to dwell on his emotions. But, sadly for Martin, this meant that he used to feel anxious when he had intense feelings because he thought it was wrong and he shouldn't feel like this. Not only did Martin invalidate the experience of his own emotions, he literally did not know what to do with the emotions. He didn't know how to cope with or tolerate them, or how to manage and regulate them using self-soothing and supportive strategies. Why would he know how to do this? The skill of learning how to emotionally nurture was not taught on the "family curriculum." Martin became unstuck when he suffered a life-threatening, traumatic event and experienced overwhelming feelings of fear and anger. The powerful feelings, although completely understandable to us, were incomprehensible to Martin because he had not been given a way to deal with them. He therefore became more distressed and self-critical when the feelings did not go away because he now believed that he shouldn't give in to feelings of fear or anger. He hid himself away from family and friends and used high levels of alcohol as strategies to try to make the feelings go away. But the avoidance and alcohol use only worked on a temporary basis. Before long Martin was caught in a cycle of flashbacks, which he couldn't avoid, and this was coupled with alcohol misuse and depression.

WAS EMOTIONAL NURTURING ON YOUR FAMILY CURRICULUM?

By exploring the relationships we had with our parents or other people who cared for us when we were young, we can begin to understand how our childhood experiences inform how we operate as adults. This can help us to gain insight into how we manage threats and our emotions, and why we might struggle with painful memories and mental suffering.

Understanding how our brains are meant to function can also help us to understand that sometimes (because of our life experiences) our brains work in a way that can hinder us from solving our mental and emotional difficulties, or indeed exacerbate these difficulties. Although our brains can go into overdrive and our emotions can become overwhelming when we feel threatened by our traumatic memories and experiences, we can also learn how to stand back from them and understand and resolve our emotional responses to life events. We can learn skills for working with our emotions that will help us deal with our traumatic experiences. We can learn to develop a compassionate mind.

Whatever the root and origins of our traumatic life experiences and our shame, we can learn how to develop our *self-soothing* system so that we can start to apply feelings of kindness and compassion toward ourselves and our own life experiences. We will then begin to learn to regulate our unpleasant threat-based emotions such as fear, anger, disgust, and shame. With a compassionate mind we can begin to develop positive connections with other people and come to recognize that we deserve a place in the world. We can also learn to tolerate and cope with our intense and sometimes frightening feelings, which will help us to navigate our way through life's challenges and which will eventually lead to a more peaceful and contented life.

SUMMARY

Remember that how we are shaped and how we developed has very much to do with the relationships we had in our early lives. This version of ourselves is the one we have become because of the life we've lived (which is not our fault). Let's think of this as one potential version of us! So, as we begin to recognize this we are able to see how often we blame ourselves for things that are beyond our control and that we are unable to change. This insight gives us hope, because we also have the opportunity to change and choose a new version of ourselves, a version that embraces kindness and self-compassion. This new version understands that we can take responsibility for the things that *we can change*. We can learn to develop feelings of self-care and kindness toward ourselves, which will in turn help us manage our traumatic experiences in a more helpful way.

Before we move on to part II of this book, let's just recap what we have learned in part I:

- How traumatic events affect our well-being and how symptoms of traumatic stress can arise.

- How our brains generate flashbacks (the specific kind of distressing memory associated with traumatic experiences) as a response to threat.

- How our brains are threat focused—which we have very little control over—and how our responses to threat are automatic.

- How we can turn off our feelings of threat by turning on our feelings of compassion.

- How our early experiences of care—which we have no control over—can greatly or subtly influence our development of self-compassion.

If we put all this knowledge, insight, and understanding together we now can see the *randomness* of our lives. We had no control over which family we were born into; no control over what life experiences we were exposed to growing up; and no control over how we were taught to deal with life's emotional challenges by our parents or the other adults in our lives. The way these experiences that are out of our control have shaped our development and brain functioning is simply not our fault. The abilities or life skills that we take into adulthood to help us deal with our life events and traumatic events have *not* been determined by us.

This is a really important insight for us because it can help us to stop blaming ourselves for the things in our lives over which we have no control. Giving up blaming ourselves is crucial to our being able to move forward in our lives and to begin to heal ourselves from our trauma. This, however, does not mean that we simply let ourselves off the hook or fail to take responsibility for how we treat ourselves and others. It's quite the opposite, as we need to find a way to stop shaming, blaming, and criticizing ourselves for the things we have done, or the things that have happened to us in the past. This can mean we need to put ourselves on the hook and take stock of what we fear by facing our past, looking at our present, and choosing our future. We cannot change a single moment that has gone before, but we can change the moment to come. By habitually being self-critical and feeling shame, we remain trapped in the threat mind-set and system. The only feelings we can experience in this state are those of anger, disappointment, anxiety, and disgust. By learning how to be compassionate we have to look reality full in the face, and we need to learn not to flinch from the facts and recognize that if we are doing things that are harmful to ourselves and others, then we need to take responsibility and change them. So, for example, it may not be our fault that we have been traumatized, but if we are misusing alcohol it is our responsibility to stop this. If we are very irritable and lash out at people, the fact that our anger system has been aroused because of trauma is not our fault—but it is our responsibility to recognize this and do the best we can to regulate our angry feelings. Simply being angry and then being full of shaming self-criticism only makes the situation worse for us. If we have hurt somebody, then rather than beating ourselves up, it's much more useful to own up to this and recognize the hurt we've caused, allow ourselves to feel genuine sorrow and regret (instead of self-focused anger or disappointment), and to the very best we can repair the damage and try to reduce the chances of doing it again. This means coming to understand our minds better; understanding what triggers our threat-focused responses and taking note of our thoughts and images; observing these; and then making choices about how we really want to act rather than letting our anger or anxiety act for us. We know how difficult this can be sometimes.

A key message is that we do not have to live out the legacy of our childhoods for the remainder of our adult lives. There are steps we can choose to take to help us on our journeys to recovery. We can opt to take on the responsibility to teach ourselves other ways to deal with our emotional world so that the rest of our lives can be as we would like, wish, and hope for them to be.

It's never too late to be who we want to be, but it requires our taking responsibility for ourselves and developing a deep commitment to reduce and alleviate our suffering and the suffering of others, with compassion.

PART II

Developing Your Compassionate Mind Skills

ABOUT PART II

Living with compassion can be quite a tough way to live because being honest and open to ourselves about who we are is difficult. It means honest and open acknowledgment of our limitations and the things that we struggle with, and when we do things that are harmful to ourselves and to others. It also means making a commitment to try to avoid doing harmful things and instead to try to do things that facilitate our prosperity and that of others. It involves giving up blaming and shaming ourselves because that traps us in the threat mind-set and system, and actually makes it less likely for us to be able to take responsibility for ourselves in a compassionate way.

People frequently confuse living with compassion with "being nice" and hiding one's negative feelings or suppressing them. That is not a helpful or a compassionate way to be. The fact of the matter is that sometimes the *truth does hurt* and we can be kind and loving in our honesty to ourselves and others. While brutal honesty is not helpful and can be cruel, suppressing and avoiding our negative experiences and difficult feelings is not helpful to our goal of recovery. There are respectful ways to be assertive and powerful, and we will learn more about this later in the book.

6

Preparing your mind for compassion: Attributes of compassion

In chapter 5 we learned that when our brains are in a particular mind-set, our attention, our thinking, our behavior, and our emotions are all affected, along with our motivations and our imaginations. Now we turn our attention to developing our skills of compassion. We will begin by exploring how to direct our attention, thinking, reasoning, behavior, and emotions to the tasks of giving ourselves care and self-soothing to help us with the development of our compassionate minds. This chapter is divided into two sections; the first section looks at the aspects and qualities of a compassionate mind, and the second section focuses on our fears about being compassionate.

Later, in part III of this book, we will use our compassionate minds to help us revisit our trauma memories and begin to learn how to turn off the threat-based emotions associated with our trauma memories to help us to move forward with our lives.

Let's focus on our compassionate minds. You may want to remind yourself of the diagram of the threat-focused mind-set and the compassionate mind-set. In chapter 5 we worked through the threat-focused mind-set and then used Jeff's story to think about what happens when we have a highly threat-focused mind or a "traumatized" mind. Just to remind us, an overall state of mind can be called a "mind-set" and the type of mind-set we are in will affect how our minds work and orchestrate a whole pattern of effects. It will direct our attention; focus how we think; urge us to behave in certain ways; texture our emotions; and influence our motivation and dreams or worries.

THE COMPASSIONATE MIND

To help us to understand our compassionate minds, we need to explore the various aspects of a compassionate mind-set by again using Jeff as an example, looking at what helped him with his attention, his thoughts, his urges to behave in certain ways, his emotions, and his motivations.

Just take a moment to remind yourself of the aspects of the compassionate mind, which are shown in the diagram below. We will then work through each aspect using Jeff's experience.

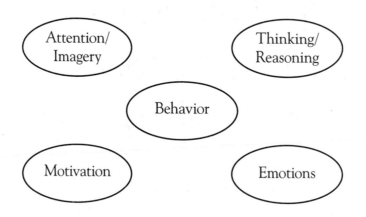

Figure 6.1: Aspects of a compassionate mind

Motivation

The aim of *compassionate motivation* is to alleviate and prevent suffering in ourselves and in others. We can achieve this by behaving in ways where the motivation encourages us to thrive and flourish over time in a manner that supports our long-term well-being. When we direct these motivations to others with the compassionate intent to help them, they will thrive too. Compassionate motivation arises because we have wisdom. We see the suffering we and others are experiencing, and we recognize that there are reasons for that suffering and there are ways in which these can be reduced and alleviated. Compassionate wisdom aids motivation because we begin to recognize that avoidance, blaming and shaming, and our self-criticism actually add to our suffering rather than alleviating it. As we gain these insights we become naturally motivated to try as best we can to lessen and heal our suffering. It can sometimes be very helpful to remember that we have these compassionate motivations inside ourselves, even if they seem deeply buried. We can cultivate and nurture them, and recognize them when they arise in us.

• *Jeff's story*

Jeff comforted an old man during the London Underground bombing experience. His motivation in doing this was one of caregiving for the well-being of his fellow victim—to try to alleviate some of his suffering. Understanding the motives, feelings, and intentions associated with that behavior helped Jeff recognize what compassionate motivation was and that he already had it in his heart—he just needed to learn to direct it toward himself.

Attention

As we now know well, when we are traumatized we have a tendency to see danger everywhere. Our threatened mind will focus us on threat, but *compassionate attention* will bring to mind the fact that we are alive and safe. A compassionate mind-set will expand the memories of our traumatic events to include thoughts that will help us to feel better about them and that are helpful to us rather than just paying attention to the highly threat-focused, fragmented memories that are our flashbacks.

• *Jeff's story*

Jeff's compassionate mind focused on the fact that Jeff survived the bomb blast. It brought to mind how, although he was dazed and scared, he still tried to help others by talking calmly to them, telling them they would be okay; helping people up and supporting them as they walked; how the emergency services, who were coordinating the rescue, shouted orders for everyone to get out of the subway station as quickly as possible; and the fact that Jeff put his arm around a weeping man to comfort him. Jeff's compassionate mind brought to his attention all the times Jeff had taken the subway and been safe, and it helped him focus on the young Muslim men he saw every day going about their daily business who were also hurt and affected by the bombings.

Thinking/Reasoning

This is the ability to stand back and think things through carefully, being both objective and caring. *Compassionate thinking* not only helps us to address our suffering but also the causes of our suffering. It enables us to understand and accept that being terrified when our lives are threatened is entirely normal. Our threat-focused brains are doing their jobs very well when they respond to a threat in the way we have described in previous chapters. Compassionate reasoning understands that flashbacks are normal after extreme emotional events and that it's no wonder we want to avoid thinking about them, because they make us feel awful all over again. Compassionate thinking therefore grounds us in an understanding that there is nothing wrong with us for the way our minds play out in response to our traumatic experiences and memories. Thinking in a compassionate way helps us to understand that it would help us if we could find a way to face our fears with understanding, and work through them with care and kindness. This form of reasoning helps us to recognize that if we are to give our brains a chance to resolve our trauma, it is possible to bring the symptoms of our trauma to an end. So, when we think compassionately about the aftereffects of trauma, we will be thinking the following:

It is absolutely not our fault that our brains are designed to keep us safe, and it is not our fault that our brains struggle to deal with traumatic events. After all, thankfully they are *not* everyday occurrences, and for most of us, it would never cross our minds (until it happens) that we could be involved in these newsworthy and often horrifying stories. Evolution has given us troublesome brains, and this is an important compassionate insight.

Many people have been faced with similar experiences as a result of trauma, and that is why books like this have been written. There's nothing abnormal, bad, or inadequate about us.

We acknowledge how unpleasant the symptoms and experiences relating to our trauma are, and acknowledge and accept that there are ways to get through them and for us to heal.

We can learn all these new insights by understanding them gradually and gently and following this process step-by-step at our own pace. If we find that we're still struggling, we can reach out to others for help, such as a GP or a therapist.

• *Jeff's story*

Jeff used to get cross with himself for not being strong enough to get over the bombings. He would criticize himself for having a "weak brain" filled with flashbacks. Learning that this was a normal way for him to respond to such trauma and that this was not his fault was very helpful to him in learning to stop his self-critical and self-blaming thoughts.

Just imagine how helpful it would be for Jeff if he adopted the way of thinking compassionately set out in the points above. How might that change him and his whole approach to his difficulties?

Imagery

Compassionate images are supportive, understanding, kind, and encouraging. When we are traumatized it is very easy to generate frightening images and self-critical ones. The good news is that we can train ourselves and our minds so that we can call compassionate images to mind that stimulate our *soothing and contentment* system. Developing compassion will not rid us of all our fears and anxieties, but it can help us to cope with them better and find a balance between the emotion regulation systems in our brains.

The exercises in this book will show us how to create these types of supportive images and to practice calling them to mind when we need them. You may remember from chapter 4 that being able to be compassionate toward ourselves is something we learn as children as a result of a healthy *attachment relationship.*

• *Jeff's story*

Jeff was able to recall some of the scenes of the aftermath of the bombing in which the emergency services rescued and comforted the victims. These images reminded Jeff that we can still be caring toward one another even in circumstances created by the worst aspects of human nature.

Behavior

This focuses on creating a new type of behavior that will help us to address the causes of our suffering. *Compassionate behavior* often requires some courage—for example, someone who is agoraphobic and frightened of going outside can start to travel a little farther from the house each day—to do things that challenge, but do not overwhelm them. Compassionate behavior is extremely important because it's the opposite of avoiding the things that cause us such difficulty. If we are able to have a kinder and more supportive understanding of our own life experiences and we learn to validate who we are and why we struggle, then we are more likely to feel able to take the challenging steps needed to help us on our journeys of recovery. Everything we do in the compassionate mind approach is to create a way of thinking that is supportive, kind, and validating and that gradually replaces our critical, frustrated, and hostile thoughts. So, to behave in a compassionate way means we have to work out what is in our and other people's best interests and to act accordingly. Bear in mind that our compassionate behavior can require us to "dig deep" so that step-by-step we can develop the courage that will enable us to learn how to behave in ways we may initially find very difficult and frightening. Compassionate behavior, however, is acting in a way that is wise so that we work out which challenges we can manage at that moment in time and which challenges we are not yet ready for. It's not about throwing ourselves into things that are overwhelming—we need to find the steps that best help us.

• *Jeff's story*

Jeff's compassionate mind was committed to alleviating his distress, so one of his tasks involved developing, step-by-step, the courage to face what was in his own mind. Jeff worked on being able to face his flashbacks and hold them in his mind long enough for him to work through his fears and find out what his memories meant to him. Also by holding them in mind, he began to recognize that, over time, they gradually lost their intensity. This is an example of compassionate behavior helping us to engage with, rather than suppress or avoid, painful inner experiences. But again, the key is to do this in a way that is not overwhelming.

Jeff also needed to develop courage to use the London subway system again. This was something his threat-focused brain found highly alarming, but his compassionate mind was able to put the threat into context, which enabled Jeff to return to subway travel and to not avoid young men with backpacks. This was hugely helpful to him, as it meant his world began to open up again and he could return to work and start to meet up with his friends once more. It was not easy for Jeff, as he was so frightened, but his commitment to his recovery meant that his compassionate behavior also involved daily practice in activating his contentment and soothing system. We will learn how to do this for ourselves in chapter 7. Compassionate behavior helped him develop ways of coping with his threat-focused feelings and manage his emotions in more helpful ways.

Emotions

Compassionate emotions are linked to feelings of warmth, support, validation, encouragement, and kindness. Basically, when the emotions of the *threat/protection* system are activated and we feel fear, anger, disgust, and so on, we seek to shift to *the contentment and soothing* system, which helps us to regulate threat so that we have thoughts of compassion, caregiving, kindness, courage, and action. Sometimes we also want to stimulate the *achieving and activating* system to provide encouragement and drive so that we have thoughts and feelings of being motivated and having energy. It's really all about how we balance our emotions and how we learn to take a breath and think about the kinds of emotions we want to create in ourselves rather than being beholden to the automatically created emotions of our threat system.

How we feel affects our thoughts, and our thoughts affect how we feel (this is a key premise in cognitive therapy). For us to find our compassionate thoughts reassuring and meaningful, it is important that they are said (in our head) with kindness and warmth. If you try to give yourself encouraging thoughts, are you able to hear those in your mind said with kindness and warmth?

- *Jeff's story*

When Jeff was working toward getting back on the subway, we noted that he would say in his head, "Come on, man, you can do this, you've done this before many times, everything is okay and you are safe." This appears to sound encouraging—until we realized that he was saying this with a tone of irritation, frustration, and mocking derision. So the words were not as encouraging after all! Jeff had to practice the art of speaking to himself in his head with the calming and soothing emotions of warmth, care, and kindness.

As demonstrated above, the emotions that we generate can affect how helpful our thoughts are. It is therefore helpful to create compassionate tones and feelings in our minds when we are being supportive, and we may need a little practice doing this.

In chapter 8 we will explore how to create these compassionate tones and feelings by using, inside our minds, our most compassionate, friendly voice and imagining a deeply compassionate person and what he or she might say to us and how he or she might say it.

In order to figure out what compassionate behavior is, we need to practice facing up to our fears, which really helps us move forward and overcome our day-to-day difficulties. This is, however, a skill, and, as with all new skills, it is best to practice slowly and gain some mastery of it before moving on to the next level. For example, it is not compassionate behavior to jump into the deep end of a swimming pool when you are terrified of water and cannot swim! Compassionate behavior is doing the things that help us to *gradually* develop our skills.

IMPORTANT QUALITIES OF COMPASSION

Professor Paul Gilbert has written extensively about the important qualities of compassion in his work on compassion-focused therapy. The concept of compassion has a long historical lineage in philosophical, spiritual, religious, theosophical, and psychological thinking. For the purposes of compassion-focused therapy, Paul Gilbert highlights the following compassionate attributes as being particularly helpful to developing our compassionate skills.

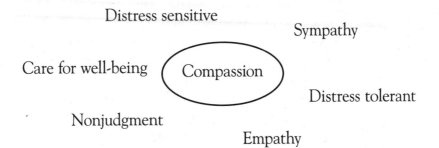

Create opportunities for growth and change
with warmth

Figure 6.2: Qualities of compassion

Let's take a look at each of these qualities in turn:

Care for well-being

The compassionate attribute of caring for well-being begins with making a decision to care for ourselves and other people—this may also mean having to commit to relieving our suffering and that of other people. Our motives when caring for the well-being of ourselves and other people can also be thought of as compassionate. This compassionate motivation contributes to the overarching aim of relieving suffering. It requires us to understand the nature of our suffering and its causes, and to wish to not suffer. As the Dalai Lama says, we all want to be happy and no one seeks suffering.

When we develop our desire to reduce suffering, then we are beginning to develop compassionate motivation and to genuinely care for our well-being. Take a moment now to sit quietly, and let's ask ourselves two questions:

Do I genuinely care for my well-being?

Do I have my best interests at heart and my mind in mind as I go about my daily business?

There may not be a clear-cut answer to these questions, but the point is to help us think about how we actually approach ourselves. We need to determine whether if, when we are suffering, we genuinely want to reduce our suffering by being caring toward ourselves? If our answer to one or both of the above questions is either "no" or "not always," then we might like to think about whether we would like to develop a caring approach to ourselves and what the value is to us in doing so.

Of course, living our lives with compassion is not obligatory; we may decide that such an approach doesn't really appeal to us at this moment, and of course that's okay. We may think, "What is the point of any of this because nothing has worked in the past," "This sounds like a lot of hard work," or "I can't imagine being compassionate to myself." These are all natural thoughts that may reflect our desire to resist change. Many people who visit the trauma clinic have voiced these same concerns; they are a natural reaction when faced with trying something new for the first time. This is particularly true if we already feel let down by ourselves because we are not living our lives in the way we would most like to due to the experiences we have been through. A method that might help us decide to try out the new techniques is to view the whole process as an experiment, one in which we have nothing to lose. Can trying to be kind and loving to ourselves be any worse than beating ourselves up and living with our trauma, with all its symptoms playing out unabated in our lives? On the other hand, we have everything to gain! If the techniques work for us, we will begin to find ways to make ourselves feel better.

Distress sensitive

To be compassionate we need to learn to pay attention and notice when we, or other people, are in distress or are experiencing certain emotions. This might sound a little strange, but sometimes we fail to realize that we are distressed, or when we feel distressed we decide we just "don't want to go there" and so we avoid our feelings. This is very common in people who have flashbacks to previous traumatic events and just want to get the memories out of their minds as quickly as possible. They don't want to think about these images or face the fear of who they think they are. We can say some unpleasant things to ourselves when we struggle with our memories such as "You weakling, get a grip" or "You are so disgusting."

In developing our sensitivity to our emotions we will achieve two things. We will become aware of what we are feeling at any given moment, especially the feelings in our bodies, and we will therefore also recognize when we are distressed. We can then decide to do something positive about our distress by employing some of the guided exercises and techniques that we will be shown later in the book. *By noticing* what we are feeling, we are also accepting and validating our own emotions and this is a very powerful way of beginning to understand ourselves and make decisions about how we want to feel and react to events in our lives.

Sympathy

This is an interesting attribute, which some people think of as wallowing in self-pity and therefore to be avoided at all cost. However, this is a misconception, as sympathy really means to be emotionally moved by pain and suffering. Many of us are brought to tears by the suffering of other people and yet remain steely-eyed and stony-hearted when faced with our own pain and suffering. The following is an example of sympathy, which has been taken from *The Compassionate Mind Approach to Beating Overeating*, with the kind permission of Ken Goss:

Suppose we see a three-year-old child happily walking down the street. We smile at her happiness—but then she trips over the curb and bangs her head heavily and is really hurt. Her laughter turns to tears of real pain. We are likely to feel a flash of tension through our body, our stomach may lurch, and we can experience flashes of different feelings all at the same time such as sadness, anxiety, and an impulse to rush over to the child with a desire to make her feel better and to comfort her in some way.

Notice how in this example all of these emotions and reactions are automatic—there was no conscious thought. Sympathy is the emotional connection to the pain of others and ourselves, and without our having to think about it, we are moved immediately. However, if we were brought up to believe that showing sympathy toward ourselves or others was somehow weak or meant we were full of self-pity, we may not always find it easy to recognize our sympathy or know how to express it. Being sympathetic toward ourselves involves being sensitive to our own pain and being moved by our own suffering. Developing sympathy for ourselves can sometimes be difficult.

People who visit the clinic are often asked, "Are you moved by how much you are suffering and in distress?" There are a whole range of responses, from "What on earth do you mean? Don't be stupid—of course not, because I deserve to suffer" to "Yes, at times it really helps to focus on the sadness of what I have been through." With knowledge and insight it is possible to learn to be sensitive and open to how we feel and also to learn to be moved by our own difficulties.

Distress tolerant

Remember the old English adage "face your fears"? Well, the truth is that fear makes us want to avoid the things that frighten us. The way to reduce our fears, however, is to face whatever it is that is making us afraid. Our desire to avoid the things that scare us is not our fault, as we know that our *threat system* makes us try to escape danger. The problem with avoiding things though is that we are likely to just cause ourselves more trouble in the long run because if we avoid feelings we don't learn to tolerate and work with them and we don't develop the skills needed to cope with difficult situations.

Using our compassionate minds we can learn to tolerate our fears and other emotions, and also to understand them and where they come from. Sometimes we have to learn how to tolerate powerful feelings, such as anger or disgust, and this can feel daunting. So learning *how* to tolerate distress is itself something we can learn. As we have said before, the key to learning is to go step-by-step rather than be overwhelmed by feelings. One of the things we will explore in this book is exactly *how* to develop tolerance for our distress and how to stay compassionate and feel stronger in the face of distress so that we don't have to keep avoiding it and trying to suppress it. We've already seen that reducing self-criticism makes a difference to our levels of distress.

Empathy

"Walk a mile in my shoes and then tell me how I feel" captures what we mean by empathy. *Empathy* is the ability to think about and understand ourselves and other people. It is probably unique to human beings because it is an ability to understand the minds of others and imagine how and why people may feel the way they do. Put simply, it is captured in statements like "I know how you feel," "I can imagine what that feels like," and "You must be angry and I can understand why, given what happened." Empathy provides us with the ability to understand why people behave the way they do, and it is also important to our self-compassion, as it also helps us understand why we behave the way we do.

As Paul Gilbert says, "We recognize that people do things for reasons" because of motivations of gain or because of emotions such as anger. Some people may even be unaware of the reasons behind their goes on to maintain that as we can understand other people's minds, so we can learn to ur own: "It's our empathy that allows us to become compassionate because it is based on a standing of how our minds and bodies work."

Empathy helps us in other ways too. It creates space for us to think and reflect; we can ask ourselves questions like "Why am I feeling like this?," "What would help me feel better?," and "What do I need to learn and develop in order to change this?" Empathy is the ability to *understand our minds and how they work*. In addition we use empathy when we make predictions about feelings—for example, "If I buy this present for Sally she will be happy." We can imagine how we're going to feel if we do X or Y or don't do X or Y. When we have empathy in a compassionate way we begin to understand how and why our minds respond so well to support, kindness, and encouragement. Our empathy allows us to reflect on and think about the value of developing these qualities in ourselves.

Nonjudgment

Whenever we teach compassion to therapists, we ask them to list the qualities that they would like their most compassionate therapist to have and nine times out of ten, the first thing they say is *nonjudgment*. It seems we all crave the same thing—not to be harshly judged for what we have done or what we are like. So what do we mean by nonjudgment? This is the ability *not* to condemn and to let go of that angry desire to attack and be critical. If we stop and examine how we look at the world, very often without even being aware of it we may condemn or criticize things or people. Obviously we must be able to go through life having preferences, desires, and hopes, but the key to nonjudgment is being able to express a preference without having to condemn or criticize either ourselves or other people. The more we criticize our responses to trauma and the way we behaved during our harrowing and traumatic experiences, the more we fuel the *threat* system. Our judgments of ourselves or other people can actually worsen all the horrible experiences that have arisen out of our traumas and our traumatic experiences.

By fostering an attitude of nonjudgment (i.e., one that does not shame or condemn), we can give ourselves a chance to reflect on and think about how best to deal with something that we find difficult or challenging, and this can be key in helping us to stop the cycle of harrowing thoughts that can exist in our tortured minds.

The components of compassion and the compassionate mind

The attributes of compassion all play important roles in harnessing and developing a compassionate mind. Moreover, notice how they all rely on and affect each other. For example, think about one of those executive toys involving a series of ball bearings hanging on separate strings. If you pull back the first ball bearing and let it go, it knocks the next one, which knocks the next one, and so on until you have a sway of ball bearings, working in unison and harmony. We can therefore imagine the ricochet and momentum created and increased with each attribute of compassion. The more compassionate motivation and momentum we can build, the easier it will be to become empathic and sensitive to our own distress.

BRINGING ASPECTS AND ATTRIBUTES TOGETHER: A MODEL OF COMPASSIONATE MIND TRAINING

This brings us to the compassion circle, the result of research, spiritual traditions, and the input of many different people. The full circle is outlined in the diagram below:

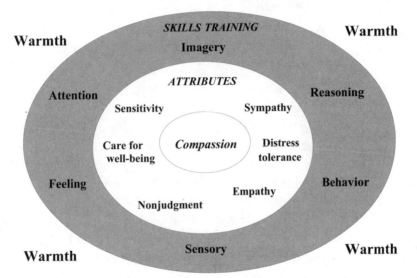

Figure 6.3: The compassion circle: Key attributes of compassion (inner ring) and the skills needed to develop them (outer ring)

Source: Adapted with permission from P. Gilbert, *The Compassionate Mind* (London: Constable & Robinson, 2009)

In the course of this book we will learn about all aspects of this model. We have already begun to look at the attributes of compassion, and in chapter 8 we will focus on developing the skills of compassion (the outer ring in the diagram above).

"HANG ON A MINUTE, THIS STUFF IS NOT FOR ME"

Even though many of the people who attend the trauma clinic can understand the values of compassion, they also sometimes feel resistant to it for all kinds of reasons. In this section we have anticipated your possible reaction, that despite recognizing the intrinsic value of compassion, there may also be a part of you that is resisting or pushing it away. We call this having a fear of compassion.

Now that we have an idea of what compassion involves, the task ahead of us is to develop a compassionate mind to help on the journey of recovery. You may have doubts about the notion of developing a compassionate mind, and you might be thinking, "Hang on a minute, this stuff is not for me." But before you decide the compassionate approach is not right for you, let's just consider some of the reasons we fear or shy away from being compassionate.

"I don't deserve compassion"

One reason we might not think the compassionate approach is for us is because we believe that we don't deserve it. Every week the trauma clinic sees people who blame themselves for their traumatic experiences. This is in spite of overwhelming evidence to the contrary. They are also highly critical of their role in the traumatic events that have happened to them. This leads them to be trapped in a cycle of self-criticism and shame (we discussed how this happens in chapter 4). A common theme is that they feel they must have done something to deserve their suffering, and it invariably comes back to thoughts of "Well it must be something about me," "I'm bad, so I deserve to be punished," or "I'm not nice so I don't deserve life to work out for me." It's understandable why our minds might go to these dark places of self-blame, because life is not fair and not everyone is involved in traumatic events that upset their lives.

When we have been involved in something traumatic, say, for example, a car accident, or we have been attacked or raped, then it's natural to think "Why me?," "What is it about me that made this happen?," "It's not fair," and "I must have done something to deserve this." The truthful answer to these questions is that life is random and there is no real reason some of us suffer more than others. But that truth is not enough to calm our threat-focused human minds, so we try to understand the reasons it happened to us in an effort to regain control and predict our worlds. Although we know there can be great cost to our well-being if we blame ourselves, we also understand that blaming ourselves for our pain and suffering also makes us think that we can do something about it. This is, of course, an illusion.

One way to overcome this difficulty is to recognize that it's not a question of whether we "deserve" to experience compassion in our lives. Compassion helps us to balance our system; it's like a lifeblood that flows through us, calming those systems that need to be calmed and helping us to face up to things that need to be faced up to. So it is not whether we deserve to live with compassion toward ourselves, but whether we want to live life fully, in a way that optimizes and enhances our existence. Compassion can help us achieve this.

When looked at in this way we can see that we all deserve compassion and we need it most when we are down and being self-critical. The problem for us, though, is that if we believe that we deserve to be punished or to suffer, we also think that we don't deserve care, kindness, and understanding.

Another reason that we may push against compassion is that as self-critics, being kind to ourselves can be abhorrent and can result in feelings of anxiety. Experiencing others being kind and compassionate toward us can produce the same extreme response. For some people, kindness feels threatening rather than comforting. There are many different reasons for this, and sometimes our own care receiving/giving memories from childhood are sadly associated with anxiety, blame, and punishment (remember the stories of Jesse, Johnnie, and Billy). Therefore, it's not surprising that we don't want to pursue compassion for ourselves.

Listed below are other reasons visitors to the clinic give for why they don't think compassion is for them; you may find these may also apply to you.

Eleven common myths about compassion

- Compassion is okay for others, but I don't deserve it.

- Compassion will not last and it will be taken away from me, so what's the point in starting it.

- Compassion is like wallowing in your own self-pity.

- Compassion is far too self-indulgent and selfish.

- Compassion is for weaklings and "wusses."

- Real men don't "do" compassion.

- Compassion is fluffy, soft, airy-fairy, and "group-huggy."

- Compassion makes you vulnerable to others who will take advantage of you.

- Being compassionate means that I will never be allowed to be cross, angry, raging, or to run away from anything or be totally selfish again.

- I cannot have any bad or negative thoughts when I am compassionate.

- Being compassionate lets me off the hook, and I don't need to take responsibility for anything that goes wrong in my life.

Do you recognize some of your own beliefs in the list above? If you do, you are not alone. I hope you will be reassured to learn that some of the thoughts you might have been experiencing—which may seem like hurdles—are also shared by other people. These, however, are misconceptions about compassion, and the problem with believing them is that they block our need to improve our well-being by developing our self-compassion skills and accepting compassion from those we know we can trust. As with all things, it helps to believe in the effectiveness of a product before you buy it. So believing that compassion will help you will, in turn, enhance your chances of benefiting from this book. I will therefore try to dispel any myths that your concerns may have created.

COMPASSION MYTHS

Compassion is the soft option

Acting with compassion toward ourselves requires us to begin to build courage, mental and emotional strength, and wisdom. It is in no way a soft option nor is it easy. It is, in fact, facing what we fear most in life and learning how to tolerate the pain—in mind and body—that our memories generate.

Compassion is the same as pity

Compassion focuses on being moved by the distress and pain we see in ourselves and in others. This is neither self-indulgent nor selfish. To be affected by these struggles that are common to all humanity is loving, supportive, and giving. We are all equal, we all struggle in different ways, and we all do what we can to cope with our lives. This is very different from our common usage of the word *pity*, which can sometimes be associated with feeling superior to other people. We have a strong aversion to being pitied, as we sometimes associate it with others looking down on us and seeing us as inferior or weak. Compassion in the form we are discussing here has nothing to do with pity, even though sometimes in the modern dictionary and in other languages the word *compassion* can be linked to pity.

Needing compassion makes you weak

Most of us have double standards when it comes to compassion. We are happy to give compassion to others (whom we don't consider to be weak for wanting or needing our help), but we are not happy to receive it from ourselves because somehow that would make us weak! Somewhere along the road, from compassion for others to compassion for ourselves, we hit a roadblock.

Compassion is easy

Compassion requires hard work and dedication. Not only do we need to develop the courage to work on our difficulties, we have to face up to who we fear we are and take responsibility for our actions and the impact they have on ourselves and on others. It takes practice and discipline to develop skills in assertiveness and boundary setting.

Myth-busting exercises

If you still have concerns about developing your compassionate mind, for any reason, it may be helpful to spend some time thinking about your blocks and working with them. Why not try the following four exercises—based on the myths outlined above—that people attending the trauma clinic find helpful:

Exercise 6.1: My personal blocks to developing self-compassion

Please check each myth if it applies to you

Myths about compassion	Applies to me	Does not apply to me
Compassion is okay for others but I don't deserve it.		
Compassion will not last and it will be taken away from me, so what's the point in starting it.		
Compassion is like wallowing in your own self-pity.		
Compassion is far too self-indulgent and selfish.		
Compassion is for weaklings and "wusses."		
Real men don't "do" compassion.		
Compassion is fluffy, soft, airy-fairy, and "group-huggy."		
Compassion makes you vulnerable to others who will take advantage of you.		
Being compassionate means that I will never be allowed to be cross, angry, raging, or to run away from anything or be totally selfish again.		
I cannot have any bad or negative thoughts when I am compassionate.		
Being compassionate lets me off the hook, and I don't need to take responsibility for anything that goes wrong in my life.		

Exercise 6.2: Overcoming your personal blocks to developing self-compassion

By each myth that you have checked off, write a few lines about what you think might make this a myth. The first one has been completed as an example. You may want to refer back to the section on why certain beliefs about compassion are myths.

Myths about compassion	Compassionate reasons as to why this is a myth
Compassion is okay for others, but I don't deserve it.	This is a double standard. Everyone deserves compassion, as we all struggle with things in our lives. The fact that I think I don't deserve compassion is just part of one version of me.
Compassion will not last and it will be taken away from me, so what's the point in starting it.	
Compassion is like wallowing in your own self-pity.	Compassion is not self pity. It is treating yourself as good as you'd like to treat others.
Compassion is far too self-indulgent and selfish.	
Compassion is for weaklings and "wusses."	Everyone has struggles. Its part of being human and does not make you weak
Real men don't "do" compassion.	
Compassion is fluffy, soft, airy-fairy, and "group-huggy."	
Compassion makes you vulnerable to others who will take advantage of you.	
Being compassionate means that I will never be allowed to be cross, angry, raging, or to run away from anything or be totally selfish again.	You can always feel your feelings
I cannot have any bad or negative thoughts when I am compassionate.	
Being compassionate lets me off the hook, and I don't need to take responsibility for anything that goes wrong in my life.	You have to s.

Exercise 6.3: Reasons for wanting to face your fears and commit to developing your compassionate mind

In this exercise, see if you can write down a few of your motivations for wanting to overcome your fear of compassion. An example has been given to start you off.

My reasons for wanting to face my fears and commit to developing my compassionate mind
1. I have been struggling with my memories for a long time and they cause me pain. They stop me from being who I want to be and leading the life I want. I now understand that I have a complicated, threat-focused brain that is doing its best to keep me safe, and I know that I have not been very good at toning down my feelings of threat. I now know that it's not my fault and that my brain has been shaped by my experiences, and knowing that this is only "one version" of me gives me hope that I can develop new skills in order to live my life with compassion.
2. I want to feel free in my daily life to claim a true identity at the core of my being of who I really am.
3. I want to be more carefree and not always have my "mood" dictate what I am capable of doing on a day to day basis
4. I no longer want to over react to what is before me and to be mindful to stay in the moment and not be overwhelmed by every small thing that comes my way. To put things in perspective.
5. I want to be able to commit to certain activities without the fear of not following through due to mood swings that put me in a negative "head space"
6. I want to share some of the things I might be good at with others that would help myself and them to improve self esteem.

Exercise 6.4: Coping with these blocks to self-compassion

Please try to list anything you could do or say to help you cope with these blocks to developing self-compassion.

Things that I can say or do to help me cope with my blocks to self-compassion:
Being compassionate feels scary and different, as I have never believed I deserved to be kind to myself. This is not for wimps, as some of the most iconic, compassionate people were strong, courageous, and brave. It will take courage and determination to work through my difficulties, but this is what I want and deserve to do for myself.

EXPERIMENT WITH SELF-COMPASSION

Finally, if you are still struggling with whether or not you feel ready to take this forward, then it might be helpful to remind yourself that you are experiencing common beliefs and obstacles to taking up the challenge of finding a new way to help you in your life. Why not therefore just commit to *trying* it as an experiment? What have you got to lose? Think of it like this: if we have weak abdominal muscles after giving birth or have stopped playing sport while we focused on our career and we now have backache, don't we want and deserve to build those muscles back up again to rid ourselves of our back pain? It is the same with compassion. Let's have a go and see if we can build and strengthen our intrinsic compassionate qualities, which we may have temporarily abandoned in our struggle to cope with our traumatic life experiences.

SUMMARY

This chapter has given us an overview of what compassion means. It is openness and sensitivity to our own and other people's distress, coupled with a desire to relieve that distress.

We have learned that compassion is made up of many components and that when we are in a compassionate frame of mind, it affects what we take notice of, how we think and reason, how we behave and feel, and what we are motivated to do.

We also explored what it means to be compassionate by looking at its specific attributes, such as caring for our well-being, being sensitive, noticing our emotions and distress, being sympathetic (i.e., being emotionally moved), and being able to tolerate and cope with our distress rather than seeking to avoid it. It includes empathy (understanding our own minds and other people's) and being nonjudgmental (halting our impulse to be critical and condemn).

Having examined some of our fears of why being compassionate might not be for us, we did some exercises to explore why we might feel this way. We then tackled some of the common themes and tried to dispel some of the blocks we might encounter when trying to develop self-compassion.

Therefore, we can move on to spending some time developing our ability to prepare our minds for compassion.

7

Preparing your mind for compassion: The beginnings of skills development

In this chapter we will focus on understanding how to prepare our minds to *function* compassionately by taking a practical approach. The way we do this in compassion-focused therapy is to use guided exercises to first prepare our minds for compassion and then to develop each of the different attributes of our compassionate minds, again using exercises (see the resources section at the back of this book). We will begin the process of turning our minds toward compassion by taking a gradual approach and introducing the idea of *mindfulness*.

COMPASSION TRAINING

Turning our minds toward compassion is no small task, so I won't mislead you into thinking this is a quick fix. Approach it more like a journey; we are training ourselves toward mental fitness. If we compare compassion training to the process of getting physically fit, there are a number of stages we need to work through:

- We notice that we are unfit.

- We care enough about our health to do something about our unfit state to improve it.

- We think we deserve to be healthy.

- We commit to getting fit.

- We overcome all our self-sabotaging thoughts, which will keep us pinned to the sofa watching television instead of taking action.

- We start exercising and keep it up.

- We start gradually to build up fitness, at a pace we can manage so that we don't put ourselves off for life!

- We commit to regular training practice for the REST of our lives to maintain our fitness after all our hard work.

With our compassionate training it is important to practice to help us learn and maintain our compassionate skills. It will help us if we can take the view that there is real value for us by training our minds for compassion by practicing a little bit each day—little steps eventually lead to long walks! Our aim for you is to learn, bit by bit, to build compassion into your everyday life and to constantly prompt yourself for it.

MINDFULNESS AND MINDFUL ATTENTION

What is mindfulness and how does it relate to our compassion training? Mindfulness is a way we learn to pay attention to the things going on around us and in our own minds so that we can be fully present in each moment. We can find our minds being pulled away from the present moment with worries, plans, and ruminations, and it is learning to recognize this shifting from the present moment that is the key to mindfulness. Mindfulness means paying attention to whatever is in our awareness right now—either something within our minds and bodies or something in our immediate environment.

Many Eastern religions, particularly Buddhism, help people to train their attention by developing skills of mindfulness. Learning to be mindful has been shown to be extremely beneficial for a range of emotional difficulties (mindfulness-based cognitive therapy [MBCT] is an example).

Therefore the skill we are training for here is *noticing* that our minds have shifted and then helping them *to return* to our desired focus.

Mindfulness is *not* "making" your mind pay attention or emptying your mind of thoughts; it is *noticing the shifting of your mind and then returning it to its focus.* As we will see later, this can be very helpful when doing our compassion exercises.

A second aspect of mindfulness is to notice how our thoughts and emotions emerge and whether there are any identifying signals that relate to our thoughts and feelings, for example, learning to identify what happens in our bodies when we have intrusive memories or flashbacks, like a hammering heart or an unpleasant buzz in our ears. Learning to notice the signals or memories and labeling the emotions and thoughts that accompany them can help us to become more observant and more aware of things emerging in our minds and bodies. This will help us to develop insight about what is distressing us about our traumatic memories.

Practical preparations

This is where we start to do some practical exercises and begin to learn some new skills on our quest for compassion to improve our lives. You may find that there are times when it is easier to concentrate than others, and it may be that to begin with you simply read the exercises and think about them in general terms before coming back to do them properly when you have more time in your day and when you can concentrate and not be disturbed. You will also find that the exercises feel more straightforward when you are calm and settled. Avoid times when you are likely to be interrupted or are feeling upset.

Because the exercises involve your following instructions about your breathing and doing visualizations in your mind, you may find it helpful to be able to record yourself reading the exercises in a calm voice so that you can play it back. This might help you maximize your concentration on the exercise.

Some of you may feel something like "But my life is always so busy and I never have peaceful time to myself, so when should I start?" It is much easier to learn and practice new skills if things feel relatively stable and calm in your life. As you get better at using each skill you will gradually be able to incorporate it as an alternative way of managing distress. So I suggest that you start by giving yourself five minutes a day. Find a good time, perhaps during the evening after you have relaxed by having a bath or have watched something on the television. Choose a time of day that suits you when you don't have other commitments and you can find a small corner of time for yourself. You will find that the original five minutes will become longer as you master the exercises and feel the benefit of doing them.

We will begin with some straightforward exercises in mindful breathing and relaxation.

Exercise 7.1: Mindful breathing

Sit quietly for a minute or two just resting your mind and not thinking about anything in particular so that you feel totally present in this moment. Alternatively, if you prefer, you can spend two minutes just allowing your attention to settle on your breathing. As you breathe in, the air comes into your mouth or nose and down to your diaphragm and then moves back out again. Concentrate on following your breath in and out.

This is a useful starter exercise because it shows how your mind is never still. It hops from one random thought to the next. The most important observation when we begin these exercises in mindful attention is to recognize that although we are capable of controlling our attention by being purposefully mindful, we don't have *control over it*. In fact, concentrating on a single thing such as your breath is quite difficult to begin with, and it takes practice to keep your attention on a specific focus. But practice makes perfect!

You may have noticed that we all have a bit of a "monkey mind"—one that jumps around all over the place, flitting from one topic to another. This is entirely normal, and it does not mean that we are particularly bad at concentrating, rather that we all have minds that are prone to switch from one topic to another in quick succession. Concentrating on one thing at a time requires a fairly big effort. This is partly because our brains are good at multitasking. However, it is also partly because we have become tremendously good at concentrating on the one single thing that dominates our lives—our traumatic experiences. When our threat system is active and we are caught in the cycle of flashbacks, shame, and rumination, it can be very difficult to concentrate on anything else; we become single-minded. Although this makes sense from an evolutionary perspective, when being safe is of paramount importance, it's troublesome for us. As a result of our trauma our *threat* system is overactive, oversensitive, and stuck in the past, still responding to threats that have long gone. So when our self-protective brains are determined to focus on our traumatic experiences, we will find concentrating on anything else challenging. But even acknowledging this will help us.

It will benefit us if we can start to develop the skill of paying attention to things that may help us and take attention away from things that are not helping us. Our goal might be then to stand back, take a few breaths, and observe our minds when we are having a flashback and experience our bodies reacting to the flashback and exhibiting signs of stress and anxiety. Put simply, if we are suffering flashbacks to a previous traumatic event, it will help to start paying attention to the fact that we are safe now.

In the following section we will explore two ways to help you do this by working on how to focus your attention on the things you would like to think about. First, we will work on developing your capacity to be *mindful* of the thoughts and feelings that you experience, and second, we will work on *developing your abilities to deliberately refocus* your attention.

Let's think about what you might experience if you are being mindful when you are experiencing a trauma memory. You might become aware that you want to get the trauma memories out of your mind as quickly as possible because they make you feel anxious. You may notice your thoughts turn to "Right, just distract yourself and they will go away" or "Have a couple of beers and that will take the edge off things." You may even then notice that you start to get angry with yourself and become self-critical and say things like "You're so weak, why can't you just get over it and stop thinking about it" or "There you go again drinking yourself silly."

When we become mindful we become a curious observer of our minds and its thoughts and emotions. We seek to change our relationships with our minds by *observing* our minds rather than getting *caught up in all the tangled thoughts within* them.

So the skill we are training for here is to be become an observer of our minds and all their frenetic activities.

We do not have to be at the whim of our emotions. By learning to become more observant we can open our minds to choices. We can choose whether or not to act on our thoughts and feelings. We can learn to:

- Slow down our minds.

- Pay attention to the present moment.

- Observe the contents of our minds and the feelings in our bodies.

So let's try to do this in the following set of exercises developed by Professor Gilbert as part of compassion-focused therapy. You may find it helpful to record yourself reading these words (or get a friend to read them) and then listen back to them. If you can't do this, you can of course read the exercise through several times so that you become familiar with the visualization you are about to try. Although the exercises involve closing your eyes, you do not have to do this. Lots of people feel very physically vulnerable when they come to treatment, and it makes them feel too unsafe to close their eyes. What I tend to suggest if this is the case is for them to stare at a blank wall instead. So please, do whatever makes you feel most comfortable.

Exercise 7.2: Mindful attention

(Begin recording)

Sit quietly for a moment and focus on your breathing. Allow the breath to come down into your diaphragm slowly and evenly and then leave your body slowly and evenly. If you find this difficult you may simply want to try to focus on the sensation of your breath coming in and leaving through your nose. Try spending two minutes simply concentrating on the experience of breathing in and out. If you don't like focusing on your breathing or you don't like closing your eyes, you could use a pebble or a shell and try to focus your attention on the experience of looking at it and feeling it.

You may notice that within just a few moments your mind will have wandered off on to something else. This is called mind wandering. If there are things that are worrying us, our minds easily get pulled into thinking about them and away from the present moment. This can also happen if there are things we are looking forward to (like a party), or if there are things that we need to do (e.g., pay a bill, or remember to call a friend), and we can find our minds skipping to them. This is very typical of how our minds are, and indeed recent research evidence suggests that it is our natural state.

One aspect of practicing mindfulness is just learning to notice when our minds wander and bringing our attention gently and warmly back to what we want to focus on. Mindfulness is not making our minds pay attention or emptying our mind of thoughts. Telling ourselves off for not being able to pay attention is not being mindful either. Indeed it is counterproductive, as noticing where our minds wander to can be very important in helping us to identify other issues that are bothering us. When our minds wander it is not a sign that we have failed to be mindful; it is a part of the very process of being mindful! It is the act of noticing and then returning the attention to the desired focus that is central to mindfulness. The very fact that you find this difficult is itself evidence that you are engaging in mindful practice!

Developing our mindful attention skills can provide us with a useful approach to help us slow down the rush to follow our impulses and to help us notice what drives these impulses.

YOUR SKILLS PRACTICE

You may wish to practice this exercise for a couple of minutes, three times each day. In the early stages you may be able to focus your attention for only ten to twenty seconds at a time. That's fine; remember that the key to mindfulness is to notice where your mind wanders to and to gently bring your mind back to the task. Just keep practicing little by little.

ACTIVATING YOUR CONTENTMENT AND SOOTHING SYSTEM

As we have been reading about in previous chapters, being compassionate requires us to be able to turn off or tone down our *threat* system. It's very tricky to access our compassionate minds when we feel so overwhelmed with threat, so it can really help us if we practice the art of actively engaging our *soothing* system, before we engage our compassionate minds, at least in the early stages.

Soothing rhythm breathing

As we saw in chapter 3, each of our three emotion regulation systems is associated with a particular physical and emotional response (see figure 2.1). The *threat* system is associated with anger, anxiety, and disgust; the *achieving activation* system is associated with drive, excitement, and vitality; and the *contentment and soothing* system is associated with feeling calm, contented, connected, and safe.

The following exercise is designed to help you *find your own* soothing rhythm for breathing rather than following a specific rate or pace. It also includes an element of mindfulness that you can use to build upon the skills we outlined in the previous section. As before, you may want to record the instructions first so that you can really concentrate on doing the exercise.

Exercise 7.3: Soothing rhythm breathing

(Begin recording)

Begin by finding a quiet place where you can sit and know that you will not be disturbed for at least ten minutes. Sit in a chair with an upright posture, don't let your head rock forward, and place both feet on the floor about a shoulder's width apart. Rest your hands on your legs.

Start by gently focusing on your breathing. Initially, just notice the air going in and out through your nose. As you breathe, notice the air coming down into your diaphragm (that's just at the bottom of your ribcage in the upside-down "V"). Feel your diaphragm move as you breathe in and out. Just notice your breathing and experiment with the pace. Breathe a little faster or a little slower and notice the difference in how your body feels. Generally, soothing rhythm breathing is slightly slower and slightly deeper than your normal breathing. It's roughly about a count of three seconds on the "in" breath, slight pause, and then three seconds for the "out" breath—but find a breathing pattern that for you seems to be your own soothing, comforting rhythm. It is as though you are checking in and linking up with the rhythm within your body that is soothing and calming to you. What you will usually find is that your breathing is slightly slower and deeper than normal. Ensure that the breaths in and out are smooth and even. For example, notice if you're breathing a bit too quickly, running out of breath, or rushing the out breath.

Now you can spend 30 seconds or so just focusing on your breathing, just noticing the breath coming down into the diaphragm, your diaphragm lifting, and then the air moving out through your nose. Sometimes it's useful to focus on the point just inside the nose where the air enters.

Even in the 30 seconds you were doing this exercise you may have realized that your wandering mind crept in with other thoughts or that you became distracted by other noises in the room. When this happens just notice that the mind has wandered and gently and kindly bring it back and focus on your breathing. At all times remember that you're not trying to force yourself to do anything, to clear your mind of thoughts, or to make yourself concentrate. You are simply noticing and gently refocusing, noticing, and then refocusing. When you first do this, it can be quite surprising just how much your mind does shift from one thing to another. This is all very normal, natural, and to be expected. In this case you are gently (re)focusing on the feelings of your breathing and your body slowing down. You might notice, for example, that you feel your body becoming heavier in the chair.

So keep in mind at all times that you are not aiming to "achieve" any specific emotional or physical state in this exercise. It is designed to help you link into your soothing system and to see what happens. Some people report that when they find their rhythm it helps them to feel calmer, slows their thoughts down, and relaxes them. Some people even use this exercise to help them get ready for sleep. This can be very helpful, but of course the purpose is to learn to train your attention with a breathing rhythm that can activate your soothing system. You are not trying to force your mind to clear itself of thoughts. All you are doing is allowing yourself to notice when your mind wanders and then gently bring your attention back to focus on your breathing. So you can use the motto "attention and return" to guide you. Notice the distractions and return your attention to your breathing. If you have one hundred thoughts, or even a thousand thoughts, that doesn't matter at all. All that matters is that you notice and then, to the best of your ability, gently and kindly bring your attention back to the breathing.

If you practice "attention and return," you may find that your mind bounces around less and less. It may become easier, but some days it will be easier than others. If you worry that you are not doing it right or that it cannot work for you, then note these thoughts as typical intrusions and return your attention to your breathing. Remember, the wandering mind is normal and indeed can provide us with very useful information to work with later on. So don't get angry with it or become self-critical; just kindly bring your attention back to the focus of your breathing. It is the act of noticing how our minds wander that is the beginning of mindfulness.

You can do these exercises at any time and in any place, such as sitting on a bus, or you can do them standing up. It's just allowing yourself a moment where you concentrate on your breathing and for your mind to come back to that single focus. The key thing is our mindful attention to the process rather than the result. This is a bit like sleeping; it's a good idea to create the conditions that will help us sleep, but if we cross a line and focus too much on our ability to fall asleep, it actually makes sleep more difficult.

SUMMARY

This chapter has developed our understanding of how we can become more mindful and create space in our minds to notice the emergence of our threat-based minds and our compassionate minds. One of the key elements of mindfulness is to *remember* to become mindful. While we can spend time deliberately practicing mindfulness (by focusing on our breathing or some other activity), its real benefit comes if we become aware that every moment of our lives could be lived more mindfully. So mindfulness is an approach that we can use in many aspects of our lives, and indeed we can practice becoming more mindful in all that we do.

We finished the chapter with some guided exercises focusing on our breathing to help us experience our *soothing system* and to practically apply being mindful.

In the following chapters we are going to be training ourselves to develop a compassionate minds and we will be exploring all the different aspects of compassion as they apply to us and to our traumatic experiences. Developing compassion won't immediately get rid of our threat-focused, traumatized minds. Like being in a canoe without a paddle on a fast-flowing river, we are learning to recognize our threatened states of mind and beginning to refocus them; we can find the paddles and start to use them to direct our canoes so that they become more under our control. So although developing compassion doesn't necessarily get rid of our troubles immediately, it can help us tolerate our troublesome and painful emotions so that we can begin to control and direct our thoughts to help us heal from our traumas.

8

Developing your skills to access compassionate feelings

In this chapter we will begin to practice developing our compassionate minds by using a series of imagery exercises, which is one of the compassionate skills we are seeking to develop. This is designed to help us soothe ourselves and to develop the compassionate patterns in our brains.

These imagery exercises can stimulate our minds and bodies into states that are compassionate, which will in turn help us to cope with our human vulnerability and frailty. People's experiences in response to these exercises vary a lot. Be aware that you may find some exercises easier or more effective than others. There are those of us who may experience self-kindness quickly, and others who may encounter quite a bit of resistance to the whole idea of self-compassion. The key thing is to remind yourself why you are developing self-kindness. So use all your learning and insight into how your brain works, and remind yourself that the purpose of developing compassion is to try to regulate your *threat* system. If you find that you are having difficulty accepting some of the ideas or finding it hard to work through the exercises, it may help if you focus on trying to absorb the more technical information of how to develop compassion. You might like to reread chapters 5, 6, and 7. This may help to reinforce your understanding of the characteristics of compassion and the value to you in cultivating a compassionate approach to your life. It may also help you overcome any residual resistance you may be experiencing.

Remember to work through the exercises at your own pace, stay mindfully observant (by noticing your thoughts but remembering to return to your focus), and above all be gentle with yourself during all your efforts. You are working out a pace that is right for you.

It can be very helpful to have a notebook in which you can write down your reactions and thoughts to the exercises. It is a great way to keep a record of any insights you may experience, and it also helps you to plot if you respond differently at different times. The extra time spent jotting down the thoughts that occur to you during and after the exercises is a good investment in you.

USING COMPASSIONATE IMAGERY

Compassion-focused exercises and imagery are designed to try to create feelings that stimulate a particular kind of brain system by using our ability to hold mental images in our minds. Images are powerful ways of changing our mental states and emotions. If we've been traumatized, we know that we can be tortured by mental images of frightening things that have happened to us or that may happen to us in the future and which are pure horror. These images also then greatly influence our emotional state. So, rather than letting these negative images and emotions hold court in our minds, we can use positive images to our advantage by deliberately choosing images that will stimulate our *soothing* system, which in turn helps to calm down our *threat system.*

We will be working a lot with imagery as a way of developing our compassionate minds. We will also find imagery a very helpful tool to use in working with trauma memories, as we can do all sorts of clever things such as bringing compassionate imagery and compassionate images into flashback memories to help make them more tolerable and less threatening.

In chapter 4 we explored the concept of shame and social threat, which relates both to who we fear we are and how we fear we exist in other people's minds. Many of the people who visit the clinic and who really suffer with shame as part of their trauma also experience profound fears relating to social threat. Some people I work with have never felt liked by others or had the belief that other people think kindly or lovingly of them. Nor have they felt "safe in their own minds," to the extent that they are severely self-critical and self-hating. It can therefore be hard for them to be supportive and validating of themselves or to have self-compassion when things go wrong in their lives. Having this constant critical battering in our heads is very unhelpful and makes us feel worse. Think what the potential effect might be, if when the critical thoughts have taken hold, we choose to deliberately turn our attention to being mindful, observing our own thoughts and feelings, and trying to refocus our thoughts onto being kind and supportive toward ourselves (thereby switching our attention to our *contentment and soothing* system).

Sometimes the way we describe switching attention to, and activation of, our *contentment and soothing* system is to use the metaphor of train tracks. There are some tracks in our *soothing* system over which trains rarely travel. The train tracks may be rusty or covered with overgrown shrubs, and in some cases they may not even have been laid down. However, if we clear the tracks that have not been used in a while and put in some new tracks, then our trains can reach our destination of self-compassion. So it is with compassionate imagery. It can be used to help clear our blockages and even give us a compassionate experience that we have never had before—just like the shiny bright new tracks filling in the gaps where the train tracks had never been laid down! Compassionate imagery can be used to activate the *soothing* system in our brains and get our train tracks to self-compassion working smoothly.

In this section we will continue to develop our self-compassion by practicing a set of exercises adapted from the Compassionate Mind Foundation website (*www.compassionatemind.co.uk*), reproduced with the kind permission of Paul Gilbert and the Foundation.

UNDERSTANDING COMPASSIONATE IMAGERY

Before we go any further it is helpful to clarify what we mean when we refer to "imagery." Mental images may be fleeting and vague. They may create a sense or impression without being a clear and distinct visual

image. Many of us, when first asked to create an image in our minds, might struggle to con
as defined as a photograph, and it may be quite natural to conclude from this that we are no
"doing" imagery exercises. But the good news is that, in fact, imagery is often fleeting and
only a vague sense or impression. For example, if we ask you to think of a bicycle, what co   .... ,....
mind? For most of us we will have a flash of an image in which we can momentarily see the key characteristics of a bicycle—two wheels, pedals, a bike seat, and so on. From this image we can immediately discern
a bicycle, but it is unlikely that the image that flashed to mind is a detailed one showing worn brakes or
reddish mud on the tires. All we need when we "do" imagery are fleeting and fragmented impressions; we
don't need crystal-clear pictures in our heads.

We often use imagery to create physical feelings as we do, for example, for the purpose of sexual
arousal. Yet, stop reading for a moment and bring to mind a time when somebody made you laugh. Close
your eyes and really remember that event; now look at yourself from the outside and see yourself laughing
and all the things going on around you. If you do this for a minute or two, notice what happens in your
body—you may have started to smile, as if your face was re-creating the emotions in the memory.

This is using imagery to bring a memory to life. When we experience a flashback or a "trauma image"
it comes from our threat system and arrives unbidden and unwanted. So, one of the purposes of the following exercises is to help you generate positive images from your *contentment and soothing* system to help
reduce the threat of the trauma image.

A SMALL (BUT IMPORTANT) NOTE ABOUT SMELL

Out of all of our five senses (sight, sound, smell, touch, and taste) smell has the fastest route to our brains.
This makes a lot of sense for evolution, as we can often smell danger long before we can see it. Smells can
also be very good triggers for emotional memories, and for those of us who suffer from smell flashbacks (as
in we smell things that aren't there and other people can't smell, which are linked to our trauma), we know
their power to activate our threat-based emotions such as fear, anxiety, or disgust. So smell can rapidly
trigger our threat system. It can also result in happy memories that trigger our *contentment and soothing*
system—for example, most of us can recall a smell (perfume, food, etc.) that makes us feel all warm inside
because it brings back such happy memories.

With this in mind, some of you may wish to begin to train your self-soothing system to be associated
with a particular scent. Can you think of a scent that you love and that makes you feel nice? Some of our
favorite scents are perfumes, essential oils, pepper, fresh ground coffee, fresh bread, freshly cut grass, and
so on. As you read the list did you notice anything? Did you have a smell memory?

If you have chosen a scent or aroma that you like and that is easy to re-create, such as perfume, aftershave, or an essential oil, I suggest you begin every exercise in the next two chapters with a big sniff at
the beginning, during, and at the end of the exercise. You will thereby maximize the opportunity for your
feelings to become associated with the smell. If this works for you we will then use the scent to trigger
compassionate feelings in your flashbacks (this will be explained in chapter 9). For the moment, just concentrate on developing the link.

SOOTHING RHYTHM BREATHING

All imagery exercises will begin with soothing rhythm breathing because it helps to slow the breathing down, focus on the out breath, and calm us. Not everyone will be comfortable with soothing rhythm breathing, so you may just want to use your normal breathing. The point of the breathing exercise is just to slow down and create space to do the exercises.

DEVELOPING YOUR "SAFE PLACE"

When we are feeling threatened, having a safe place to go to in our minds can be a very helpful, calming experience. I often spend quite a lot of time with traumatized visitors to the clinic helping them to develop safe place imagery. I can then help them use this to tolerate and end their flashbacks and turn off their threat systems by creating feelings of "safeness" and calm, which soothes them. Safe place imagery is especially useful if our traumatic experiences involved fear and physical threats to our safety.

You may find you already have a safe place, as many of us remind ourselves of being in a better place or recall happy memories from the past when we are feeling sad or upset. The safe place exercise builds upon this natural way that we activate our soothing system. Feeling safe and calm can help us think about our memories with more compassion. We may find we can tolerate them and bear them more easily and so have less need to engage in less helpful behaviors to end our distress.

Some people have clear ideas about places they like or places they feel safe in, but others don't; and sadly some of us have never felt physically safe. So before you start you may want to think about the sorts of places you could feel safe in. The place does not have to actually exist; that's the wonder of the human mind—we can create fantasy images and they still affect our brain chemistry. Here are some helpful prompts to aid your creativity:

- What would your safe place be like?

- Would it be outside or inside?

- What would the weather be like if it was outside?

- What colors would there be around you?

We are aiming to create a place where we will feel safe, calm, and contented. This can be a real place or it can be somewhere we invent. The act of really thinking about what sort of place helps us feel safe can be an important part of this exercise; some of you might never have thought about this before. Try to engage in the exercise with curiosity and interest, as if you're an artist creating something for the first time, seeing if you like "this" here or prefer "that" there.

If using a real place, try not to use one that has other feelings such as grief and sadness associated with it. You may find that these feelings are activated by the imagery exercise, which will not be helpful (at least not at this time) because the purpose of the exercise is to access feelings of safeness.

We can also distinguish between genuine feelings of safeness and freedom as opposed to safety. For example, someone might say they feel safe if they can lock themselves behind steel doors. That is understandable, but it traps you inside and doesn't give any sense of freedom and joyfulness in the place you find yourself. So "safeness" means you are safe to *move around* anywhere you want; it is a place of liberation where you don't have to worry about anything.

We are learning to focus our minds on deliberately creating images and exploring the value of these images in terms of how they help us to feel safe.

Exercise 8.1: Imaging your safe place

(Begin recording)

Begin by finding somewhere comfortable to sit and where you will not be disturbed for at least ten minutes. Engage in your soothing rhythm breathing (see exercise 7.3). Focus on your breathing and allow the breath to come down into your diaphragm slowly and evenly and then leave your body slowly and evenly. Just concentrate on the experience of breathing in and out.

Feeling safe

When you feel ready, try to create a place in your mind that could give you the feeling of safeness and calmness. You're not trying to make yourself feel safe, you're only trying to imagine a place that could make you feel nice and safe, calm and contented. You can close your eyes if you feel okay with this. If not, focus your attention on the image in your mind or the picture or reminder of your safe place. Alternatively, you can focus your attention on your pebble or shell and imagine your safe place without closing your eyes.

When you feel you've developed an impression of a safe place, work through your senses of sight, touch, and hearing, and imagine what details they will add to your safe place. Start with what you can see, for example:

What colors are around you? Are they dark or light?

If you are outside, where are you?

Are you on a beach? What kind of beach? Is it sandy, pebbly?

Are you in a garden, in the country?

Are there trees or other plants around?

What does the sky look like above you?

Now move on to your sense of touch:

Are you in the safe place and can you see yourself? Or are you just looking out at everything?

What are you doing and what can you feel?

Are you walking? If so what are you walking on?

Are you lying or sitting down? What does it feel like?

Now think of any other sensations such as a gentle cooling breeze or the warmth of the sun on your face.

What can you hear?

Is there the sound of water, perhaps the ocean lapping, a stream babbling, or a waterfall?

Can you hear any birdsong or the sound of bleating sheep, cooing pigeons, or the gentle drone of traffic far away?

Remember that, quite naturally, your wandering mind will take you away from this place after just a few seconds. So just notice when it goes, and then gently return your attention to the element of your safe place image you find most appealing. When you have that specific image back, gently expand it to re-create the other parts of your safe place.

Some people find it helpful to imagine seeing themselves in their safe place; to imagine the look on their face, and how they would sit or lie when they are feeling safe, relaxed, and contented. Other people prefer just to imagine their safe place and their feeling of being in it. It is okay to do either.

There is no "right or wrong" about your safe place. It is just a place where you feel safe, and you may find that different images work better at different times of the day, or when you are experiencing different levels of distress.

After a little practice you may find an image that really works for you. Remember, it is not going to be in complete "HD 3D surround-sound and smell-o-vision," so the more reminders you can develop to help you focus on your image the better. When you have a safe place, you might find it helpful to write your own script to help you recall and stay in your safe place. You might even want to record this to make your own CD that can be played back.

Feeling wanted

In the compassionate mind approach we add an important part to our imagery, which again is designed to stimulate your soothing and compassion systems. After you've been imaging your safe place for a few minutes and when you're ready, just imagine that this is your creation and therefore this place really welcomes you and wants you to be here and wants to offer you safeness and rest. The feeling of being wanted by a place may seem strange, but try to see how you do. Focus on feeling in harmony with this place. You might find that if you imagine seeing yourself with a gentle expression of contentment or compassion on your face this helps with feeling in harmony with your safe place.

You might also have trouble having a feeling of harmony with your safe place. Don't worry about this; with time and practice these feelings will come. At all times remember that nothing is being forced here. You're not trying to make yourself feel safe in this image; you are engaging in a gentle, curious exercise to see how a sense of safeness might develop over time. As you practice this exercise you may find that your safe place changes as you continue to explore what it is that could make you feel safe.

Some people can become quite sleepy when they do this exercise, and some even use it to help them sleep. That's okay too. However, the main aim of using the imagery in this context is to bring our soothing system online so that we can begin to think about our difficulties a little more easily than we can if we are caught up in the achieving and activating or threat system. With this aim in mind, perhaps remind yourself to use an "alert" posture so that you don't go to sleep. Try to make a conscious effort to sit upright in a chair, with the small of your back touching the chair and your mind aware of the upright posture you have adopted.

DEVELOPING YOUR COMPASSIONATE MIND THROUGH IMAGERY

The following compassion-focused exercises are focused in four main ways:

- Developing the inner compassionate self. In these exercises we will be focusing on creating a sense of a compassionate self, just like actors do if they are trying to inhabit a role.

- Compassion flowing out from us to others. Here we focus on the feelings in our bodies when we fill our minds with compassionate feelings for other people.

- Compassion flowing into us. Here we focus our minds on opening up to compassion, to stimulate areas of our brains that are responsive to the kindness of others.

- Self-compassion. This is focused on developing feelings, thoughts, and experiences that direct our own abilities for compassion toward ourselves.

Developing the inner compassionate self

As we have seen, we all have the capacity to experience and act upon different mind-sets. We are men and women of many parts. In the next set of exercises we are working to develop the compassionate part of ourselves. Our compassionate self has a number of key qualities:

WISDOM

There are many important aspects to wisdom. Wisdom is the way in which we learn from our experiences and how that changes us and how we can gain deeper insight into the nature of things. From reading the previous chapters, you now have the understanding that all of us just find ourselves here, with a very troublesome brain that has evolved over many millions of years without our choice or design input. We can therefore begin to open our hearts to the reality of our lives without shaming or blaming ourselves.

The experiences we are having now have also touched many millions of others. We are not alone, and this sense of common humanity allows us to see that we are all caught up in the same struggles. This can be helpful in those moments when we feel something especially bad about our experiences. So open up your mind and heart to our common humanity and use the wisdom that is there for you. You are not the first to suffer in this way and sadly you will not be the last.

A second insight is that our sense of self and memories come from our own experiences of life. These are the relationships and situations we were born into. A third insight is that our emotions and thoughts come and go; nothing is permanent and everything changes. This is the nature of all things.

Of course the most important aspect of wisdom is recognizing that you are suffering and that you don't want to suffer any more. Coming to understand the causes of your suffering and the role your threat system has in this is very important in changing the way your mind works. It may be a difficult path that you see behind and ahead of you, but you now have the wisdom and insight to recognize the link between your threat system and your trauma memories. You now know the value of developing your soothing system to regulate and tone down your threat system. This new wisdom is crucial because it starts you off on your journey of healing.

Our compassionate selves know that we had no choice over the design of our bodies and brains or the lives we found ourselves born into. We just found ourselves on this planet, doing the best we can with the brains and bodies we inherited. Working with some of what goes on in our minds—those powerful emotions, mood shifts, unwanted thoughts or images, and painful memories—can, through no fault of our own, be difficult. Our wisdom understands that all these things that we did not choose can be at the root of our suffering through no fault of our own.

AUTHORITY AND STRENGTH

People often confuse compassion with weakness, but there can be no compassion without some degree of authority and strength. Compassion is not just nice wishes and sentiments. The way in which we translate our wishes into actions is very much related to the development of fortitude and courage. It can offer us an inner sense of confidence and authority, which comes from wisdom. Strength helps to give us a commitment and determination to try to face and heal suffering. When we imagine our inner strength, we might imagine ourselves as older or bigger than we are; we can imagine ourselves coming through our difficulties.

MOTIVATION WITH WARMTH

Developing compassionate motivation is a crucial aspect of our work. We become motivated to do something about suffering because we understand it; we have new wisdom and we can see a path forward, and this strengthens our intentions. Here we focus on our intention to relieve suffering in a gentle but firm way. This warmth is like an open friendliness. This type of kindness is not (just) about being nice but having a real desire to be helpful with a gentle, warm, friendly, and open voice and manner.

RESPONSIBILITY

With motivation comes a desire to take responsibility. We now begin to see that because compassion is about sensitivity to suffering, we have a commitment to think about it. That commitment is about standing up and taking responsibility to relieve suffering by courageously engaging with it and also not to cause harm (e.g., by being harshly critical to ourselves and others). Here we focus on facing, rather than turning away from, life's challenges. It involves recognizing that although something is "not our fault," we can make a commitment to ourselves and others to do our best to work on it, even with small steps at a time. So responsibility is not about blaming or criticizing (because that is usually focused on things in the past), but rather it is about genuinely wanting to act in ways that are helpful and based on our wisdom, strength, and warmth (focusing us on the future).

These are the qualities at the center of our concept of a compassionate self. Next, we're going to practice focusing on each of these qualities and imagining we have each of them in turn, noting what they feel like and any effect they have on our bodies.

Exercise 8.2: The compassionate self

(Begin recording)

This exercise is designed to help you focus on the feelings associated with creating compassion in yourself. It helps when we come to offer ourselves, or others, compassion if we have a little idea of what it feels like. As we do this exercise and the ones that follow, keep in mind that it doesn't matter if you feel you have these qualities or not. It is the act of imagining that you have them that is important. This is the type of approach that Method actors use to get into a role. They imagine themselves to have the characteristics of the character they're playing. In this way they are stimulating certain qualities in the mind and body, which in turn makes their acting convincing. For that short time they "become" the character they imagine themselves to be and often "stay in character" even when they are not performing. Of course, when they come out of the role they may not want to be anything like the character they played (particularly if they are Hannibal Lector!). In these compassion-focused exercises it doesn't matter whether you feel you currently have compassionate characteristics or not, or even desire to have them; it's about putting yourself into the mental state of imagining that's important. The extent and degree to which you practice this will have a bearing on how naturally it develops and whether it starts to feel more natural.

Take each of the qualities we just described in turn—wisdom, authority and strength, motivation with warmth, and responsibility—hold them in your mind and imagine yourself having them. Work through each quality steadily and slowly. You may find some qualities easier to imagine than others, and this is perfectly normal. Try to notice how each quality affects your body differently. Does your body feel different when you focus on strength and when you focus on kindness? Remember that you may just get glimmers of things because your mind wanders or you can't really focus. This is very typical of learning something new, just like if we were trying to learn to play a piano we'd be all fingers and thumbs to start with. Regular practice will help, and remember that being mindful is observing our thoughts wandering and gently bringing them back to focus on the quality we are exploring at the time.

To begin the exercise, find a place where you can sit quietly and not be disturbed for at least ten minutes. Once again, focus on your soothing breathing rhythm, giving yourself a chance to slow down and create the space for undertaking the exercise. When you feel that your body has slowed down (even slightly), you are ready to practice imagining that you are a very deeply compassionate person. Think in turn of each of the qualities you would ideally have as a compassionate person, trying to spend at least one minute focusing on each quality—longer if you can.

Now focus on your desire to become a compassionate person and to be able to think, act, and feel compassionately. Focus on the first quality of being wise. Imagine being a wise person, with a wisdom that comes from your understanding about the nature of our lives, minds, and bodies. You are wise enough to know that much of what goes on inside us is not our fault but is the result of our evolution and experiences over which we had no control.

When you are ready and have a sense of your wisdom, you can switch to imagining the quality of having strength that comes with a sense of maturity and authority. Explore your body posture and make sure you are sitting or standing confidently and assertively, in a way that matches your idea of being strong. Your facial expressions should also reflect what it feels like to be confident.

Keep your head upright rather than letting it drop forward; your sitting posture or standing posture is one of confidence. Remember, you are imagining yourself as a person who understands your own difficulties and those of others in a nonjudgmental way, and has the confidence to be sensitive to distress and to tolerate suffering.

When you have a sense of your wisdom and strength, focus on the qualities of warmth and gentle friendliness. Imagine being warm and kind. Create a compassionate facial expression. Try to imagine yourself speaking to someone and hear the warm tone in your voice. Now reach out with that warmth and feel what it might be like to offer it to another. Remember you are imagining yourself filled with warmth and gentleness.

Next, move on to imagining feelings of responsibility. Imagine that you have lost interest in condemning or blaming and that you now want to do the best you can to help yourself, and others, move forward. Hold on to your compassion and facial expression of warmth, but just focus on this experience of taking responsibility and committing yourself to a compassionate path of self-development.

Finally, imagine yourself having all of these qualities and incorporating them into the way you are with yourself and others.

When you have finished, bring yourself gently back into the room. You might want to write down what it felt like to have these qualities and how it might affect the way you want to act in the future.

Exercise 8.3: You at your best

(Begin recording)

Another way you can access and practice your compassionate self is to spend time reminding yourself of a time when you felt compassion and/or acted in a compassionate way. When we are struggling with difficult things in our lives it can be easy to forget that we have the capacity for compassion, so actively bringing memories to mind of when you have been compassionate to others—no matter to what degree—can help you to remember that you do have compassionate qualities and to bring these qualities to the fore.

One way to think of your compassionate self is as "you at your best." You can begin by practicing your soothing rhythm breathing, or your safe place image, and then bring to mind a time when you were kind and compassionate to somebody and you were satisfied with how helpful you were. Focus on the feelings it created when you were kind to somebody. Remember your feelings of kindness and what it's like to feel a genuine desire to want someone to feel better and to flourish. The aim is to focus on your kindness and feelings of wanting to help as you bring your attention to your own compassionate qualities.

Try not to focus on times when you have been compassionate with someone who is very distressed, especially when you are just starting this exercise. The reason for this is that we want you to focus on the act of kindness, not become upset remembering somebody's distress. It may help to write down the specific memory and "risk assess" it to make sure it is not distressing. Otherwise you can end up focusing on your distress, and maybe your inability to alleviate it, rather than bringing your attention to your own compassionate qualities.

Using your example, develop your image of you at your best by seeing how you can call to mind the compassionate qualities of wisdom, strength, warmth, and courage as demonstrated in your example from your own life. Focus on your body position, facial expression, and tone of voice as you offer your wisdom, strength, warmth, and courage. Spend sufficient time on this exercise to really be able to explore it and reflect on the experience.

Your sense of self

Paul Gilbert reminds us that the whole point of Buddhist meditation is to develop *the sense of self* and gain enlightenment. Buddhist practices are about developing key qualities of the self (such as mindfulness and compassion), which in turn give us new insights into the "nature of the self." The compassionate self can also be what we would like to become. If we want to be good at sport, playing the piano, cooking, or analyzing poetry, we recognize that we need to spend time on these activities and practice them. The more we practice, the closer we move toward becoming what we want to be.

The same is true of developing compassion; we need to spend time practicing our exercises and actively living the compassionate attributes. We can make a decision to become more like the compassionate selves of our imaginations. We can practice what we would like to become by imagining enacting, thinking, and playing with those compassionate qualities. If we have an argument with somebody, we can make a decision to slow down and be observant (mindful) of the thoughts and feelings flowing through us and reflect with the compassionate self on how we might deal with that situation more compassionately. We can decide what sort of person we would like to be and practice being that.

COMPASSION FLOWING OUT FROM YOU TO OTHERS

The idea here is to focus on your desire to help others and your feelings of kindness and warmth toward them. Keep in mind that it is your behavior and intentions that are important—the feelings may follow.

There are three exercises in this section. In the first, you simply remind yourself of the qualities of the compassionate self and imagine your compassion flowing into someone you care about, giving him or her three key compassionate messages. In the second, you will be focusing your compassion on helping an individual you care about who is struggling with something in his or her life and whom you would like to support using your compassionate self.

The final exercise can be a little trickier for some people because we will be exploring receiving compassion, and some of us may struggle with this to begin with. Don't be put off; just keep gently trying.

Exercise 8.4: Focusing the compassionate self on others

(Begin recording)

To practice this, find a time and place when you can sit quietly without being interrupted for at least ten minutes. Once again, remember to begin with your soothing breathing rhythm even if you only take a few deep and slow breaths. Now remind yourself of being "'you at your best" as we did in exercise 8.3. Some days this will be easier than others—even just the slightest glimmer can be a start.

Next, focus and bring to mind someone you care about (for example, a partner, a friend, a parent or child, an animal, or even a plant). When you have them in mind, focus on directing toward them three basic feelings and thoughts:

May you be well.

May you be happy.

May you flourish.

It can often help to actually name the person. So it would be "May you be happy, Deborah." It is also important to recite these words in your head on the out breath rather than the in breath, because compassionate feelings are linked with the parasympathetic nervous system, which is accessed on the out breath. We should also note that these are only examples and you can choose different words such as "'May you be safe" or "May you overcome your difficulties or be free of suffering." So the exact wishes you send to this person depend on your inner feelings for them, but the three we've given you here are good starting points.

Keep in mind that it is your intentions that are important—the feelings may follow. Be gentle, take time, and allow yourself to focus on the desires and wishes for the other person/animal/plant. Maybe picture them smiling at you and sharing these feelings. Okay, that's tricky if you are thinking of a plant, but imagine the plant as "happy" to receive your compassionate wishes. Spend time focusing on this genuine desire of yours for "the other."

Remember to be mindful: if your mind wanders, that's not a problem—just gently and kindly bring it back to the task. Try to notice any feelings you have in yourself and your body that emerge from this focusing exercise. Don't worry if nothing much happens at a conscious level; the act of trying is the important thing. It's like getting fit—it may take some visits to the gym or training sessions before you consciously notice feeling different, but your body will be responding immediately.

Exercise 8.5: Compassion flowing out to others

(Begin recording)

In this exercise we are going to imagine kindness and compassion flowing from you to others, but in this case they will be facing a difficulty in their lives that you want to help them with. As with exercise 8.3, try not to choose a time when that person (or animal) was very distressed because then you are likely to focus on that distress. It can help to prepare by jotting down the name of the person or animal you want to help, and the difficulty you want to help them with. Before you start, try to make sure that the issue will not be so distressing for you that you cannot do the exercise.

Begin with your soothing rhythm breathing or your safe place image exercises to help you get in a compassionate mind-set. Try to spend at least one minute on each element of the exercise.

When you feel ready, bring to mind a time when you felt compassionate toward the person (or animal) you have in mind.

Imagine yourself expanding, as if you are becoming calmer, wiser, stronger, more mature, and better able to help that person. Pay attention to your body as you remember your feelings of kindness.

Now imagine expanding with warmth and imagine it flowing from your body over the other person. Feel your genuine desire for this other person to be free of suffering and to flourish.

Now focus on your tone of voice and the kind of things you would want to say or do to help him or her.

Think about your pleasure in being able to be kind.

To finish, focus on combining all of these qualities in your compassionate self and imagine them flowing into the other person or animal: your desire to be helpful and kind; the sense of warmth; feelings of expansion; your tone of voice; the wisdom in your voice and in your behavior.

When you have finished the exercise you might want to make some notes about how this exercise made you feel.

COMPASSION FLOWING INTO YOU

Although many of us can see how being offered, and being able to accept, compassion can be helpful for other people, we can find this quite difficult to accept for ourselves. Our compassionate minds have both the capacity to give and to receive compassion from others. As we have seen, our capacity to receive compassion is crucial to activating our soothing system, and hence to helping us manage difficult events and emotions. In the following exercises we will practice allowing compassion from others into our lives.

The first exercise is focused on helping us to remember times when other people have offered us compassion. When we are distressed our threat system naturally focuses on things that are dangerous to us, and this may mean that we "forget" that some people in the world have been compassionate to us. The key here is to nurture these memories and use them as a basis for helping us to engage with those in our lives who can be compassionate, to recognize compassion when it is offered to us, and to use it to help us.

Sadly, sometimes people cannot remember other people being particularly compassionate toward them. This can occur for a variety of reasons, perhaps because they are so distressed that it is hard to activate the memory or maybe they have had very few experiences of other people being compassionate toward them. Sometimes people struggle to activate these memories because compassion has been conditional. It has come at a price that the person doesn't want to think about. For example, the people they recall have been very unpredictable, offering compassion one moment and hostility the next. It may also be that memories of compassion from another are too painful to bring to mind because that person is no longer around, so recalling them activates grief rather than helps them to focus on being offered compassion.

So activating a memory of being offered compassion can be tricky. If we have experiences that have made this difficult it is not our fault, nor need it be associated with a sense of failure or personal inadequacy. It is simply the way it is! It does, however, become our problem, as we have to build up an image of compassion that flows from others into us from scratch. The second exercise is designed to address this by developing an image of someone or something that can offer us compassion throughout our lives, a compassionate companion we can always rely on. It is possible to do this even if we have limited experiences of compassion from others by drawing on the innate wisdom about compassion that we used in the previous exercise.

Exercise 8.6: Using your memories of compassion from others

(Begin recording)

Here we are aiming to activate a memory of someone being compassionate toward you. This memory shouldn't be of a time when you were very distressed, because you will then focus on that distress rather than on the compassion. The point of the exercise is to concentrate on the desire of another person to help and be kind to you. Try to spend a minute or so on each phase of the exercise.

To begin, engage in your soothing rhythm breathing for a minute or so until you can sense your body slowing down. As you feel this, prepare for your compassionate imagery by allowing your body posture to become compassionate. For example, have an open chest and shoulders and take on a half-smiling expression.

When you feel ready, bring to mind a memory of a time when someone was kind to you.

Create a compassionate expression on your face and a body posture that gives you a sense of kindness and a warm glow of gratitude as you recall the memory.

Explore the facial expressions and body position of the person who was kind to you. Sometimes it helps if you see him or her moving toward you or see his or her face breaking into a smile.

Focus on the important sensory qualities of your memory. First, spend one minute just focusing on the kinds of things this person said and the tone of his or her voice. Then focus on the emotion in the person—what he or she really felt for you at that moment.

Now focus on the whole experience, maybe whether he or she held you, touched you, or helped you in other ways such as standing by you or talking to you. Notice how he or she created a feeling of being soothed and connected to you, and notice your sense of gratitude and pleasure at being helped. Allow the experience of soothing, connectedness, gratitude, and joy in being helped to grow. Remember to keep your facial expression as compassionate as you can.

When you are ready, gently let the memory fade, come out of the exercise, and make some notes on how you felt. You may notice that bringing these memories to mind has created feelings of compassion inside you, even if they are just glimmers. What came up for you? Was there anything that surprised you? What would you like to work on to take your practice forward?

CREATING PERFECT NURTURING IMAGERY

When we experience compassion and kindness from another, when we feel and sense another mind is focused on us with benevolence, it can have quite a powerful positive impact on us. There are systems in the brain that are very responsive to receiving kindness from others. So we want to develop exercises that will help trigger these systems, because they create a sense of soothing and also an inner security. Of course, we all want compassionate relationships with real people too, and these exercises are not meant to replace those relationships. They are designed to stimulate the brain to help you with your feelings and emotions. Developing these aspects of the brain can also help us to feel safe enough to create and foster compassionate relationships with other people in the outside world. To use another sporting analogy, practicing in the gym is not the same as playing the real game. But it can help us when we do play the game for real.

Exercise 8.7: Creating a perfect nurturer

In this exercise, we're going to create your perfect nurturer. If you could imagine or create someone who would capture everything you want from somebody totally focused on your welfare, what qualities would he or she have?

Now some people may of course dismiss this with thoughts like "I don't deserve that" or "If anybody got really close to me and knew me from the inside, they wouldn't like me." However, for this exercise the point is to imagine that you are the recipient of complete compassion from another mind without judgment in the present moment.

Whatever image comes to mind that you choose to work with, note that it is your creation and therefore your own personal ideal—what you would really like from feeling cared for. It is not uncommon for people's first image to be that of an inanimate object (like a tree or a color). Some find that they would like their perfect nurturer to be humanlike; others prefer an animal or even a fantasy character (like a fairy). There are those who bring to mind a fictional character from a book or film (e.g., Gandalf from *The Lord of the Rings*), while others prefer to invent their own companion. You can use people you actually know, although in my experience this can be a little complicated. Often, the people we know are not compassionate all of the time—after all they are only human, like us! We can also end up choosing people who have been very caring but perhaps are no longer with us, such as a teacher, friend, or relative who may have passed away or whom we no longer see. Thus our image can get mixed up with feelings of grief and longing for them, which can distract us from the aim of the exercise, which is to experience compassion from our perfect nurturer.

Whatever your perfect nurturer looks like, it is important that you try to give her or him certain qualities, which are outlined below. These are superhuman—complete and perfect—compassionate qualities that are there for you to practice creating and bring to mind. They include:

- a deep commitment to you: a desire to help you cope with and relieve your suffering and to take joy in your happiness

- strength of mind that is not overwhelmed by your pain or distress, but remains present, enduring with you

- wisdom that has been gained through experience and true understanding of the struggles we go through in life (we all "just find ourselves here" doing the best we can)

- warmth, conveyed by kindness, gentleness, caring, and openness

- an acceptance that is never judgmental or critical but understands your struggles and accepts you as you are, while at the same time being deeply committed to helping and supporting you

You can use worksheet 1 (Developing my perfect nurturer imagery) to help you with this exercise. One of the key experiences is that your image really wants you to be free of suffering, and/or to be able to deal with your difficulties and to flourish. It knows that we all just find ourselves here, living as we do, trying to make the best of our minds and lives. It understands that our minds are difficult, that emotions can run riot in us, and that this is not our fault. The key to this exercise is not the visual clarity. Indeed some people don't really see their images in any clear way at all. Rather it is the focus on and practice of compassionate desires coming into you. Here you are practicing imagining another mind wishing you to flourish.

Before you begin your imagery work, please complete worksheet 1.

WORKSHEET 1: DEVELOPING MY PERFECT NURTURER IMAGERY

How would you like your perfect nurturer to look? (For example, describe her or his physical appearance, size, color, etc.)

What would you like your perfect nurturer to sound like?

Soothing?

Calm?

Low?

Soft?

Strong?

What does your perfect nurturer smell like?

Can you use your compassionate scent?

Does your perfect nurturer have a texture (e.g., soft, smooth, strong)?

When you are struggling with your memories, what would you like your perfect nurturer to offer you in the way of comfort?

Unconditional acceptance?

Nonjudgment?

Warmth, care, kindness?

Strength and wisdom?

Genuineness?

Hope?

When you have completed the worksheet you are ready to begin.

(Begin recording)

Sitting in a place where you won't be disturbed, first engage your soothing rhythm breathing and adopt a compassionate expression. Then bring to mind your safe place. This may now be the place where you wish to create and meet your perfect nurturing image. You can choose to meet your image in another place; that's okay too. The key is to create the feelings of being safe and soothed before you meet your perfect nurturer.

Imagine your image appearing in your safe place; he or she may be materializing from the mist, walking through a door, and so on. Picture him or her sitting or standing beside you. You may want to touch him or her or be held by him or her, and that's okay; only allow your perfect nurturer to be with you in a way you feel comfortable with and that helps you to feel safe and soothed.

To begin with, simply practice experiencing what it is like to focus on the feeling that another mind really values you and cares about you unconditionally. Now focus on your image, which is looking at you with great warmth. Imagine that he or she has the following deep desires for you:

That you be well.

That you be happy.

That you be free of suffering.

Allow yourself to sit with and open up to these experiences of compassion, in the knowledge that you can always rely on your perfect nurturer to offer you his or her commitment, strength, wisdom, and acceptance.

You may notice that your mind wanders, perhaps to memories of times when people have not been compassionate toward you. This is perfectly normal. Just gently bring your mind back to focusing attention on experiencing compassion from your nurturer.

Try to do this exercise for about ten minutes, and then gently bring yourself back into the here and now and jot down what you felt during the exercise.

Difficulties you may encounter

It is common for people to struggle to develop this image of the perfect nurturer. You might have thought, "Yes, but this is not real; I want somebody real to care for me." That is, of course, very understandable and doing this exercise could even make you feel sad. That is because your intuitive wisdom recognizes that you are seeking a connection with another person.

The aim of imagining a perfect nurturer is to help you develop the compassionate aspect of yourself that you can direct toward other people but may find hard to direct toward yourself.

Of course it is desirable to find people who are caring and to be able to accept their compassion. Sometimes these people will be in our lives, but we can't allow their compassion in because we struggle to accept it. At other times people are not as available to us as we would want, even if we could accept their compassion.

Your perfect nurturer allows you to practice receiving compassion at a pace and in a way that feels safe for you. It can also be available to you whenever you need it, and it understands what you need to feel safe and when you are struggling. Try not to see your perfect nurturer as an either/or choice but as quite different processes between the compassion you give to yourself and the compassion you'd like other people to give to you, both of which can be useful in helping us manage our emotions and life's challenges.

SELF-COMPASSION

This may be the hardest of all of the exercises we have introduced so far. Many of us struggle to offer ourselves compassion, and we will explore this in a little more detail in the next chapter. However, for now we are simply going to try to practice self-compassion using the skills we have learned in the exercises so far.

People can find it difficult to jump straight into offering themselves compassion. This is where your perfect nurturer can be really helpful. You can focus the attention of your companion's compassion on a difficulty in your life you need help with—ideally one that is not overwhelmingly distressing, otherwise you might get caught up in this. As you become more confident using your compassionate companion to support you, you can always increase the level of difficulty that you bring to him or her.

Of course we know that your perfect nurturer is not real; it simply represents the kindest, strongest, wisest, and warmest parts of you that can help you when you are struggling. However, it can be a useful bridge until you are able to offer yourself compassion directly. Try the exercise below.

Exercise 8.8: Getting help from your perfect nurturer

(Begin recording)

First find a place and time when you can sit quietly without being interrupted. Then, engage your soothing rhythm breathing and compassionate expression. Bring to mind the safe place where you want to meet your companion. Try to spend at least one minute on each element of the following exercise.

Imagine spending some time with your companion and experiencing his or her compassion flowing over and around you. You may want to touch him or her or be held by him or her—this is fine. Only allow your compassionate companion to be with you in a way you feel comfortable with and that helps you to feel safe and soothed.

Next, focus on your perfect nurturer, who is looking at you with great warmth. Imagine that he or she has the following hopes and wishes for you: That you be well. That you be happy. That you be free of suffering. Allow yourself to sit with and open up to these experiences of compassion, in the knowledge that you can always rely on your perfect nurturer to offer you his or her commitment to you, his or her strength, wisdom, and acceptance.

Next, imagine telling your perfect nurturer about the struggle that you are having. Imagine his or her facial expression and body posture as he or she listens to you with concern and acceptance.

If you can, imagine what he or she would say to you to help you have the courage, wisdom, and strength to face your difficulties. Perhaps he or she will come up with other ways of seeing things or suggest other ways to help you. Perhaps he or she cannot. It doesn't really matter; the key is to experience his or her warmth and kindness, strength and wisdom, and to allow you to express the things that are worrying you or the feelings that you have without being judged or criticized.

You can finish the exercise by again imagining the compassion flowing from your companion into you. Allow yourself to take pleasure in the feelings of safeness, comfort, and connectedness for a while, and then gently bring yourself back into the room.

You may want to note down how this felt and any new understandings or ways of coping that you have learned from your companion.

Exercise 8.9: Being the focus of self-compassion

This exercise is similar to Exercise 8.5. The only difference is that you, rather than someone else, are the focus of your compassionate attention.

(Begin recording)

Find a time and place when you can sit quietly without being disturbed. Now try to create a sense of being a compassionate person. When you can do this, bring to mind a picture of yourself. Sometimes it can help to use a photograph or look at your face in the mirror. If you have a strong sense of self-dislike or self-criticism for the way you are now, it may be helpful to use an image of you when you were younger. It can be easier to be compassionate with our childhood self.

When you have an image in mind, focus on directing toward yourself three basic feelings and thoughts:

May I be well.

May I be happy.

May I be free of suffering.

Keep in mind that it is your behavior and intentions that are important—the feelings may follow. Maybe you can picture your compassionate self smiling back at you and feeling joy and gratitude.

Your wandering mind is likely to be very active during this exercise, particularly at first. This is normal, so just gently and kindly bring it back to the task.

When you have finished, note down any thoughts or feelings that you are left with or that you want to take away from the exercise.

Exercise 8.10: Focusing self-compassion toward yourself

(Begin recording)

This is the final exercise in this chapter and is the most advanced so far in terms of self-compassion. It is a variation on exercises 8.5 and 8.8. In this case you are practicing offering yourself compassion for a specific dilemma or difficulty in your life. As with exercise 8.8, try to resist the temptation to choose something that is very painful for you at the moment. You can work your way up to this as you grow in confidence with the exercise.

In this exercise we are going to imagine kindness and compassion flowing from you toward yourself. It can help to prepare by jotting down the issue you want to work on. You may also want to look in the mirror as you do the exercise.

Begin with your soothing rhythm breathing or your safe place. Try to spend at least one minute on each element of the exercise.

When you feel ready, bring to mind your compassionate self. Imagine yourself expanding as if you are becoming calmer, wiser, stronger, more mature, and able to help.

Pay attention to your body as you remember your feelings of kindness.

Now imagine expanding the warmth within your body and feel it flowing over and around you. Experience your genuine desire for yourself to be free of suffering and to flourish.

Now focus on your tone of voice and the kind of things you would want to say or do to help you with the problem you are facing. If it helps, you can imagine having a conversation with yourself.

Next think about your pleasure in being able to be kind to yourself and to accept your own kindness.

To finish, focus on combining all these qualities of your compassionate self and imagine them flowing into you. This includes your desire to be helpful and kind; your sense of warmth; feelings of expansion; your tone of voice; and the wisdom in your voice and in your behavior.

When you have finished the exercise you might want to make some notes about how this felt for you and what you want to take away from it, what insights you have gained, or what you have learned about yourself.

START YOUR DAY THE COMPASSIONATE WAY

Ideally, practice "becoming the compassionate self" each day. If life is busy, start by learning what Professor Gilbert has called "compassion under the duvet." When you wake up in the morning, try to spend a few minutes practicing becoming your compassionate self. As you lie in bed, bring a compassionate expression to your face and focus on your desire to be wise and compassionate. Remember, inside you, you have the capacity for wisdom and strength, but you have to create space for it. Even two minutes a day, if practiced every day, may have an effect. You can also practice when you stand at the bus stop or when you're just lying in the bath. You may then find you'll want to practice for longer periods of time or even perhaps find places where you can train more. Whenever you are aware of it, even sitting in a meeting, you can use soothing breathing and focus on becoming the wise, compassionate, calm, and mature self.

MEMORY PROMPTS

The key thing to remember is to practice little and often. Here are some memory prompts for you:

While doing any of the exercises, you may choose to hold a semiprecious stone that feels nice in your hand. Carry it with you so that when you touch it in your pocket or purse, it reminds you of the kind of person you want to be.

Stand a little card next to your bed with a note on it about compassion so that before you get up in the morning you can remind yourself to be compassionate today.

Put a candle at the end of your bath and use it as a reminder to engage your soothing breathing rhythm and refocus on your compassionate self as you enjoy a soak. After all, how often do we lie in a relaxing bath when our minds are all over the place. This is a good time to become mindful, to be observant, and to focus on compassion.

One inventive visitor to the clinic bought multicolored socks that she called her compassion socks, and she would wear them to remind herself to constantly focus on her inner wisdom, strength, and true desire to be confident in a compassionate way. The memory prompts you use can be original to you, as long as they help you.

SUMMARY

The exercises covered in this chapter are designed to help you to develop and foster your capacity for compassion, and to learn to direct your compassionate attention toward yourself and others. It will take time and effort on your part to work on these exercises; however, it will be useful if you can learn to "act" from the perspective of your compassionate mind before we move on to helping you revisit your traumatic memories. You will find it helpful to always be able to return to your sense of the compassionate self if you struggle with any of the work on dealing with your difficult memories. As I've said throughout this book, never go faster and further than feels comfortable. If, at any time, you get stuck or overwhelmed with painful feelings try to come back to your safe place or imagery, and if you feel comfortable doing so use your favorite compassion flow exercise.

At this stage you may not "feel" compassionate, particularly toward yourself, but the foundations of those "train tracks" are being laid. These feelings are normal, particularly if you have limited experience of compassion from others or if you have learned to be a harsh self-critic. These feelings can emerge eventually, usually for other people or things first, before we have them for ourselves. It is also normal for these feelings to come and go, particularly when we are distressed. The key is to continue to use the exercises to gradually build up this "mental muscle." As you do, your brain will gradually change to improve your capacity to give and receive compassion.

It is possible that these exercises may arouse strong feelings or memories. If this happens, the key is to compassionately accept them as the part of you that may need to be cared for.

You have now reached the end of two chapters of hard work. Congratulations on your dedication to the cause (you) and your commitment to alleviating your suffering—you deserve a certificate.

PART III

Using Your Compassionate Mind to Soothe Your Traumatized Mind

ABOUT PART III

In part I of this book we explored how to think about traumatic memories and the difficulties in soothing our threat-focused emotions. We explored the randomness of our lives and how our early experiences have shaped our development and brain functioning. Most importantly, we learned that often what happens to us in life, and our reactions to events, is simply not our fault because we did not choose our genes, how our brains have evolved, or our early life experiences. However, we can use the abilities of our "new brains"—reasoning, wisdom, and logic—to understand the sources of our suffering and to learn to control our "old brain" instincts of self-protection. Using our "new brains" we can work actively with our compassionate attributes to heal our trauma. It therefore becomes our responsibility to move forward in our lives by making insightful and compassionate efforts for change.

In part II we turned our attention to developing the skills needed to nurture a compassionate mind. We looked at preparing our minds to function compassionately by orienting our attention, thinking, reasoning, behavior, and emotions to the tasks of caregiving, self-soothing, and self-encouraging in the development of a compassionate mind. We used imagery to stimulate particular states of mind and emotions and used exercises to learn to feel soothed and compassionate toward ourselves.

In this final part we will use the attributes of our compassionate minds to help us revisit our trauma memories and experiences. We will look at our life stories and develop a kinder and more compassionate view of our lives that will put our traumatic experiences into a compassionate context, thereby helping us move forward with our lives.

9

Using compassion to understand your life story

MAKING A COMPASSIONATE COMMITMENT

You may recall that the first stage of compassion training is to make a commitment to be sensitive to when we (and others) are suffering and to our desire to help to alleviate it. It can therefore be helpful to write down some of the reasons developing compassion and beginning to engage with our trauma memories can be helpful.

When you do this, keep in mind how compassion can strengthen and encourage us to keep going when things are difficult. Just as a caring, supportive friendship can help us in times of difficulty, the same is true for our inner sense of self. Our inner compassion can strengthen our resolve and ability to cope in times of inner difficulty.

Another useful approach to seeking compassionate commitment is to sit comfortably in a chair and bring our compassionate selves to mind and then focus on how wonderful it would be to help that traumatized part of us. Don't focus on the stress but on the pleasure and joy of being helpful and supportive. Allow yourself to really build a commitment to engaging the aspects of your experiences that can feel tricky for you to think about.

Always remember that you will be going at your own pace—the idea is to compassionately move forward, not to overwhelm yourself. That is why no matter what you are doing, you can always come back to the sense of the compassionate self and remind yourself of your kindness and your wish to heal and improve.

GING FLASHBACKS

ng at our traumatic memories in more detail it will be helpful to think about how to manage uur flashbacks, as we may find that when we begin to work on our traumatic experiences our flashbacks feel more frequent. This is quite normal, so don't worry. Things are not getting worse, but rather you are choosing to face the things that scare you in order to give yourself a chance to think about things differently. This may mean that you are beginning to face your memories and by doing so you are giving up some of your avoidance and safety behaviors. It may therefore feel as if your memories are more frequent or more intense for a while. This makes sense if you consider how you may have been avoiding your memories and things that remind you of your past up until now.

So it will be helpful to learn ways to enable us to feel more in control of our flashbacks until such time as we feel able to work directly with our trauma memories.

Below are some things we can do to try to feel more in control of our memories. Remember how in chapter 3 we learned that our flashbacks were a part of trauma memories and were generated by our threat system? When we are having a flashback our threat system is aroused and the goal of managing flashbacks is to try to tone down our threat system and activate our self-soothing, supportive, and encouraging systems. We learned ways to do this in part II and so now we can put them into practice.

It's in the past

First, let's remind ourselves that the traumatic event is in the past. It has already happened, we survived, and it is now over. It's only because of the way trauma memories are stored in our brains that we feel as if the event is happening all over again. Our minds and bodies give us the sense that we are back in the trauma, "reliving it."

If this happens, perhaps try saying the following to yourself out loud:

"This is just a memory. Painful though it might be, it is not happening to me now. That was then—this is now. This happened in the past. I am safe."

And then repeat:

"This is now and I am safe now."

The present and back to reality

As noted above, a key way we can manage our flashbacks is to ground ourselves back into reality. Some of you may already be aware that you tend to dissociate a bit when you have a flashback or a nightmare, and we explored this in chapter 1. When dissociation happens we tend to become less and less aware of what is going on around us and more focused on our feelings, bodily sensations, and images. By focusing on what's happening in our minds and bodies we tend to miss all the external things that help our brains work out that we are not back in the trauma.

• *Amanda's story:*

Amanda would begin to feel nervous when she saw someone who looked like the rapist. They had the same color hair and roughly the same build as her attacker. What Amanda did to deal with these situations was to make a conscious effort to ground herself back in the here and now.

The following may help you bring yourself back to the present and help your brain confirm that you are not "reliving" the trauma:

Notice three factual things in your environment. For example, you may remind yourself you are in your kitchen rather than back at the scene of an attack because you can smell the dinner cooking. Remember to use all of your five senses (sight, sound, smell, touch, and taste).

Remind yourself of things that have changed since the event. If you have had your birthday you can say to yourself, "I am 45 now and I was 44 when I was in a car accident." Or you may have changed your physical appearance, so, "I have long hair now but it was short when I witnessed the robbery."

Remind yourself that "Today is April 14, 2011, I am at work, it is 10:55 a.m., it is spring, it is sunny outside." You may also take this further by writing down that the traumatic event took place in winter, in the afternoon, last December.

By doing this you learn that although you may *feel* afraid, you are, in fact, in a situation that is not dangerous. Imagine you are like an investigator evaluating the situation.

Using your compassionate scent

This is a good time to bring your compassionate scent into play. We used this a lot in part II as we trained our self-soothing system to become associated with a favorite pleasant scent.

Grounding objects

Many people also find that objects associated with safe memories can help their brains recognize that they are in the present. Some visitors to the clinic even carry their objects around with them in their pockets. For instance, Amanda had always loved shells and the noise they made when she put them to her ear. The shells reminded her of happier times in her life and generated warm feelings of safeness in her mind and body. So she found her shells incredibly useful when she had flashbacks to the rape and her childhood. She would use her shells to help her get out of her threatened mind and into her compassionate mind. This helped her remember that she was not back in the traumatic moment.

Grounding techniques

It can also help to practice your soothing rhythm breathing while repeating your grounding statements and then move on to using your safe place imagery exercise. Remember too that it can be very useful to engage in grounding techniques. For example if you are sitting, feel your body in the chair and the sensation of being held by the chair. If you are standing, pay attention to the solid ground beneath your feet. Sometimes fixing your vision on something that keeps you in the here and now or rubbing your thumbs across your fingers can work to make you feel connected to the present moment. A combination of deliberately slowing the breath to help engage the *contentment and soothing* system and directing attention to the "here and now" by focusing on some grounding sensory experiences can be very helpful.

Recall too that in the beginning of a new practice—be it soothing rhythm breathing or imagining your compassionate self—don't make it too difficult. Like learning to swim or drive a car, start with what feels easy and build up to more difficult things as you build confidence. The more you have practiced these techniques by themselves—so that you are familiar with them—the easier it will be for you to put them to work.

Jeff, who was caught up in the London subway bombings, found it helpful to rebalance his sense of the here and now by using the past tense.

JEFF'S "NEW" THOUGHTS

Flashback thinking	Remembering it is in the past
I'm going to die.	I survived the bomb blasts.
There's an enormous bang and flash.	I heard the enormous bang of the bomb going off, and I remember that I saw a flash of bright white and yellow light.
I can hear screaming.	At the time people were very scared and some were badly injured. Lots of people screamed in terror.
I can smell burning.	At the time the air smelled of burning and explosives. I can still remember this smell.

The key with this is to constantly remind yourself that the event is in the past. Perhaps you might find it useful to write your flashbacks as thoughts using the past tense.

Flashback thinking	Remembering it is in the past

If your family or friends notice that you are becoming distressed, perhaps you could ask them to remind you that it is a memory and the trauma is not happening again. Much depends on your taking responsibility for working out what is helpful to you.

"I'M REALLY STRUGGLING TO SLEEP"

Unfortunately, poor sleep is a common complaint of people who have been through traumatic events. Some of us even turn "night into day" in our efforts to avoid sleep, staying awake for most of the night and falling asleep only in the early hours. The prospect of sleep can become quite frightening, as this seems to be the time when the memories and images of our traumatic events come back to haunt us. We may struggle to get to sleep as we lie in bed thinking about how our lives have changed and wondering if things will get better. Nightmares may wake us up and make it difficult to get back to sleep again. So on top of everything else we are dealing with, we may be tired, irritable, and low on energy.

Below are some suggestions that may help you get a better night's sleep. We use these suggestions at the trauma clinic and although some do take perseverance, they can make a difference to people's sleep patterns.

Sleep rules

1. Bed is for sleeping and sleeping happens at nighttime:
    Try to keep your bedroom and bed for sleeping only and avoid sleeping in the day.
    Develop a routine before bedtime such as having a bath or listening to some relaxing music and go to bed at around the same time each night. Try to wake up at about the same time each morning.
    If you cannot sleep after thirty minutes, get up and try an activity such as listening to music. Do this for about fifteen minutes and then return to bed and try to sleep. Repeat this as often as necessary until you fall asleep.

2. Be kind to yourself:

    Do not go to bed hungry but try to avoid spicy food late in the day.

    Avoid caffeine after 4:00 p.m. and remember that caffeine is also found in tea and fizzy drinks like cola. You can buy decaffeinated versions of these drinks if needed.

    Although alcohol can initially make you feel sleepy, it actually acts as a stimulant and is likely to interfere with your sleep, so it is best avoided.

    Make your bedroom a nice place to sleep. Try to make the room smell nice with scented oils or flowers, or perhaps invest in some new bedsheets to make bed seem more inviting.

3. How to cope with nightmares:

    Having a card with the tips previously covered under "It's in the past" earlier in this chapter may help ground you back in the moment. For example, one of the cards by your bed may say, "I am safe, it is May 2011, and I am in my bedroom." Read it when you wake from a nightmare to remind yourself where you are.

    Having a picture by your bed that reminds you of the present can also be useful. If waking from a nightmare, it will help your brain focus on the "here and now" and calm your threat system quicker.

    Taking a scent to bed (e.g., on a handkerchief or in a container) and having it ready can also be a useful way to help your brain remember where you are following a nightmare. It can also help you fall back to sleep.

NIGHTMARE IMAGERY RESCRIPTING

It is very common for us to suffer from nightmares as well as flashbacks in the aftermath of traumatic experiences. Sometimes the nightmares are directly related to daytime flashbacks and are reruns of the actual traumatic experience. At other times, nightmares can be about something quite different but still be very scary. For instance, you may have a nightmare in which you are running for your life, although this has never happened to you. Nightmares tend to be very intense, and it's common for us to wake up in the middle of them with the feeling that we have been reliving the trauma. On waking we may notice that we feel very aroused and scared, and it can take a few minutes to realize that we were dreaming. It is common for us to feel disoriented and to be unable to fall back asleep. We may even notice that the feelings of fear and anxiety caused by the dream stay with us for some time. It may be useful to keep your compassionate scent and other grounding objects by your bed and use them when you wake up from a nightmare. This will help you access feelings of safeness and begin to calm your threat system down. You can remind yourself that you are safe and well. You may need to get up and do something to distract yourself and that's okay too. As you work through your trauma memories you may find that your nightmares diminish.

The added burden of nightmares is, of course, that we can lose considerable amounts of sleep. Sleep can be affected because we wake up and then can't get back to sleep, or we can put off sleeping for fear of having a bad dream. Some people even put off falling asleep until the early hours of the morning and then sleep during the day to make up for it. This can result in their feeling disconnected from friends and family, as they are asleep when everyone else is awake.

Nightmares are very distressing for most visitors to the trauma clinic, as they begin to dread going to sleep. It's as if they can never get any respite from their memories. One of the ways I teach them to deal with their nightmares is to rescript their dreams. This might sound a little strange but for some people it can really help. Basically, we work out a different ending to their nightmares or different scripts to their stories and then rehearse them when they are awake. The following are the stages of nightmare rescripting; you may find this helps you too.

Changing the end of nightmares

Keep a notebook by your bed and write down your nightmare next time you have one.

At some point during the day, try to find some time to work on this nightmare. Even thinking about it can make you feel scared, so it's important that you look after yourself during this exercise and access your compassionate mind.

Engage in some soothing rhythm breathing and give yourself some time to bring some compassionate feeling to your body. You may want to use "you at your best" imagery for this exercise (see exercise 8.3).

Once you are ready to begin, think about what the most frightening part of your dream was, what made it the worst part, and how it made you feel.

Think about what you would like to see happen in the nightmare to give it a different ending and to make you feel less frightened. Remember, you have a good imagination, so you can write whatever script you want for your dream. The key thing to focus on is the fact that you want to end your distress and fear, so your compassionate rescript will have compassionate behavior in it.

Once you have come up with a different ending that works for you, try to write out the new dream with the new script. This does not have to be very long at all and sometimes it only takes a few lines.

If you feel able to do this, try to close your eyes and imagine your new dream. Remember to stay in your compassionate mind. It might be helpful to use your compassionate scent at this point to remind yourself of your compassionate feelings of "safeness."

The more you rehearse, the better chance your brain has of remembering your new dream. I might therefore ask visitors to the clinic to go over this new dream several times.

At nighttime, make sure you have your grounding objects by your bed and perhaps a copy of your written-out new dream. You may want to rehearse it again before going to sleep.

Some will find that the rescript reduces or changes the nightmare, but if you still wake up from the same nightmare then quickly use your compassionate scent and remind yourself of your new ending.

Keep practicing and use this technique alongside all the other sleep rules outlined above.

MARTIN'S RESCRIPT

Martin, the traffic police officer whom you may remember from earlier, used to have a reoccurring nightmare several times a week. In the nightmare Martin would see himself and his female colleague being attacked by a man. He would dream that he was desperately trying to fight this man off but that he couldn't find the strength to overcome him. His dream would then shift to him seeing his colleague, unmoving, on the ground, and at this point he would wake up screaming and in a cold sweat.

Martin's colleague survived the actual attack that was the root of Martin's dream, and he did a lot to help protect her at the time and was able to overcome the attacker. He was even commended for his bravery after the fact. But all this was forgotten in his nightmare, which seemed to capture his worst fears about himself: that he had not done enough to protect his colleague. During one of our sessions, Martin worked out a new script for his nightmare in which he saw himself overpowering his attacker and then saw his colleague getting up off the ground. He ended the dream with his colleague smiling at him and thanking him for helping and protecting her. He rehearsed and practiced this new script, and it had a significant impact on his nightmare, which disappeared.

Now, although Martin was able to use actual facts to rescript his nightmare, this does not have to be the case. We can let our imaginations come up with fantastical things that never happened, and they can have the same effect on our brains. It does not seem to matter to our brains if they happened or not; they respond anyway. So just as we can *scare* ourselves with fantastical things that have never happened to us, so we can *reassure* ourselves with fantastical things that did not actually happen. We have very creative brains.

WHAT'S NEXT?

As you have read, one of the reasons our traumatic experiences keep us stuck in the past and unable to move forward in our lives is because the trauma memory has become a powerful trigger to fuel our threat systems. Essentially, we become scared of our own minds and our trauma memories. It's therefore understandable that we try to avoid thinking or talking about the past, as it causes us to feel bad, scared, ashamed, guilty, and angry. While we can see this avoidance makes us feel better in the short term, we probably already know that it doesn't make the memories go away and in the long term things can just get worse. In fact one of the patients at the trauma clinic aptly described it as being stuck in a hamster wheel, going round and round but getting nowhere!

We need to find a way to move on in our lives, and to do this we need to process the trauma memories so that they can become "unstuck." We need to learn to tone down the threat system, engage with our compassionate minds, and begin to put the memories away in our past, where they belong, and get on with the business of living our lives in the present moment.

ENGAGING OUR COMPASSIONATE MINDS

Before beginning any work on your trauma stories and memories, remember to engage your *contentment and soothing* system and use your compassionate mind. Hopefully by now you will have been able to practice the exercises in chapters 5 and 6 and are beginning to feel confident about accessing your compassionate mind. Just to recap, begin with soothing rhythm breathing. By this stage, you may find your compassionate scent has the ability to fill your body and mind with feelings of calm and soothing warmth. In this state of being, remind yourself of the qualities of compassion you hold true, such as:

Nonjudgment

Wisdom

Strength

Kindness

Perhaps say out loud (or even look in the mirror and say) that you genuinely care for yourself and your well-being and that you wish yourself well. Focus on what it feels like in your mind and body to say these words to yourself.

Remember that being compassionate to yourself is a state of mind, just as feeling threatened is a state of mind and that states of mind are related to physiological responses in the body that govern behavior, thought processes, and attention, all of which are compatible with our needs and goals at any one time.

The key skills of a compassionate mind are as follows:

Motivation

Attention

Thinking/Reasoning

Imagery/Fantasy

Behavior

Emotions

It may help if you make a flashcard detailing the attributes of your state of mind. This way you can carry it around and read it when you need to remind yourself to use your compassionate mind.

As an example, Amanda's reminder card looked like this:

My Compassionate Mind
When I am being compassionate to myself, my:
motivation is to care for myself and find a way to end my distress.
attention is focused on things that are going well for me and on the fact that I am doing the best I can to manage things; my friends and family who love me and want me to feel better about myself; the fact that things are gradually getting better for me.
thinking/reasoning is to think of more supportive and kind ways to help myself. What happened to me was not my fault, and I know now that I did not deserve to have this happen to me. It was very difficult for me to endure.
imagery/fantasy is to recall my compassionate image of a big yellow sun radiating heat and warmth for me; it is smiling and supportive.
behavior is to use my compassionate scent when I'm feeling low and spend some time practicing my soothing rhythm breathing. It also helps me to share with my partner what is going on in my mind as he makes me feel better about things.
emotions are feelings of warmth and safeness in my body. They flow through me as a calm green stream of energy.

Perhaps now, if you would find it helpful, you could fill in your flashcard (worksheet 2).

WORKSHEET 2: MY COMPASSIONATE MIND

My Compassionate Mind
When I am being compassionate to myself, my:
motivation is to care for myself and find a way to end my distress.
attention
thinking/reasoning
imagery/fantasy
behavior
emotions

UNDERSTANDING YOUR LIFE STORY WITH COMPASSION

Having reminded ourselves how to access our compassionate states of mind, let's see if we can revisit our life stories and begin to develop empathy for our nonintentional lives. With all the knowledge gained in this book, I hope this will help you to understand that your difficulties are simply not your fault. In part I, we learned that not only do we have complicated threat-focused brains that are poorly designed for the task of twenty-first-century living but that we have also had random lives and been brought up by people learning to be parents. Our brains have been shaped and conditioned to respond to threats in certain ways, so the things that happened to us in childhood and how our brains responded to these events were beyond our control and were not our fault. We take these coping skills with us into adulthood and continue to do the best we can to deal with events that happen in our lives.

Remember this is only *one version of you*. Try saying out loud:

"I did not intend for my life to work out like this. This would not have been the script I would have written for my life."

What did that feel like? Were you able to connect with the compassionate sentiment in these words? Perhaps repeat these words again and see if you can focus on the sadness and kindness in the message directed at you.

"I did not intend for my life to work out like this. This would not have been the script I would write for my life."

You may notice when you say these words that your critical voice creeps in to tell you, "Yes, *but it is your fault, it's different for you, you've only got yourself to blame."*

Don't worry if this happens; try to remind yourself that it is hard being compassionate, especially if we are not used to it. It can make us feel anxious and scared and as if we are letting ourselves off the hook. It might be helpful to remind yourself that your critical voice is in fact a safety strategy, albeit an unhelpful one! Perhaps remind yourself that you are taking responsibility for your life by facing your fears and ending the cycle of self-blame and self-criticism. We all deserve help, kindness, and understanding when we commit to making changes in our lives and taking responsibility for ourselves.

Taking responsibility for your life

Taking responsibility for yourself and your life is different from blaming yourself for things that have gone wrong. In fact, we can begin to take true responsibility for ourselves when we stop blaming ourselves for things that are not our fault. Sometimes this can be a tricky concept for us to grasp because, as adults, we choose to behave in certain ways to respond to things we find threatening in our lives that can make us feel ashamed and guilty. We then tend to beat ourselves up, mentally, for the way we have behaved, and this further fuels our sense of shame. You may remember from chapter 3 that our self-criticism keeps us trapped in a cycle of shame and self-blame. The compassionate mind approach helps us to understand that we all do things in our lives that cause us sadness and distress. We can behave in ways that are unhelpful and damaging to our health (such as smoking, drinking alcohol, or taking illicit drugs), and we can do hurtful things to others and our loved ones. Yet there are understandable reasons we learned to be fearful of things and why we learned to deal with our fears in certain ways.

By exploring our pasts and our childhood memories with kindness, nonjudgment, and wisdom, we can begin to gain insight and understanding about who we are and why we respond in the way we do to things that happen in our lives and, in this case, particularly to traumatic events.

Let's use these insights and develop an understanding of why we are struggling with things in our lives. We will work through Amanda's life story to illustrate the compassionate approach, and then perhaps you may like to try the suggested exercises so that you can build your own compassionate story.

An overview of Amanda's story

When Amanda came to see us at the trauma clinic she was feeling very ashamed and overwhelmed by her traumatic memories of being raped some months previously. She blamed herself for the attack, although it was clearly not her fault. Amanda was unable to stop blaming herself, and she would become overwhelmed with feelings of shame when she thought about the attack and how it made her think about herself. The other difficulty Amanda had was that she really did not like herself very much. This was a long-standing issue for Amanda, as, sadly, she had also been abused as a child. This experience had left her with strong feelings of being somehow bad and dirty. She had always believed that the childhood abuse was her fault too.

What happened to me and how I reacted
A few months ago I was raped by a coworker. This was a very distressing and frightening experience for me. Since then I have been really struggling to cope with things, as I often feel overwhelmed with my memories of the attack and I also have horrible flashbacks. These make me feel ashamed, and I feel that it is all my fault. I think that I deserved to be raped because I am not a nice person. I often think things are my fault because I am bad. I was also abused in my childhood, which has always made me feel dirty and ashamed. It feels as if bad things always happen to me.

Now write down a short description of your own trauma story in worksheet 3, below. You do not have to go into a lot of detail, but just write about your reactions to your traumatic event as Amanda did.

WORKSHEET 3: WHAT HAPPENED TO ME AND HOW I REACTED

What happened to me and how I reacted

What are the key childhood experiences and memories that help you understand this version of yourself?

We began to look at Amanda's difficulties from a compassionate perspective by using our knowledge of this approach. Amanda's early experiences of abuse and poor parenting had left her with real fears about not being liked by others. Her threat-focused brain became sensitive to being hurt and rejected. Amanda remembered that she was blamed for a lot for things that happened as a child. Her mother was very critical of her and was emotionally cold and not protective. Taking the blame felt "right" because she must have done something wrong for her mother to be so mean to her. She therefore reasoned that if it was her fault, she could change and make her mother love her more.

Amanda realized how frightening this was for her as a child and how confusing it was to be touched inappropriately by her uncle. Her caregiving system understandably activated feelings of anxiety and fear rather than soothing and safeness. Her mother was not very good at making Amanda feel safe when she was sad and scared. Whenever her uncle was "nice" to her, he physically hurt her. Whenever she sought comfort from her mother she was absent and unable to respond in a warm and caring way. Amanda was criticized and blamed a lot as a small child, so she felt it must have been her fault. Amanda also realized how sad she was that her father died when she was young. She had never really been able to talk about her feelings of grief, as her mother would become upset and get cross with her. Amanda even wondered whether her mother's lack of interest, emotional coldness, and criticism were due to her own feelings of grief and loss. By using her compassionate mind, Amanda surmised that perhaps all these experiences had sadly made her "believe" that she was bad and naughty and deserved bad things to happen to her (including her belief that she deserved to be raped), but in fact none of them were her fault at all.

My key childhood experiences and memories that help me understand my fears and my reaction to my traumatic event
My father died when I was young. My mother was cold emotionally, not there for me, and critical of me. She used to blame me for things all the time. I did not feel loved or liked by her. My uncle abused me for a period of time. He told me that I was naughty and that it was my fault.

Now reflect on your own childhood and important experiences that have shaped this version of you by filling in worksheet 4. These memories may help you understand your reactions to your traumatic event. Remember to be kind to yourself, as this is not an easy thing to do. Often our lives are filled with lots of sad memories and experiences, and it is important that we can grieve for the things we have lost, whether that is lost opportunities, lost innocence, or lost relationships. Perhaps remind yourself that you are facing your past because you want and deserve to have a compassionate future. Your compassionate, wise mind knows that you have suffered and how hard it can be to face the past.

WORKSHEET 4: MY KEY CHILDHOOD EXPERIENCES

My key childhood experiences and memories that help me understand my fears and my reaction to my traumatic event

What do you fear about who you really are and who others think you are?

Moving on, let's see what key fears emerged for Amanda from her childhood experiences. How was her threat-focused brain shaped by her experiences? Well, Amanda was very self-critical and described having a constant critical commentary in her head. She was very afraid that other people would come to know what happened to her and also blame her and think she was bad. It did not cross her mind that other people might feel compassion for her and feel sad that she had endured such distressing events in her life. It never occurred to her that she was not to blame for the things that had happened to her.

My key fears are:
External fears: What might others do to me? What might others think of me?
I think people know what happened to me. They think I brought this on myself. They think I deserved this. No one likes me because they know what happened to me.
Internal fears: What do I think of myself? Who do I think I am? What will happen to me?
I think that I am bad. I think there is something wrong with me. I must not let others know who I really am.

See if you can identify your key fears and what is going on in your own mind (internal) and what you fear is going on in other people's minds (external). This will really help you understand some of your behaviors and what you struggle with, because if we know what frightens us, we can see how we might avoid it. That is a natural response to threats after all. Try to fill in worksheet 5, following.

WORKSHEET 5: MY KEY FEARS

My key fears are:
External fears: What might others do to me? What might others think of me?
Internal fears: What do I think of myself? Who do I think I am? What will happen to me?

What do you do to keep yourself and your world safe?

We know our threat-focused brains want to make us safe, as that's what they are designed to do. So beyond our conscious control our threat-focused minds will be motivated to seek safety and get rid of threats and things that frighten us.

Once we had been able to work out what Amanda feared about herself and other people, we tried to see if we could make sense of the way she behaved and to link these behaviors back to her motivation to avoid her worst fears. First, we realized that the only time Amanda ever got any respite from her tortured mind, which bombarded her with critical thoughts (internal threats), was when she drank too much and made superficial cuts to her arms. That was when she could escape her own mind for a period of time. Of course, another problem arose from this: Amanda would get angry at herself for drinking and cutting and she felt even more shame. She was stuck in a cycle of shame and self-blame. Furthermore, because Amanda was so concerned that other people would also blame her and not want to be her friend, she went to great lengths to avoid getting close to people. She developed a "social act" designed to hide from the world the person she feared she really was. Have a look at Amanda's responses following.

My strategies that I use to keep myself safe from:
My internal fears/threats
Drink too much every night
Make superficial cuts to my arms
Overeat at times
My external fears/threats
Avoid getting to know people
Avoid making friends
Don't tell people the truth about my life

Think about what you do to keep your world safe. Try to be honest but kind to yourself as you think through the way you manage your threats, and remember it takes courage and strength to face our pain and we are doing this because we are committed to recovering from our experiences. Try to fill out worksheet 6.

WORKSHEET 6: MY STRATEGIES THAT I USE TO KEEP MYSELF SAFE

My strategies that I use to keep myself safe from:
My internal fears/threats
My external fears/threats

WHAT ARE THE UNINTENDED CONSEQUENCES OF YOUR BEST EFFORTS TO STAY SAFE?

Sadly for Amanda, she had been using her safety strategies "successfully" for some years, and now things had become even more difficult for her, especially since the recent rape. This was because she did not feel she could tell anyone about what had happened to her, as she was terrified they would say it was her fault. She could not cope with the shame of other people knowing. We looked together at some of the unintended consequences of her safety strategies and filled in the chart below.

The unintended consequences of my best efforts to keep myself safe
Feel isolated and lonely
Being disconnected from others
Physical health problems from alcohol
Overweight
Embarrassing scarring from self-harming
Unable to tell anyone about the rape or go to the police
I don't know how to make myself feel better about the rape, as I have no one to talk to about it

Do some thinking about the long-term costs of your safety strategies. They may take away the pain in the short term, but, sadly, the effects of keeping our worlds safe often stack up and cause us further harm. But remember, do not beat yourself up again; your compassionate, wise, and caring mind knows how hard this has been for you and that there were good reasons you stumbled across these safety strategies and they worked for a while. The cost is now outweighing the benefit, however, and they may be keeping you stuck and unable to move forward with your life. See if you can fill in worksheet 7 below.

WORKSHEET 7: THE UNINTENDED CONSEQUENCES OF MY BEST EFFORTS TO KEEP MYSELF SAFE

The unintended consequences of my best efforts to keep myself safe

GETTING TO KNOW YOUR INNER BULLY

The final piece of the jigsaw puzzle in Amanda's story was to try to understand her self-blame and distressing cycle of self-criticism. What we needed to unravel was why Amanda blamed herself for things that went on in her childhood, and for the rape, when they were clearly not her fault. We know from an evolutionary perspective that humans have an innate ability to submit to dominant others as a safety strategy. But where did she learn to speak to herself in such a critical way? Had others spoken to her like that throughout her life? Could she give her inner bully a face, and was it connected to key memories in her life? Would she consider it acceptable to speak to others the way she spoke to herself, in her mind, on a daily basis? Together we explored the idea that maybe her inner bully was actually one of her safety strategies. Perhaps if she blamed herself for the rape and thought it was her fault, then that meant she could change things and stop it from happening again. Perhaps if she "got to herself first" then others would not be able to hurt her because, after all, Amanda reasoned, "They wouldn't be telling me anything I didn't know already was true."

We talked about her flashback memories to both the rape and childhood sexual abuse and realized that every time she thought about these events, her head became filled with distressing thoughts such as "I am bad, I am disgusting, and it's my fault these things happened to me." This, of course, just made her feel worse and even more ashamed because she thought she had brought it all on herself.

The other thing that Amanda's inner bully would do is criticize her when she used her safety strategies. It sounded something like this: "There you go again. You're so weak, you can't stop drinking, can you? Get some self-control!" So Amanda's bully would take every opportunity to "beat her" while she was already down!

See below how Amanda explored her inner bully by linking its development to key experiences in her past.

Getting to know my inner bully
What does my inner bully look like?
A wizened old man
What does it say to me?
You're weak, you deserve this, no one likes you.
What does it make me feel like?
Rubbish, anxious, and unsafe
Can I remember key memories when I learned to talk to myself like that?
Yes—childhood memories of the abuser and also of my classmates
Has anyone else in my life spoken to me like that?
Yes—I can clearly remember the occasions and I can see them in my mind.
Does my bully have my best interests at heart?
NOT AT ALL
What is my bully trying to do to me? Help me or hinder me?
Destroy me
Would I speak to other people the way my inner bully speaks to me?
Never
If not, then why not?
Because it's horrible and unkind
What makes me accept what the bully says without question or without defending myself?
I never did have a choice.

Perhaps you have an inner bully, or you may just be becoming aware that you do as you read this chapter. Why not try to fill in the sheet below to see if we can shed some light on what your inner bully is up to and the relationship you have with it, because it is probably playing a big part in keeping your difficulties going. Again, remember to take care of yourself, as bullies are designed to be scary! Remind yourself that your compassionate, wise, and kind mind knows all about the bully, where it comes from, and what it is trying to do to you, but your compassionate mind wants it to stop now since it does not have your best interests at heart. Your compassionate mind has your best interests at heart and wants what's best for you. Try to fill in worksheet 8, following.

WORKSHEET 8: GETTING TO KNOW MY INNER BULLY

Getting to know my inner bully
What does my inner bully look like?
What does it say to me?
What does it make me feel like?
Can I remember key memories when I learned to talk to myself like that?
Has anyone else in my life spoken to me like that?
Does my bully have my best interests at heart?
What is my bully trying to do to me? Help me or hinder me?
Would I speak to other people the way my inner bully speaks to me?
If not, then why not?
What makes me accept what the bully says without question or without defending myself?

THE COMPASSIONATE WAY TO MAKE SENSE OF YOUR TRAUMATIC EVENTS

So how did Amanda put this all together and develop a compassionate insight into her life and traumatic event? By completing the exercises above, Amanda was able to develop an alternative way of being with herself in her mind. Rather than blaming and condemning herself for the things that had happened to her, she began to feel an acceptance of what she had been through. She knew that she had not asked for these things to happen to her and that there was sadness in realizing that she found herself in these situations through no fault of her own. She began to understand why she blamed herself for things including the rape, and she found it helpful to think of her blame as a safety strategy and to remind herself that her threat-focused brain was only doing the job it was designed to do. Amanda began to get in touch with the sadness of her life. She commented that she felt "sadness" for herself, which for once did not feel self-indulgent or pitying. She noticed the stirrings of feelings of warmth, care, and support for herself.

Amanda was able to develop a compassionate reframe for herself about the rape (see below), which focused on what we call her compassionate, KUWS:

Knowledge

Understanding

Wisdom

Strength

Here is Amanda's compassionate reframe of her traumatic experiences:

Old self-blaming meaning	You're not a very nice person and you brought this on yourself.
	You've only got yourself to blame.
	If other people knew what you were really like, they wouldn't want to know you.
New compassionate reframe *Knowledge* *Understanding* *Wisdom* *Strength*	I understand why you want to blame yourself; it makes sense given what you have been through in the past and how hard you have found it to be kind to yourself.
	It's understandable that you are so sad and distressed but this is not your fault.
	Focus on the warmth, care, and kindness you have for yourself.
	Allow yourself to accept the support you have for yourself.
	Allow yourself to feel the warmth you have for yourself in your body.
	This is not your fault.

By filling out worksheet 9, try to see if you can develop a kinder, more compassionate view of your life and your reactions to your traumatic event. Remember, focus on the insights you gained from the above exercise *and bring in your compassionate KUWS.*

WORKSHEET 9: MY COMPASSIONATE REFRAME

Old self-blaming meaning	
New compassionate reframe *Knowledge* *Understanding* *Wisdom* *Strength*	

WHAT WAS THE OUTCOME FOR AMANDA?

Once Amanda was able to develop and use her compassionate mind skills, we revisited the memories of the rape. Whereas before, when Amanda thought about the rape she would have thoughts like "You are dirty and deserve this," now she was able to say (and feel it to be true), "It is so sad that you have suffered like this. You don't deserve this. Focus on the feelings of warmth and kindness you have for yourself." This new emotional experience became meaningful to Amanda because it seemed to trigger a physiological response in her body, which felt warm and soothing.

Amanda was then ready to revisit her troublesome and distressing flashbacks. We decided that we would use her compassionate imagery to help her tolerate her memories, and you can see how we did this in chapter 10.

SUMMARY

Let's recap what we have learned in this chapter before we move on to work more directly with our traumatic memories and flashbacks. We have begun to apply the information we gained from parts I and II, and together we have developed a compassionate understanding of your life story by using the work we did with Amanda, by way of illustration. Hopefully now you have begun to engage your compassionate mind to look at your own story and can see how, through no fault of your own, this version of you has contributed to the difficulties you are having in dealing with your trauma. We have looked at what your key fears are, for yourself and your world, and we have begun to develop an understanding of all the behaviors that have been designed by your threat-focused brain to keep you safe. Last and most important, we revisited your trauma story with a compassionate mind and developed a kinder, more compassionate view of your life and your reactions to your traumatic life experiences.

10

Using your compassionate mind to resolve your shame-filled flashbacks

In this chapter we are going to turn our attention to working through troublesome flashbacks. You may remember from chapter 3 that flashbacks come from a type of trauma memory that our brains store after a traumatic event. Our complicated and threat-focused brains respond to flashbacks and other trauma memories as warning signals. So, when we recall a trauma memory, our brains can respond to that inner event as if we are still in danger, even though in fact the original traumatic event is long over.

Do you remember these characters in your brain: the amygdala, the hippocampus, and the frontal cortex? Flashbacks to highly frightening and distressing experiences mobilize the amygdala, which responds as if it is in grave and current danger again. This causes our brains to secrete stress hormones that anesthetize the hippocampus. This is troublesome because, as you may remember, the hippocampus is the "gatekeeper" to really useful information in the rest of the brain. The anesthetized hippocampus affects the frontal cortex (where our self-soothing skills, compassionate minds, and safe memories are stored), our problem-solving skills, and our long-term memory stores. If the hippocampus is not working properly it becomes difficult for our brains to work out that the "flashback" is a memory of a past, traumatic event and it is not happening to us now. We find it hard to access our compassionate minds and self-soothing because our threat-focused brains will always prioritize a threat (e.g., a flashback). So that leaves us rather stuck, as our brains are unable to process the emotional memory related to our traumatic experiences and as a result the emotional trauma memory remains fragmented and cannot be integrated. Our brains continue to think the memories are threatening.

Our brains essentially respond automatically to certain stimuli, which means that we are left to deal with the consequences. These consequences might not be very pleasant, as they are frequently associated with high levels of stress hormones, which can make us feel agitated, anxious, and hyperaroused. How we then seek to understand our experiences can lead us to dark places in our minds, places that are filled with self-criticism, self-blame, and strong feelings of shame.

Those of us who feel shameful about our traumatic histories and struggle to self-soothe can find it very helpful to develop a more compassionate and supportive perspective of our traumatic experiences. However, this ability does rely on our frontal cortex (or conductor), and so that is why we spent part II of this book developing the frontal cortex's abilities to self-soothe and to think compassionately. Remember that through no fault of our own some of us don't get taught these important skills in childhood (think back to Jesse, Jhonnie, and Billy, whom we met in chapter 4).

We know people often describe feeling ashamed, inadequate, and dirty as a consequence of their traumatic experience. We also know that when we are self-critical, our threat systems are activated, and this keeps us stuck in a threat-focused brain!

WHAT'S THE WAY FORWARD?

We want to use our compassionate minds to help our flashback memories become normal, less threatening memories that belong to our past. In order to do this, we need to keep our threat-focused minds from dominating the show and instead use our compassionate minds to tolerate and make sense of our flashbacks. They then become less threat focused and shameful, and in turn we can begin to put them to rest in our long-term memory stores.

In the rest of this chapter we are going to practice the following:

Engaging our compassionate minds.

Developing compassionate self-talk to deal with our self-criticism and self-blame.

Using our perfect nurturer imagery to support us as we revisit our shame-filled flashbacks.

Working through our other threat-based emotions such as disgust and anger.

ENGAGING YOUR COMPASSIONATE MIND

We need to start by engaging our compassionate mind to feel peaceful and calm. You may find it helpful to go back to part II and reread chapters 6, 7, and 8. You may already find that your compassionate scent is enough for you to feel that your body is filled with the self-soothing sensations of peace and calm. You may also have some favorite compassionate flow exercises you like to do (exercises 8.7 and 8.8 in chapter 8). Whatever works best for you is what matters! We will be using perfect nurturing imagery in this chapter too, so perhaps remind yourself of your image by getting out your written description, drawing, or smell and practice visualizing it. Don't worry if you don't like using this type of imagery, as it doesn't work for everyone; you can still do the exercises without it.

Try to begin by engaging some way of slowing down such as with your soothing rhythm breathing and then move on to compassionate flow exercises (exercises 8.7 and 8.8 in chapter 8). Take a moment to remind yourself that your compassionate mind wishes you well and wants you to be content and happy. You did not deserve what happened to you and you are not to blame. Having spent some time working with your compassionate life story in chapter 9, take a moment to remind yourself that this is only one version of you and that you have learned to take the blame for things that are not your fault. This is a safety strategy, and perhaps you no longer need it in your life, as it causes you pain and distress.

DEVELOPING COMPASSIONATE SELF-TALK TO REPLACE SELF-CRITICISM

You may recall that chapter 3 looked at how our self-criticism maintains our flashbacks so we get caught in a vicious loop. This is illustrated in the diagram below.

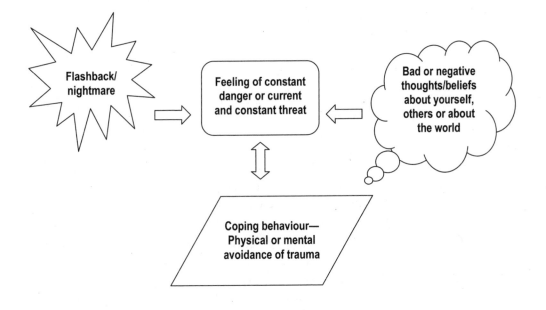

Figure 10.1: What keeps our flashbacks going?

What we are going to practice now is identifying our own loops. You will be able to use some of the work you completed in chapter 9 to help you do this. Let's use Amanda again to illustrate how to do this. Think about what you would put in the empty boxes. Your trauma may be much less serious than a rape, but regardless of how "major" the event is, it is serious to you and may trap you in a vicious circle. Whatever you do, do not dismiss your trauma if you think it is not as "serious" as the ones outlined here. These are examples that illustrate that even very major trauma can be helped with compassion.

Amanda's vicious loop

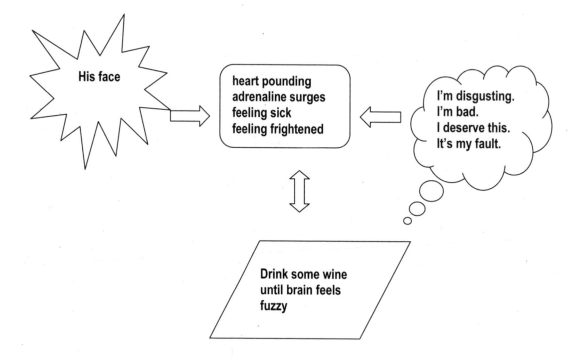

Figure 10.2: What keeps our flashbacks going?

Can you see Amanda is stuck in a vicious loop of distress? Every time she has a flashback to the rape she feels intense emotions of fear and disgust. She feels like she is "reliving the event," as her emotions are so powerful. Remember at this moment Amanda's amygdala is center stage and her threat-focused brain is engaged. This feeling triggers all sorts of threat-focused thoughts, and Amanda says to herself that she has only got herself to blame for the attack. She thinks she is a bad person who deserves bad things to happen. These very thoughts make her feel even worse and more ashamed of herself, and so now she is fueling her threat-focused mind with even more threat emotions! Her only way of ending the state of distress and shame is to have a glass or two of wine. This helps her block out her thoughts and makes her mind a bit fuzzy, which is preferable to feeling terrified.

Now see if you can fill in the boxes in worksheet 10 and explore your own possible vicious loop.

WORKSHEET 10: MY VICIOUS LOOP

Take a moment to reflect on what you I have earned about yourself and your flashbacks. Are you trapped in a loop too?

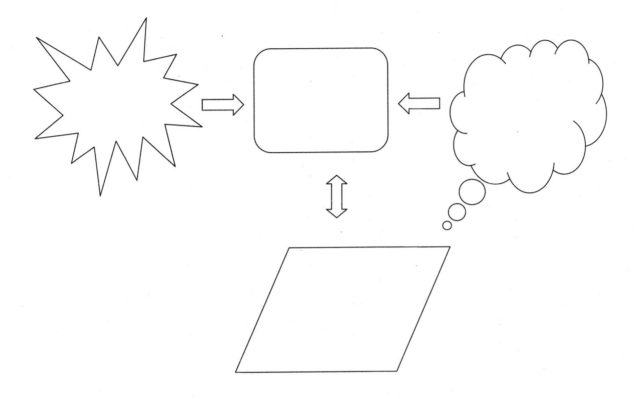

COMPASSIONATE REFRAMES AND WORKING WITH YOUR FLASHBACKS

If we turn our attention to developing other ways to think about ourselves and our trauma experiences, we can begin to break the vicious loops of distress we have created through no fault of our own. Do you remember Jeff from chapter 5 who was involved in the London subway bombings? Just to remind you:

Jeff was caught up in the London subway bombings and was a passenger on one of the trains when the bomb was detonated. He felt the force of the bomb, was injured, and was rescued by firefighters. At the time of the blast Jeff's brain became very threat focused because his life was in danger. He felt intense fear. His thinking was rapid and threat focused because he was trying to work out how to survive. This was an overwhelming experience for him and his amygdala. In the days and weeks after the bombing, his brain tried to make sense of the experience, but every time Jeff's mind flashed back to the event, he was overwhelmed with intense feelings of fear again. His brain responded to the images and memories (flashbacks) as if he were in real and present danger and so released lots of the threat focused hormones such as cortisol and adrenaline. This "anesthetized" Jeff's hippocampus and blocked access to the thinking part of the brain where there is sense, meaning, context, and self-soothing. Put simply, Jeff's experience of the flashbacks was that he was back at the traumatic event rather than simply remembering it, so he then became trapped in a mind that was reliving the horror of the bombing with all of its intensity and without any of the relief of knowing that the horrors belonged to an event in the past. His mind-set during these terrifying flashbacks was threat-based, which meant a whole host of other reactions were orchestrated at the same time, namely, that his attention, thoughts, feelings, behavior, motivation, and images all became threat focused too.

What did Jeff need to work on in order to end his vicious loop and resolve his flashbacks?

In order for Jeff to resolve his flashbacks and move on with his life, two things were needed to help him: he needed to develop and access his compassionate mind and replace his critical threat-focused thinking with compassionate self-talk, and he then needed to be able to "reframe" his traumatic experience and his flashbacks from a compassionate perspective.

What is a compassionate reframe?

The compassionate reframe is about developing an alternative perspective on an event such as a trauma or a way of being toward yourself that is accepting, warm, caring, understanding, encouraging, and supportive. For example, this is a compassionate reframe:

I understand why I want to blame myself. It makes sense given what I have been through in the past and how hard I have found it to be kind to myself. It's understandable that I am so sad and distressed, but this is not my fault. I can focus on my deep intention to help myself and to alleviate my suffering with warmth, courage, and concern.

Remember that when Jeff was traumatized, every time he thought about the bomb blast, his memories would trigger a whole host of threat-focused thoughts such as:

Jeff's thinking and reasoning were very focused on how much danger he was in. He would consider all the possible harm he could come to outside his home and would think about how unsafe the London subway was. Jeff would think about how terrifying it was to face his own death and would mull over the fact that he should have "known" that something bad was going to happen. He would dwell on how he behaved after the blast and would worry that he did not do enough to help the injured. Jeff thought that he should be stronger and get over this, and he would criticize himself for being "weak and not coping." Jeff would worry about what other people would think of him if they knew how "selfish" he had been in the aftermath of the blast, when he did not help other injured passengers.

So does it make sense to you that if Jeff was able to think differently about his traumatic experience and himself, particularly in a way that was nonshaming, supportive, and caring, then his memories would no longer be threatening to him? He would have ended his vicious loop. That would mean that his brain would no longer need to respond to the memories as if they were threats and the whole threat system would calm down. This would give Jeff's hippocampus a real chance to use information from his frontal cortex to put the memories into some other more helpful context.

This was our task. Let's work through how we did this, and then you can try it with your own flashbacks. We have broken the work down into three steps.

STEP ONE

First we started by asking Jeff to write down a brief description of his main flashbacks, how they made him feel, what thoughts they triggered in him, and what he then did to cope (essentially this is his vicious loop in chart form rather than using the diagrams we filled in earlier in this chapter). Have a look at Jeff's chart below.

JEFF'S FLASHBACKS

Flashback description	How it makes me feel	What it makes me think about myself and others	What I do to cope with the flashback and how it makes me feel
1. I can hear, feel, and see a massive white and yellow flash and bang. My heart is thumping, pounding, and it takes a moment to register the panic around me. People are screaming for help and moaning. I can smell burning and see that some people have been hurt. I feel as if I can't breathe, and I am beginning to panic and have a strong urge to run. I am terrified now and I think I'm going to die. Someone is asking for water, but I can't answer, as I've got to get out.	Utter terror and helplessness Scared Sad Angry Guilty	This is it; I'm going to die. Other people will be disappointed and sad, as I did nothing to help others. How dare the bombers ruin my life. How pathetic am I not to be strong enough to get over this.	Avoid London subway system. Avoid walking in the vicinity of the subway stations. Avoid watching television or reading the papers in case something reminds me of the events. Avoid young Muslim men. Do not leave the house.
2.			
3.			

Now see if you can fill one in for yourself. You may have only one or two key trauma memories, or you may have more than four; just try to make sure you identify all of them and write down a brief description of each one.

WORKSHEET 11: MY FLASHBACKS

Flashback description	How it makes me feel	What it makes me think about myself and others	What I do to cope with the flashback and how it makes me feel
1.			
2.			
3.			

STEP TWO

Next we asked Jeff to engage his compassionate mind to fill in the following chart. You may want to go back and reread chapter 6 to remind yourself of the different states of mind.

JEFF'S CHART

My traumatized mind's response to my flashbacks	My compassionate mind's response to my flashbacks
Motivation: To survive at all costs and get out of danger ASAP.	What is the motivation of your compassionate mind? To find ways to alleviate my distress and suffering through my KUWS (Knowledge, Understanding, Wisdom, and Strength).
Attention: Focused on possible dangers, alert to young men of Muslim appearance and unattended bags.	What would compassionate "'attention'" attend to or focus on? This is a rare event. All the other times I have used the subway (thousands of times) nothing has happened. I have lots of Muslim friends whom I love and care for. Most Muslims were appalled by what happened that day. Once I escaped the subway station I spent time helping the walking wounded.
Thinking/Reasoning: How dangerous and unpredictable the world is, I could be in danger all the time, the prospect of dying is terrifying. I am a weakling and ought to be strong and get over this. I am selfish, as I did not act to help to others.	What would compassionate "thinking" reflect? I would remind myself that this was a terrible ordeal and anyone would have been terrified. My brain went into threat mode and I acted automatically in the moment. This is a difficult thing to "get over" and most people will never experience anything as frightening. I am doing the best I can to work through things and my memories.
Imagery/Fantasy: Flashbacks to the carnage—people screaming, the burning smell, the flash of the blast.	What compassionate images do you have? My lion, which is my perfect nurturer, walking by my side, protecting me. Images of people offering kindness and care. Humanity coming together in the aftermath to help and support one another.

Behavior: Avoid things that make it worse, such as newspapers and TV. Avoid people who will ask about it, avoid going on the subway, avoid leaving the house. Use alcohol to numb my mind and help me fall asleep.	**What would be a compassionate way to behave?** To talk to my family and friends and tell them that I am struggling. Ask them to help me ride on the subway again. Begin to make contact with my Muslim friends again, who are equally appalled by the bombs.
Emotions: Terror, helplessness, panic, anger, guilt, shame, sadness.	**What feelings would be associated with being compassionate?** Warmth in my body, "safeness," strength, and courage.

It's now your turn to engage your compassionate mind. Let's see if we can try to break your vicious loop by replacing your self-criticism and self-blame with compassionate self-talk.

Fill in worksheet 12 following, remembering your KUWS (Knowledge, Understanding, Wisdom, and Strength), and just take a moment to check that you are still in your compassionate mind-set. Perhaps take a few moments to breathe in your compassionate scent and focus on the feelings of self-soothing in your body. Remind yourself that your compassionate mind's motivation is to alleviate your distress and to be nonjudgmental, kind, and caring. If it helps, fill in your traumatized mind's responses too, as we did with Jeff.

WORKSHEET 12: MY COMPASSIONATE RESPONSE TO MY FLASHBACKS

My traumatized mind's response to my flashbacks	My compassionate mind's response to my flashbacks
Motivation:	What is the motivation of your compassionate mind?
Attention:	What would compassionate "'attention'" attend to or focus on?
Thinking/Reasoning:	What would compassionate "thinking" reflect?
Imagery/Fantasy:	What compassionate images do you have?
Behavior:	What would be a compassionate way to behave?
Emotions:	What feelings would be associated with being compassionate?

STEP THREE

The final task we asked Jeff to complete was to engage his compassionate feelings by using his compassionate scent; next we asked him to reread his flashback and then read the compassion response only. Finally we asked him to write a compassionate reframe of his experience. His form looked like this:

JEFF'S COMPASSIONATE REFRAME

My flashback:

I can hear, feel, and see a massive white and yellow flash and bang. My heart is thumping, pounding, and it takes a moment to register the panic around me. People are screaming for help and moaning. I can smell burning and see that some people have been hurt. I feel as if I can't breathe, and I am beginning to panic and have a strong urge to run. I am terrified now and I think I'm going to die. Someone is asking for water, but I can't answer, as I've got to get out.

My compassionate reframe of my flashback:

I survived a terrifying ordeal when I was involved in the London bombings. Sadly, others died and I was not able to help them. I was able to help some people when we got out of the station, and this fills me with a sense of courage and warmth and common humanity. We were all doing the best we could to help and support each other. That feeling of kindness and care from others will always stay with me. This experience has had a life-changing impact on my life, and I have found courage I did not know I had to face my fears and get back out there living the life I want to live again. I am surrounded by loving family and friends who support me and want the best for me, and I am now able to put memories of this sad day in the past where they belong, not forgotten but much less frightening. I survived.

And finally, it's your turn. Try to develop your own compassionate reframe for your flashbacks. As always, remember to engage your compassionate mind by revisiting the compassion exercises in chapter 8 before beginning this exercise. Use worksheet 13 to guide you.

WORKSHEET 13: MY COMPASSIONATE REFRAME

My flashback:

My compassionate reframe of my flashback:

Remember to do this for each of your flashbacks, and really focus on the feelings of warmth, care, and kindness that you are generating in your body as you complete this exercise.

Take some time now to reflect on how you feel about things and what new insights you have gained from doing these exercises. You deserve a "well done" for completing them, as it takes strength and courage to face things that terrify us, including our own minds.

USING PERFECT NURTURING IMAGERY TO REVISIT SHAME-FILLED FLASHBACKS

For one reason or another some of us find it difficult to just use our own self-talk as part of our compassionate minds. This is often the case with those of us who really struggle with compassionate flow to ourselves (e.g., offering compassion to ourselves). It was for this reason that we developed perfect nurturing imagery, so let's just briefly recap this form of imagery, and then perhaps you can revisit the instructions for creating a perfect nurturer outlined in chapter 8. Perfect nurturer imagery is a specific form of compassionate imagery and is based on a fantasy notion of an inner helper created especially to meet our needs perfectly—the need for caring, kindness, emotional nurturing, strength, and connectedness. It is created to be beyond human failing and can never let you down or fail to say what you need to hear when you are distressed. It has your best interests at heart, and care for your well-being is paramount to it. There is no right or wrong in perfect nurturer imagery, and it's up to you what image you come up with. Some people develop images of animals such as lions; see Jeff's example above. Others conjure up angelic images or a mother-earth being, while still others come up with cartoon-like characters. It really can be whatever works for you and is most memorable.

We use perfect nurturer imagery with people at the trauma clinic for the specific purpose of helping them access the compassionate mind, where they can feel the positive effect associated with a sense of safeness. The other nice thing about this imagery is that it can increase feelings of being connected to others and of not being alone (it's a bit like having an imaginary friend!). If you like, you can use your image to help you reframe your self-criticism or respond to your inner bully. Just remember to make sure that you can experience feelings of compassion first (by using your scent) before you bring your image to mind and certainly before you tackle your self-critical thinking.

What we really want to explore now, however, is how you can use your image in your flashbacks to help resolve feelings of shame and self-blame. What's important here is to make sure that your scent triggers your image, as we want to use your scent to help you access the feelings when you need them.

After helping Amanda to develop her compassionate skills and her using them to good effect to help her work through the rape, she was still struggling with thoughts of being bad and of deserving bad things to happen to her. Although she had successfully resolved her self-blaming thoughts and feelings about the rape, she still struggled to come to terms with her memories of childhood sexual abuse. We realized that these memories still had a powerful influence on how she felt about herself and Amanda remained unconvinced by her compassionate mind when it came to her memories of sexual abuse. She found it very difficult to stop blaming herself for what happened. So we decided to try something different to help her resolve this battle. We agreed to see if using her perfect nurturing imagery would help her access feelings of self-soothing and strengthening, and enable her to accept a compassionate perspective on her memory of abuse.

We will take you through what we did with Amanda, and then perhaps, as before, you can try to see if it helps you with your flashbacks. You can use perfect nurturing imagery with any of your flashbacks and with any type of trauma experience. It just so happens that Amanda's was a memory from her childhood.

Using perfect nurturer images to work with Amanda's shame-filled flashbacks

Once Amanda was well rehearsed in the art of accessing the compassionate mind by using her perfect nurturer image and associated scent, we agreed to revisit her painful memory of childhood abuse. However, this time Amanda included her perfect nurturing imagery in the flashback to help bring the compassionate feeling into her mind. We enabled Amanda to do this by following three steps that we have outlined below. Perhaps you can try to follow them too.

STEP ONE

As we did before with Jeff, we started by asking Amanda to write down a brief description of her main flashbacks, how they made her feel, what thoughts they triggered in her, and what she then did to cope.

Have a look at Amanda's chart following:

AMANDA'S FLASHBACK

Flashback description	How it makes me feel	What it makes me think about myself and others	What I do to cope with the flashback and how it makes me feel
I was about seven or eight years old. My uncle came to visit us one Sunday. He told my mother that he would like to put me to bed and read me a goodnight story. I remember him looking at me when I got into my pajamas. He then touched me when I was in bed.	Scared, disgusted, yucky, and ashamed.	It's my fault because I didn't say anything or ask him to stop. I'm dirty. Other people will think differently about me if they knew what happened—they will think I'm bad too.	I start to scratch at my arm. I want to take a shower to clean myself. I try to distract myself. I drink some wine if this happens in the evening.

Now you can go back to the chart you filled in earlier in this chapter and work on a flashback that you are finding particularly troublesome or having difficulty shifting feelings of shame or self-blame associated with it.

STEP TWO

Next, I discussed with Amanda what she would need to focus on in the flashback to help her feel safe and soothed. In order to do this we first conjured up her perfect nurturer image in her mind, using her scent as a trigger to feeling the compassionate mind emotion, and then asked a series of questions including: What would she like her perfect nurturer to say and/or do in the flashback to support her? How would she like to feel in the memory? Amanda had worked out how she wanted her perfect nurturer to support her and help her feel soothed and safe in the flashback.

Using my perfect nurturing imagery
Briefly describe your image:
My image is a big purple flower with a yellow center. The petals are like the ones on Gerbera daisies, and they move and sway and envelop me. The yellow center has a face with a half-smile and kind, caring eyes. It makes me feel strong, protected, and warm.   **Scent:** Lavender oil
What would you want your perfect nurturer to say to you to offer you strength and courage?
I'm right here for you. Your uncle should not be doing this to you. It's wrong and he is the adult; his actions are his responsibility. This is not your fault. You have been very brave to endure this.
How would you like your image to support you in the flashback?
To tell me that it's not my fault and to ask me to feel warmth, care, and comfort radiating from my nurturer to me.

What would you want your image to do for you? Remember, before you start to fill in worksheet 14, it is helpful to bring your image to mind (we did this exercise in chapter 8) and trigger the compassionate mind by using your compassionate scent.

WORKSHEET 14: USING MY PERFECT NURTURING IMAGERY

Using my perfect nurturing imagery
Briefly describe your image: Scent:
What would you want your perfect nurturer to say to you to offer you strength and courage?
How would you like your image to support you in the flashback?

STEP THREE

We then asked Amanda to complete the following tasks:

Rehearse and repeat what she wanted her perfect nurturer image to do for her in the flashback so that it became familiar to her.

Use her lavender oil to conjure up her perfect nurturer image.

Tell her perfect nurturer image about her flashback, what happened, and how it made her feel.

Allow her perfect nurturer image to speak to her and offer her strength, comfort, and wisdom (the compassionate reframe).

Write down what words of wisdom and strength her perfect nurturer image offered her.

The words Amanda's perfect nurturer offered her are found below:

My perfect nurturer's compassionate reframe of my flashback
Amanda, I hope you can feel the care and compassion I have for you at this moment. Focus on that feeling, as I want you to know that this abuse was not your fault. You were a child and your uncle is responsible for this. I am so sorry you had to suffer this, as you must have been frightened and alone. You have so much strength and courage now, and you can move on from this event and begin to love and care for yourself as I love and care for you. Let go of the blame, as this was not of your making. Move on now and live the life you deserve to live.

Amanda found this exercise very helpful. She was surprised how much better she felt when her perfect nurturing image was there for her offering comfort and strength. She was also surprised to see how much she believed now that the abuse was not her fault.

It's now your turn to see if your perfect nurturing image can help you feel differently about your self-blame. What I would like you to do is follow the five stages outlined in step three above:

Rehearse and repeat what you want your perfect nurturer image to do for you in the flashback.

Use your compassionate scent to conjure up your perfect nurturer image.

Tell your perfect nurturer image about your flashback, what happened, and how it made you feel.

Allow your perfect nurturer image to speak to you and offer you strength, comfort, and wisdom (the compassionate reframe).

Write down the words of wisdom and strength that your perfect nurturer image offered you.

What is really important to stress here though is to make sure you have engaged the *contentment and soothing* system before you bring your flashback to mind. This is because it will be much harder for you to bring the compassionate mind to your threat-focused mind, as we know it doesn't like to relinquish center stage that easily. It will be much easier for you to do it this way and much more tolerable for you! So when you are ready, complete worksheet 15 below.

WORKSHEET 15: MY PERFECT NURTURER'S COMPASSIONATE REFRAME OF MY FLASHBACK

My perfect nurturer's compassionate reframe of my flashback

Take some time now to reflect on how you feel about things and what new insights you have gained from doing these exercises. Well done for completing them. Remember, as before, it takes strength and courage to face things that terrify us and to make a commitment to move on with things in our lives.

A COMPASSIONATE NOTE ON DISGUST

Before we end this chapter we just want to spend a little time thinking about disgust. Lots of people who are traumatized often have to witness things that make them feel disgusted. This is especially the case with emergency personnel who have to attend accidents, for example. Sometimes people have to endure disgusting acts that others do to them. It's quite difficult to describe disgust, but we all know what it feels like. It can be a very visceral feeling in our bodies. It's an automatic feeling of revulsion coupled with a desire to rid ourselves of the feeling. We may even feel the need to be sick. So, for example, a disgusting smell might make us automatically grimace and turn our heads away or cover our noses. Similarly, a disgusting feeling in our bodies, triggered by a flashback, might cause a strong desire in us to want to cleanse our bodies or rid ourselves of the feeling.

Visceral rescript

The feeling of disgust can be very distressing. If it is triggered by our trauma flashbacks, we can find ourselves very upset and feeling sick and desperate to rid ourselves of the feeling. Martin the police officer, who we met in earlier chapters, used to suffer from disgust-filled flashbacks. This was related to his job as a traffic officer, and over the years he had attended many horrific road traffic accidents. He would often have flashbacks to scenes that made him feel disgusted. We helped Martin manage his flashbacks by using a technique that we call a visceral rescript. Let's work through this technique together, as you may find it helpful if you too have intense feelings of disgust.

It's important to say one very important thing before we start. You may have been subjected to disgusting acts and felt disgusted, but this does not mean that you are disgusting. Your threat-focused brain will trigger the feelings of disgust automatically in response to certain things, because that is what it is designed to do. This will cause you to feel disgusted, but again this does not mean that you are disgusting.

STEP ONE

Below we will look at how Martin worked with his disgust flashback. We won't go into too much detail about his flashback, as you might feel disgusted when you read it. Suffice it to say, Martin had a strong disgust response to his memory.

The flashback in brief:
Attending the scene of an accident, where the car had caught fire and people died. Thinking a piece of human remains was in his mouth.
What does disgust feel like to you?
It feels like a sickly, revolting feeling. It feels like a mental and bodily grimace, a recoiling in my body. It feels like a muscle cramp.
Where do you feel it in your body?
I can feel it in my nose and at the back of my throat. It travels down to the pit of my stomach.
Can you give the feeling a color?
Yes, it is sickly greenish yellow.
Does it have a smell?
Yes, it's putrid and burning meat mixed together.

Let's start as we did before and identify the flashback that makes you feel disgusted. Then, see if you can answer the following questions using worksheet 16 as a guide.

WORKSHEET 16: EXPLORING MY DISGUST FLASHBACKS

The flashback in brief:
What does disgust feel like to you?
Where do you feel it in your body?
Can you give the feeling a color?
Does it have a smell?

STEP TWO

We then asked Martin to think about a compassionate antidote to this feeling by using all his knowledge of the compassionate and soothing feelings. We spent some time developing this feeling in his body using visualization. This is what he came up with:

Compassionate antidote to disgust
What does compassion feel like to you?
It feels warm, safe, calm, strong, and open.
Where do you feel it in your body?
I feel it in the middle of my chest and above my abdomen, as if it's a ball of energy.
Can you give the feeling a color?
Yes, a definite mix between purple and turquoise—so that makes it purquoise!
Does it have a smell?
Yes, my compassionate scent is Old Spice aftershave.

I want you to think now about what a compassionate antidote to disgust would feel like in *your* body. So I really want you to think about what compassion feels like in a visceral sense. Really try to develop this feeling of compassion in your body. You may find that visualizing and imagining this will help to strengthen the feeling. Close your eyes and imagine. Perhaps you can think back to how you felt when you did your compassion flow exercises in chapter 8, and then complete worksheet 17.

What's important to focus on when you are doing this exercise is that you spend some time imagining the new compassionate feeling in your body. You will need to put some quiet time aside, begin with your soothing rhythm breathing, and then see if you can fill your body up with your compassionate feelings. Perhaps even imagine your body from top to toe changing to your compassionate color. Your compassionate scent will really help you here too, so breathe in a big lungful of it.

WORKSHEET 17: COMPASSIONATE ANTIDOTE TO DISGUST

Compassionate antidote to disgust
What does compassion feel like to you?
Where do you feel it in your body?
Can you give the feeling a color?
Does it have a smell?

STEP THREE

This is the part of the exercise for which you'll need your compassionate courage and strength. What we would like you to do now is to see if you can bring to mind your disgust flashback and tolerate it in your mind for a few minutes, while at the same time your body is filled with the compassionate feeling.

How did you do? Perhaps spend a few minutes writing down any key insights from this exercise. Martin found this exercise very calming, and with practice he noticed that his disgust flashbacks became less potent and frightening when he used his compassionate feeling. Martin also carried around a little cloth with his compassionate scent on it. He would then sniff this whenever he had a smell flashback that made him feel disgusted. He soon found that the disgusting smell memory did not linger. You may want to try this too and keep some of your compassionate scent on you for when you need it.

SUMMARY

In this chapter, we have continued to develop and use our compassionate minds to help us work through our self-critical thinking and self-blame. We have used the life stories of Amanda, Jeff, and Martin to illustrate how we can end the vicious loops of self-attack, develop compassionate reframes to our flashbacks, and use our perfect nurturing imagery to support us in more troublesome flashbacks. We then spent some time thinking about the feeling of disgust and how we can use a compassionate body feeling to work through our disgust-filled flashbacks.

I hope that you have found these exercises as helpful as Amanda, Jeff, and Martin did. I hope you continue to use them to help you resolve your flashback memories in a way that allows you to free yourself of shame and self-blame.

11

Using compassionate letter writing to bring compassion to your trauma story

We are now going to continue to develop our compassionate perspective on our traumatic experiences by developing a specifically compassionate written account of our trauma experiences. Although loosely based on the idea of exposure, helping us to engage with, rather than avoid, painful feelings, we are going to add the compassion-focused aspect. So we are going to write a compassionate letter to ourselves about our experiences but not go into the details of what actually happened. Visitors to the clinic often write a detailed account of their traumatic experiences as part of their therapy, and we call this developing a narrative account. Some, however, choose to tolerate their traumatic experiences out loud and bring their new insights into the story in order to reframe the meaning of their trauma. Both approaches can be very helpful in developing a new account, bringing new meaning to previously distressing events.

Chapters 9 and 10 provided a number of exercises to help you begin to think about your traumatic experiences in a wise, insightful, and compassionate way. Remember the reason for this is because that compassionate focus will bring important processing systems in your mind to the problem of your trauma and will help you soften it. In chapter 8 we developed a compassionate account of our life experiences in order to shed light on our fears and safety strategies. One of the important insights gained from chapter 8 was that our struggles are understandable and not our fault. Using the compassionate story we can begin to appreciate the nonintentionality of our life path and move toward accepting that compassion helps us in our lives. We can then offer compassionate understanding to our feelings of self-blame for the sad things that have happened to us. We give up blaming and shaming ourselves, and we allow ourselves to take firm responsibility for healing and change.

In chapter 10 we explored how to work with our critical voices and our flashbacks using our compassionate mind-set and compassionate imagery.

The purpose of these exercises is to help us bring compassionate insight to our traumatic experiences. So now let's move on to develop our skills by writing a compassionate letter to ourselves. The focus here is on our compassionate orientation to the trauma, not the distress embedded in it, and this is why we do not dwell on the details of the event. Remember, this is your own personal journey to recovery, and you can take things at a pace that feels comfortable for you. A compassionate letter does not need to contain details of the traumas if you do not wish it to do so. Treat yourself with care and kindness.

COMPASSIONATE LETTER WRITING

Some people find writing down their worries and concerns helps them work through things. Writing can be very helpful, as it gives us a chance to get our thoughts "out of our heads" and reflect on them. By reading our thoughts we can often gain new insights about ourselves, our experiences, our feelings, and our behaviors. This technique is often used in cognitive therapy, when people jot down negative thoughts and then write out a more helpful perspective reevaluation. So it's important to see that writing isn't just about rehearsing negative things over and over but about being able to stand back from them and try to evaluate them in more helpful ways. When you write something, you can ask yourself questions such as How could I have improved the situation? What would be helpful for me now? How might I cope with this better in the future? What might I say to a friend who experienced a similar situation?

We are going to focus on writing a letter to ourselves in a style that offers us support, understanding, and kindness to help us deal with our traumatic events. We call this approach *compassionate letter writing*.

We use compassionate letter writing, as it helps us develop our skills of compassion by becoming motivated to improve ourselves, developing a sensitivity and openness to our experiences, and learning how to tolerate distress and be nonjudgmental. Developing these skills gives us insight into our blocks to becoming self-compassionate, and we can hear that "yes but" voice in our heads. Remember that different parts of you always have different thoughts and beliefs about the trauma. The key for you is to choose to focus on that wise, strong compassionate self that wants to help you.

Although we are going to use compassionate letter writing as a way to develop a written account of your traumatic experiences, many also use the letter as a way of developing a new relationship with themselves. You may find both helpful. If you want to further develop your skills of compassionate letter writing, you may want to read the chapter on it in Paul Gilbert's self-help book, *The Compassionate Mind* (see the resources section at the back of this book).

Going with the flow of your thoughts

Don't worry too much about what you are going to write; in other words, don't think about things in advance. Just take your time and go with the flow of your thoughts. Start writing regardless of whether or not you know what you're going to put down on paper. There is no perfect letter or perfect way to do this, there is no right or wrong, and it's okay to take your time and rewrite things until you find what works for you. It may help if you remember that the purpose of this letter writing is to help you activate your compassionate self, which comes with a particular kind of feeling, wisdom, and desire to be helpful in regard to your traumatic experience.

Letter writing can be very powerful and poignant for people. Some find themselves moved by sadness for themselves as they write. This can be an important part of their journeys as they begin to focus on the sadness of their experiences rather than on their shame. Acknowledging and grieving for your pain can be important in healing the hurt and finding a way to move on from things. Your compassionate mind may already be thinking that this could be upsetting for you, and so you may want to think about what would be a compassionate thing for you to do after you have finished your letter. Consider what that might be for you, perhaps calling a friend or going for a walk.

STEPS TO COMPASSIONATE LETTER WRITING

Try to find a quiet, safe space and set aside a good hour where you will not be disturbed. You may not be able to finish the letter in one sitting, and you may want to go back to it and change it.

Step 1: Compassionate motivation

Before you begin to write your letter, remember that the motivation of your compassionate mind is to alleviate your distress and suffering with kindness, courage, warmth, and strength. You may already be noticing merging feelings of anxiety or distress as you begin the task of writing to yourself about your experiences. This is an understandable reaction, and if it happens to you, try to focus your mind on the compassionate feelings in your body and perhaps use your compassionate scent to trigger this state in your body.

Step 2: Getting into the right mind-set

As with all the previous exercises we have done, remember to access your compassionate sense of self by using your compassionate imagery before you begin. Doing this helps us to tap into the soothing and contentment system that is so important in helping us regulate threat. So first, always spend a moment just trying to engage your soothing breathing rhythm, which helps you focus on the importance of slowing down your mind. Remember to always focus on the out breath and pay attention to your posture so that you begin to command a stance of dignity and authority. Allow yourself to create a friendly facial expression; this is important because the muscles in your face feed back to the systems in your brain that register soothing and "safeness." Remember that your voice will be calm. Spend just thirty seconds creating this sense of self. Using our own minds to write a letter allows us to create a compassionate frame of mind within ourselves. We can use some of our exercises in chapter 8 to help us with this.

Alternatively, if you prefer, you can imagine your perfect nurturing image writing the letter to you. Some people find it easier to accept compassionate thoughts from an imagined fantasy than from themselves, even though they know they created the perfect nurturer.

If you are using the perfect nurturer to write your letter, then spend a little time imagining that person or image being with you. You might want to use your compassionate scent or some of your imagery exercises to elicit the emergence of your compassionate mind. We want to be able to access the feelings of wisdom, strength, kindness, and warmth as we sit down and begin to write our letters. Remember that your image was created for you by you and has your best interests at heart. It offers you the courage to face your pain.

When you can feel your compassionate mind gradually emerging and taking shape, you can begin to work through the various steps of letter writing outlined below. Remember to be kind to yourself, as this is your journey, and you may take several weeks to work through it. This is okay, and you can pace it in a way that helps you.

Ideally we will not begin letter writing until we feel confident that we can bring our perfect nurturer images to mind, even if only as a fleeting experience.

It may be helpful to remind yourself that your compassionate mind will draw attention to things in your life that will aid you, will help you to think through your difficulties with courage and kindness, and will enable you to behave in ways that are supportive to your well-being.

It's worth noting that it can be difficult to access and activate our compassionate minds and this is not our fault. What's important is that we can focus on the intent our minds have to help alleviate our distress.

Step 3: Experiencing safeness

As we write our letter, it is important to remind ourselves that we are safe, that the trauma is in the past, and that it can no longer harm us. Perhaps remind yourself of where you are right now and that you are safe; look around you and feel the floor beneath your feet supporting you, and if you're sitting in a chair, feel your chair at your back holding you up; notice the colors and textures around you. Maybe you're sitting at a table or looking out of the window. Focus for a few moments on the feelings in your body that are triggered when you concentrate on your "safeness" in this place right now. Writing your letter from a place of "safeness" and warmth will help you begin to tolerate what are sometimes intense feelings and the distress associated with your traumatic experience. If at any time you feel too distressed or overwhelmed just come back to feeling where you are right now, focusing on your breath, focusing on the feelings of sitting in the chair or looking out of the window. Sometimes you can move in and out by writing for a while and then coming back to the present moment, and then writing again. Do whatever helps you.

Step 4: Are you ready to start?

Write your letter from the perspective of the compassionate self or imagine a compassionate other writing to you. The compassionate self understands, validates, empathizes with, and supports you unconditionally. It is wise and knows that life is very difficult and all of us just find ourselves here. It understands that traumatic experiences are sadly common and can be overwhelming. It is the part of you that can develop confidence in this understanding and also this deep motivation to be caring and supporting. This is when you begin to recognize that compassion is not about soothing away or getting rid of unpleasant feelings—it is not a kind of ascension to some wonderful state of goodness and grace. True compassion is developing the courage we need to engage with the painful things within us in a very concerned and helpful way. Compassion recognizes that thinking about doing things differently or understanding ourselves in new ways can be painful and we can resist it for all kinds of reasons so it won't rush your letter; or ask you to make changes that you are not ready for.

Step 5: Start by recognizing your wisdom, courage, strength, and resilience

It's not uncommon to find it a struggle to think of the first paragraph of anything we might write. In order to help you overcome this block why not try to follow the suggested structure below, as this has helped many get started with the compassionate letter.

I always suggest that people start their letters by making statements to validate their suffering and what they've been through. Let's work through this with an example from Amanda, whom we have met before.

Dear Amanda,

I am writing this letter to you, as I know that you are struggling at the moment and have suffered much in the past from your traumatic experiences. I'm writing this letter to offer my help and support as you find your way to work through your difficulties and move on in your life. I would like you to know that you didn't choose to be here, you didn't choose to have your history, and you certainly didn't choose to have a brain that is primed for fear or primed to dwell on things you are finding difficult.

The first part of our letters can help us tune into our own internal wisdom, courage, strength, and resilience. It's interesting that just simply taking the time to give space to this part of yourself can allow it to gradually emerge. If we are stuck in these feelings, it can be hard for us to be able to recognize these qualities in ourselves, and so it can be helpful to at least remind ourselves that we have them, even if we can't feel them. Your letter might go on to include something like this:

Remember that none of us chooses to be traumatized—and that goes for all human beings who right now are suffering from the effects of trauma. The most important thing right now is to step back from your trauma and think about what it is you really need in order to heal and come to terms with your experience. The problem with trauma is coping and dealing with so many different emotions spinning around in your mind: anxiety, terror, but perhaps also anger and disgust and disappointment and confusion. It's no wonder things are difficult for you to deal with. So we can just go one step at a time and recognize that none of this is your fault and that this is how our brains are designed to respond to threatening situations. It's been difficult watching you suffer in the way that you have and blaming yourself for the things that have happened to you. I want to tell you that you have shown great strength and courage to endure such suffering and my heart goes out to you. Your wisdom and courage will help you find a way through your pain.

You may not even believe your compassionate image at this point, but it is important we help activate that part of your brain that focuses on your compassionate competencies, courage, and ability to tolerate and manage distressing and difficult things.

Step 6: Add empathy and understanding

It is important that our letters allow us to express empathy and understanding of the struggles that we have experienced in the past and how our traumatic experiences have affected us. We need to understand that the struggles we are having are part of a common human experience and relate to our histories. They are not our fault, but they are our responsibility in the sense that we have to find ways to manage them, ideally without attacking ourselves.

So it may help you to focus on what you know about your brain, your personal history, the situation you find yourself in, and the ways that you have learned to cope with difficult things.

The next part of your letter may focus on the empathy and understanding you have for why you blame yourself for your traumatic experience.

I know how difficult it has been for you to cope with the aftermath of the rape, and I understand why you have a tendency to blame yourself for the sad things that happen in your life. I have been impressed by your courage and honesty as you've looked back over your life and looked at the experiences in your childhood that have made you not like yourself. It takes courage to do this and you are showing brave commitment to your recovery. The thing is it's just not your fault that you were bullied at school and it's not your fault that your parents weren't very good at teaching you how to manage your emotions to self-soothe. You were often blamed as a child, and because of this you tend to blame yourself for things that go wrong in your life. It is therefore understandable that you blamed yourself when you were raped; you thought it was your fault and that you deserved it. I can understand why you want to blame yourself, as it makes you feel more in control and you have a complicated threat-focused brain that keeps thinking you are still in danger. But you are not. You are safe, and despite all that you've been through, this was not your fault. You did not deserve to suffer in this way.

Your strength and determination have kept you going, and I'm impressed by the way you have managed to look after yourself and your family and provide a loving home. You are doing the very best you can, and I want you to remember the kindness and the warmth in the comfort that I feel for you. You are not alone in your suffering. You can commend yourself for your efforts and how well you have done in committing to recovering from this attack. I want to remind you that none of this is your fault, that you did not intend for your life to be like this, and you would not have written this script for yourself if you had a choice.

Step 7: Understand the unintended consequences of the ways you have coped

Now the letter might move on to think about some of the unintended consequences of the way you have coped with threat. You can remind yourself of yours by revisiting your compassionate story, which we developed in chapter 9.

Amanda, whatever you did to cope as a child and as an adult was the best you could do at the time, given everything else that was going on in your life. I know you feel sad that your relationship with your husband has suffered because of the rape and you find it difficult to be close to him. It's understandable why you avoid physical contact because it reminds you of the rape, and I know you don't want it to be like this forever. You are taking brave steps to sort out these difficulties, and with time, things will improve. Just go one step at a time. You also have faced up to the fact that you have been drinking too much and putting your health at risk. I know you are sad about this, but it's understandable that you have wanted to escape your mind and your memories. It's been tough for you, and it is also understandable that you bully yourself and think how "weak willed you are" when you drink. But one of the unintended consequences is that you are now so good at bullying yourself that you end up even more miserable, alone, and isolated. It also stops your thinking about your rape in a more balanced and helpful way, which just adds to your feelings of shame.

Step 8: It's not your fault, but it is your responsibility

The letter might now move on to making a statement about taking responsibility for change in our lives. In order to help us do this, the key to a compassionate approach is to remind ourselves that we didn't ask to be born into the circumstances or relationships we grew up with, and certainly did not ask to experience traumatic life events.

It's not your fault that you want to run away and hide, avoid your memories and flashbacks, blot your mind with beer, and avoid your husband. These are understandable and normal reactions to frightening things, and it's not your fault that you didn't have an opportunity to learn different ways to manage such difficult, complex, and conflicting emotions and life's challenges. Remember, you didn't choose to be here, you didn't choose to have your history, and you certainly didn't choose to have a brain that is primed for fear or that dwells on things you are finding difficult.

But you also realize the pain these behaviors cause you, as they come at a cost to your well-being. You do want to find other ways to cope with the threats you experience now, and I know you can and will work to find other ways to cope when you feel afraid, ways that are better for you and more supportive of your future goals.

Step 9: Describe what you need to help you cope with your memories

The next step in letter writing focuses on understanding what you need to help you cope with your emotions and memories. This has two elements: what you needed in the past to help you find different ways of coping with the events that were not your fault and what would help you to cope differently now.

Throughout your whole life, you haven't really known how to cope with the complex and conflicting emotions that our brains are designed to provide, particularly in the context of your traumatic experience. In addition, desperate wishes to try to get it right led you to be very focused on yourself and to self-blame when things went wrong. None of this is your fault. But today you are recognizing how tricky our brains can be and that self-criticizing is understandable but not helpful. So the key really is thinking about what you need to help support yourself and offer comfort when you are struggling with your flashbacks and your self-blaming thoughts. You are working hard at developing your capacity for compassion, which will help you face, tolerate, and work through your fears. Being raped was not something you wanted to happen, and it was not part of the life plan you would have written for yourself had you had the choice. This is not your fault and focusing on this fact helps you deal with your feelings of self-blame. It also helps you when you remind yourself that you are not a bad person who has deserved these things to happen to her. You are choosing to live your life with compassion, and it's not weak to want help from others, as it takes great courage to show vulnerability. It's a great strength to be able to reach out to others when you feel so vulnerable. Remember that you have a choice about how you want to feel about yourself and whether you want to believe bad things about yourself. Others have labeled you for their own interests and not yours. If those people did not have your best interests at heart, why bother to listen to them? This is not about whether you are a good or bad person; this is about who you are trying to become and the choices you have in what you believe about yourself.

Step 10: Final statement of courage and commitment to a future without suffering

I tend to encourage people to end their letters with a commitment to their future. This helps them think about a life after their traumatic experiences. It also helps them to explore the reasons they can think and act differently in the future.

You are learning about yourself all the time. Although you still have these emotions and fears that come into your memories, you can now use your self-soothing skills to help you manage your feelings better. You now know you are developing the capacity to be a compassionate person and you can seek out the comfort of your husband and friends when you are struggling in the future. Your compassion will allow you to engage with, tolerate, and compassionately move forward. Your vision for your future does not need to include the Amanda who feels ashamed of who she is, as you may choose to be the Amanda who is strong and safe and has survived. You can choose a future now that includes reconnecting with your husband and enjoying the close relationship you once had and both want again. Just go one step at a time.

Now that we have worked through the ten steps of writing a compassionate letter to ourselves about our traumatic experiences, you might want to try to compose your own. As I won't be able to read it for you, please try to make sure it is a compassionate letter and includes all the points discussed above. I say this, as sometimes visitors to the clinic have written letters about their experiences that are far from compassionate. Remember, this is not a letter to beat yourself up with; we know you are already very good at doing that and you don't need further practice. This is a letter to develop your compassionate mind, and the motivation is to take self-blame and distress away from your traumatic experience.

Step 11: Pay compassionate attention to your letter

Professor Gilbert talks about the importance of "hearing" your compassionate letter, as many people can write a very compassionate letter to other people or even themselves but cannot feel it to be true.

There are ways in which we can enhance our ability to emotionally connect with our letter, and we explore these below.

We can start to feel the compassion in our letters by imagining the flow of compassion into ourselves. This will help you to have the experience of being cared for and supported by another person in a warm, kind, nonjudgmental, and helpful way. Start by imagining kindness and compassion flowing from you back toward yourself. When you feel ready, bring to mind your compassionate self. Imagine yourself filling up with feelings of calm, wisdom, strength, and warmth. Imagine the flow of compassion coming into you and being all around you. Now focus on the genuine care you have for yourself and the fact you really do desire to be free from suffering. Shortly you will begin to read your letter out to yourself, so spend a few moments focusing on the compassionate tone of your voice. Imagine your voice sounding calm, soft, and soothing. Also notice the tone of wisdom and concern. You know that you are doing your best to get through things and cope as well as you can. Focus on what that feels like.

When you are ready you can begin to read your letter aloud to yourself. Some people find it helpful to actually read the letter out loud while looking in the mirror so that it feels as if they are really having a conversation with themselves. This way you could even smile at yourself in the mirror and focus on how warm it feels to offer yourself kindness and compassion. You may even want to record this and use it when you are in need of self-compassion. If you feel uncomfortable with the idea of recording yourself, you can practice reading your letter aloud and notice which parts touch you, help you feel soothed and understood, and which parts are helpful. This can offer you more useful insights into where some of your blocks might be in developing your compassionate mind.

Another thing that I sometimes do with visitors to the clinic is read their letters back to them as if they were listening to someone else's story. This can be very helpful in promoting their feelings of warmth, care, and sadness with regard to their suffering, as it gives them some distance from their own tendencies to self-criticize. You may also find this helpful, but it is important to choose someone who makes you feel safe and who cares for you. Please don't do this if it will make you feel unsafe and anxious to share your thoughts with another, as this will defeat the object of the exercise.

LOOKING AFTER YOURSELF

This is a powerful exercise, and you are likely to find yourself getting in touch with upsetting and sad feelings. Although we can appreciate that we have to go where our pain is to find healing and growth, doing so can leave us feeling exhausted and drained. So remind yourself of the reasons you want to do this and that you are committed to your recovery. Remember to take care of yourself and engage in your compassionate behavior after you have finished this exercise.

ELEVEN STEPS TO DEVELOPING A COMPASSIONATE LETTER

Here is a helpful summary of the key stages in your letter writing to help you with your own composition. Before you begin to write, focus your mind on the compassionate feelings in your body and get into a compassionate mind-set by bringing your compassionate imagery to mind, using your compassionate scent, and slowing your mind down with soothing rhythm breathing. Allow yourself at least an hour to write your letter, and plan something soothing or distracting to do when you have finished.

1. Start by noticing and validating your distress and remind yourself of your motivation to alleviate the suffering associated with the trauma.

2. Bring to mind your compassionate focus and remind yourself of your compassionate thinking, behaviors, and feelings.

3. Remind yourself that you are safe now and access feelings of "safeness" using imagery.

4. You are ready to start if you are feeling safe and you are in the compassionate mind-set.

5. Begin your letter by recognizing your courage, your resilience, and your ability to cope, both recently and in the past.

6. Remind yourself of what you have been through and how you have a threat-focused brain that has been shaped by your experiences.

7. Spend time acknowledging the impact and cumulative effect your safety strategies have had on your life and your well-being.

8. Use your insight and understanding to appreciate that what happened to you is not your fault but it is your responsibility to commit to recovering from these events.

9. Think about what you find helpful in coping with your trauma memories.

10. Make a final statement of courage and determination to lead the compassionate life you want and deserve.

11. Spend time making your letter real to you by developing feelings of compassion as you read your story aloud to yourself.

SUMMARY

In this chapter we explored using compassionate letter writing to develop an account of our traumatic experiences. The purpose of this exercise is to help us bring a compassionate reframe to our feelings of self-blame, which will help us to alleviate the feelings of fear and shame associated with our memories.

By taking time to complete the exercises in chapters 9 and 10, you may have found new insights and given new meaning to your traumatic experiences. You can use these to help you in your letter to bring compassion and care to your traumatic memories and to yourself.

12

Moving on in your life with compassion

Now we are at the end of the book and somewhere on our journeys to develop our compassionate minds.

As you have worked through the chapters and completed the exercises that seemed relevant to you, you may have already experienced some changes in how you are feeling about yourself and your traumatic experience. You may even have had some "lightbulb" moments, when things have suddenly clicked into place for you or made sense. Some may have read the book and been at the "I see what you mean, but I just can't feel it to be true for me" stage. This is a common feeling, and it may take some time for your compassionate feelings to develop. Try to stick with your compassionate practice; the more you practice, the easier it will become for you to access the feelings. Remember that you are developing your capacity for compassion. Some of you will think "This stuff is not for me." That's okay too, and whatever stage you are at, remember this is a journey of self-discovery. But try to keep practicing, and in time you will be able to move a little further on in your journey. If you feel you are being helped by these ideas, then keep at it, and perhaps you may want to consider exploring some of the ideas with a therapist. No two journeys will be quite the same. Reading about other people's experiences throughout the book will have given you insights and ideas about how to understand your experiences and manage your traumatic memories with kindness and compassion.

TEN KEY INSIGHTS TO A COMPASSIONATE APPROACH TO TRAUMA

Below I have summarized what I think are the ten key messages or insights you can take from this book, although you may have different or additional ones. Take a moment to read over the ten points, and then think if there are any others that you would like to add to the list.

1. The majority of us will be exposed to traumatic events in our lifetimes of varying degrees of severity and duration. Some of us will find it difficult to come to terms with what has happened to us and may even develop symptoms of PTSD. Some of us will blame ourselves for what happened and for the symptoms of anxiety, depression, and irritability that go with PTSD. We can suffer from painful feelings of shame and be very self-critical about our traumatic experiences and our own reactions to it.

2. We can understand our reactions to traumatic events by accepting that human beings have threat-focused brains that have evolved over millions of years and are not the best design for current-day living! It's not our fault that we are designed by nature in such a way that we run into these problems. Also, we can be highly sensitized to becoming traumatized because of how we experienced our early lives.

3. Flashbacks and nightmares are a common and distressing experience for those who have been traumatized. Our brains treat flashbacks as a threat so we become frightened of our own memories. As it can be too upsetting to have to "relive" our traumatic experiences over and over, we may use elaborate avoidance strategies to try to limit our exposure to the flashbacks. We may avoid the people who love us, hurt ourselves, misuse alcohol or drugs, or feel as if we are always on our guard and looking out for potential danger.

4. Our reactions to threat (feelings of anxiety, anger, disgust, and sadness) are not only normal but are important in helping with the brain's foremost mission to keep us safe. We behave in certain ways when we are threatened, and this is also not our fault but just a part of our safety strategies. What's important is that we can regulate or calm the threat-related emotions.

5. Our own self-criticism and self-blame keep us stuck in vicious loops of distress. Our brains respond to self-criticism as if it is a social threat, and we fear how other people will think of us. We care about what other people think because we have a social brain that is designed by evolution to care. But self-criticism makes our flashbacks feel even more frightening, as these pieces of memory convey to us that the events are our fault. So we fuel our threat systems with more threat when we blame ourselves, and this keeps us stuck in the "hamster wheel" of our traumatized minds.

6. We can regulate our threat-based emotions by experiencing the emotions governed by the *content-ment and soothing* system, where we feel peaceful and calm but also feel the support and encouragement needed to engage with that which is frightening and upsetting. One reason compassion can be so helpful is that it balances our threat-sensitive brains.

7. Through no fault of our own, some of us find it difficult to access and use the *contentment and soothing* system or find the inner support, understanding, encouragement, and validation that we need. We are too locked into our avoidance, self-criticism, and shame. Learning how to be inwardly understanding, supportive, and self-reassuring is a skill that we usually learn in our attachment relationships as we are growing up. However, if this wasn't part of our childhood experiences, it is a skill we can learn through training and practicing a compassionate mind focus, just as we can develop strength in our physical muscles.

8. Developing a compassionate mind involves using the *contentment and soothing* system to organize our minds. The motivation of a compassionate mind is to alleviate distress and suffering, and we can do this by paying attention to our reasoning, behaviors, and feelings. Compassion is not about being soft. We have to go to where our pain is in order to find healing, and this takes strength, fortitude, and courage. Indeed, it is important to keep in mind that when we talk about soothing, this is not soothing something away. Instead, it is about creating an inner space where we can do psychological repair work. Compassion is not about ascending away from pain and trying to become some angelic-like being. Compassion is about descending into the pain of our lives in order to be helpful and healing. Anyone who thinks compassion is soft or weak has misunderstood the concept.

9. When we are motivated to alleviate our pain and suffering we can use our compassionate minds to help us cope with traumatic life events. We can understand our life stories with compassion and begin to recognize that this is only one version of us. Through letting go of our self-blame, we can begin to use our compassionate minds to develop another version of ourselves and move on from our traumas.

10. When you notice that you are in the threat mind-set, take a moment to remember life is better and more bearable when we look at it with the compassionate mind.

See now if you can think about your personal journey through the book by filling in worksheet 18.

WORKSHEET 18: MY PERSONAL INSIGHTS ABOUT COMPASSION AND TRAUMA

My personal insights about compassion and trauma
1.
2.
3.
4.

WHAT CHANGES HAVE YOU NOTICED IN YOURSELF?

Perhaps it's time to take a moment to think about any changes you have noticed in yourself since using the exercises in this book. They may not be big changes just yet, and that's okay. Remember though, that a little drop of water in the ocean can create ripples and if there is enough momentum, ripples can create waves. So before you know it, you may find yourself riding on the crest of a compassionate wave of change! So no matter what stage you are at right now, think back to where you have been and the differences that are in your life at the moment. Then write them down in worksheet 19.

WORKSHEET 19: THINGS THAT ARE DIFFERENT IN MY LIFE NOW

Things that are different in my life now
For example:
I am less hard on myself.
I am beginning to notice when I am in the threat mind-set.
My flashbacks seem less scary.
It's good to know I am not alone in this.

WHAT EXERCISES HAVE YOU FOUND THE MOST HELPFUL?

Spend some time now thinking about the exercises in the book and which of them you found most helpful. You may remember that part II of the book was dedicated to developing compassionate skills. We looked at how to develop mindful, soothing breathing, then we went on to complete a series of exercises aimed at developing our flow of compassion, and we finished by developing perfect nurturing imagery. In part III we developed a compassionate story of our lives and then used our skills to work with our trauma memories, self-criticism, and feelings of shame.

Which exercises did you find the most helpful for you? See if you can list in worksheet 20 following, the ones you would like to continue to use.

WORKSHEET 20: HELPFUL COMPASSIONATE EXERCISES

Compassionate exercises that I find helpful and will continue to use
For example: Soothing rhythm breathing, imagining my safe place, perfect nurturing imagery, and compassionate skills development.

THE NEW VERSION OF YOU

Now it's time to think about the "new version" of you. You know the "old version" of you because you have been living with yourself for some years now, but what about this "new version," the one that you can develop the capacity to be and the one that perhaps isn't a legacy from your childhood experiences? Remember, you have a choice in this and you can use all your insights from the first part of this book and all the exercises and worksheets from the second and third parts to see if you can think of a way you would like to commit to being a more compassionate version of yourself.

Try to use this exercise as a recap and summary of what you have learned about yourself from reading this book, and remember that this is about developing your capacity to be compassionate, wise, and nonjudgmental.

What would a compassionate version of you be like? Let's think about this together. It might be helpful to see if you can answer the following questions on worksheet 21.

WORKSHEET 21: THE COMPASSIONATE VERSION OF ME

The compassionate version of me

If I were compassionate to myself

How would I think about myself?

For example, I would think that I like myself and that I care about my well-being. I would know that I am trying my best to get through life, causing as little pain as I can to myself and others.

How would I think about other people?

For example, that we all struggle because life is tough and we all have complicated human brains. Others are also doing what they can to cope with their lives. Perhaps I can offer compassion to them too.

How would I behave toward myself when I was struggling?

For example, I would engage my compassionate mind, and I would act in ways to help take away my distress. I would be kind and understanding, perhaps talk it through with a friend.

How would I behave in my life in general?

For example, I would try to be mindful of who I am and my hopes and fears. I would try to treat myself and others with care and kindness. I would try to behave in ways that are supportive and are in my best interests.

What things would I have in my life?

For example, good supportive friends, a social life, and a job that I actually enjoy.

What things would I want for my future?

For example, contentment, a compassionate mind, and a continued belief that I deserve a life free from pain.

A COMPASSIONATE COMMITMENT TO YOURSELF

You can see from the exercise above that we used the word "would," which help us to work out those things in our lives that we do not have but which we would like to have. If we "would" like things to be different then there is every possibility that "I would" can become "I am." It takes a compassionate commitment to work toward this version of ourselves, and we can commit to do our best to try if that's want we want. That's all we can ask of ourselves. But we already know this journey is hard and can be painful, so we will need all the help and support we can muster from ourselves and from others.

A COMPASSIONATE FIRST-AID BOX

Something that many people find useful is to make up compassionate first-aid boxes to remind themselves of what they need to do to help access the feelings of contentment and soothing associated with their compassionate selves. Here are some of the popular items that people choose to put in theirs:

Compassionate scent, for example, a bottle of perfume or a scent-soaked cloth

Compassionate objects such as stones or shells

Drawing of a perfect nurturer

Something in their favorite color

Copy of new compassionate version of themselves exercise

Pictures of loved ones smiling

Important letters

Copy of compassionate story of their lives

Compassionate letter to themselves

Hopefully this list has given you some ideas about what you could put in your box. Why not fill in worksheet 22 below to remind you of the things you want? Then see if you can collect them—and spend a bit of time reminding yourself what the compassionate mind feels like.

WORKSHEET 22: MY COMPASSIONATE FIRST-AID BOX

My compassionate first-aid box

LOOKING FORWARD

I hope that this approach has helped you to learn to compassionately change your relationship with yourself and your traumatic experience. I hope this allows you to be free to live the life you want for the version of yourself you want to be.

If you are struggling with the ideas in this book but want to make changes, then please do think about seeking professional help. There are lots of therapists who are very experienced in working with trauma and who will doubtless be able to support and guide you through your recovery.

There are also many resources you can use to help you become more self-compassionate and to help you work on your traumatic experience. You will find some of them listed in the resources section.

So on that note I wish you well and

May you be well.

May you be free from suffering.

May you be happy.

May you treat yourself more compassionately.

Useful resources

BOOKS

Fennell, Melanie. *Overcoming low self-esteem: A self-help guide to using cognitive behavioural techniques.* London: Constable & Robinson, 2009.

Gilbert, Paul. *Overcoming depression: A self-help guide using cognitive behavioral techniques.* 3rd ed. London: Constable & Robinson, 2009.

Gilbert, Paul. *The compassionate mind.* London: Constable & Robinson, 2009; Oakland, Calif.: New Harbinger, 2010.

Herbert, Claudia, and Ann Wetmore. *Overcoming traumatic stress: A self-help guide using cognitive behavioural techniques.* London: Constable & Robinson, 2008.

Rothschild, Babette. *8 keys to safe trauma recovery: Take-charge strategies to empower your healing.* New York: W. W. Norton & Co., 2010.

SUPPORT GROUPS

The following are support groups or caring organizations that you might also find helpful.

The Samaritans (Tel: 08457 90 90 90; http.samaritans.org.uk). They offer 24-hour support over the telephone for anybody in crisis.

Cruse (Tel: 0870 167 1677; www.crusebereavementcare.org.uk). They offer counseling, advice, and support throughout the UK for those who are bereaved.

National Center for PTSD: www.ptsd.va.gov/. Information for veterans with lots of good resources.

Veteran Crisis Line: www.veteranscrisisline.net/. Veteran crisis line for immediate help.

International Society of Traumatic Stress Studies: www.istss.org. ISTSS has lots of good resources and links: www.istss.org/UsefulLinksAndResources/3607.htm

National Child Traumatic Stress Network: www.nctsnet.org. Lots of good resources and links for children.

National Institute of Mental Health: www.nimh.nih.gov. NIMH has resources for the public.

References

Chapter 1: Understanding your reactions to traumatic life events

American Psychological Association. *Diagnostic and statistical manual of mental disorders* (DSM IV-R) (Washington, D.C.: Author, 2000).

Chapter 2: Understanding your responses to traumatic events: your brain, your motives, and your emotions

Brewin, C. A cognitive neuroscience account of PTSD and its treatment. *Behaviour Research and Therapy, 39*, 373–93.

LeDoux, Joseph. *The emotional brain: The mysterious underpinnings of emotional life* (London: Weidenfeld & Nicolson, 1998).

Chapter 3: Understanding your trauma memories: flashbacks, nightmares, and intrusive thoughts

Ehlers, A., and D. M. Clark. A cognitive model of post-traumatic stress disorder. *Behaviour Research and Therapy, 38*(4), 2000, 319–45.

Harman, R., D. A. Lee, and C. Barker. The role of self-attack and self-soothing in the maintenance of shame-based PTSD. *Clinical Psychology and Psychotherapy, 17*, 2010, 13–24.

Chapter 4: Understanding shame and self-criticism in relation to traumatic events

Gilbert, P. *Human nature and suffering* (Psychology Press, 1989).

Gilbert, P. What is shame? Some core issues and controversies. In *Shame: Interpersonal behaviour, psychopathology, and culture* (New York: Oxford University Press, 1998), 3–38.

Chapter 5: Understanding your need for compassion in your life

Bowlby, J. *Attachment: Attachment and loss, Vol. 1* (London: Hogarth Press, 1969).

Gerhardt, S. *Why love matters: How affection shapes a baby's brain* (Hove, U.K.: Brunner-Routledge, 2004).

Chapter 6: Preparing your minds for compassion: attributes of compassion

Gilbert, P. *The compassionate mind* (London: Constable & Robinson, 2009; Oakland, CA: New Harbinger, 2010).

Chapter 7: Preparing your mind for compassion: the beginnings of skills development

Gilbert, P., and S. Proctor. Compassionate mind training for people with high shame and self-criticism: Overview and pilot study of a group therapy approach. *Clinical Psychology and Psychotherapy*, 13, 2006, 353–79.

Krakow, B., and A. Zadra. Clinical management of chronic nightmares: Imagery rehearsal therapy. *Behavioural Sleep Medicine*, 4(1), 2006, 45–70.

Lee, D. A. The perfect nurturer: A model to develop compassion within cognitive therapy. In *Compassion and psychotherapy: Theory, Research and Practice* (London: Routledge, 2005).

Chapter 8: Developing your skills to access compassionate feelings

Ehlers, A., D. M. Clark, F. McManus, and M. Fennell. Cognitive therapy for post-traumatic stress disorder: Development and evaluation. *Behaviour Research and Therapy*, 43(4), 2005, 413–31.

Grey, N., K. Young, and E. Holmes. Cognitive restructuring within re-living: A treatment for peritraumatic emotional "hotspots" in post-traumatic stress disorder. *Behavioural and Cognitive Psychotherapy*, 30(1), 2002, 37–56.

Chapter 9: Using compassion to understand your life story

Grey, N., K. Young, and E. Holmes. Cognitive restructuring within re-living: A treatment for peritraumatic emotional "hotspots" in post-traumatic stress disorder. *Behavioural and Cognitive Psychotherapy*, 30(1), 2002, 37–56.

Kennerley, H. *Overcoming childhood trauma* (London: Constable & Robinson, 2000).

Lee, D. A. The perfect nurturer: A model to develop compassion within cognitive therapy. In *Compassion and psychotherapy: Theory, Research and Practice* (London: Routledge, 2005).

Wheatley et al. "I'll believe it when I can see it": Imagery rescripting of intrusive sensory memories in depression. *Journal of Behavior Therapy and Experimental Psychiatry*, 38(4), 2007, 371–85.

Chapter 10: Using your compassionate mind to resolve your shame-filled flashbacks

Lee, D. A. Compassion focused cognitive therapy for shame-based trauma memories and flashbacks in PTSD. In *A casebook of cognitive therapy for traumatic stress reactions* (London: Brunner-Routledge, 2009), chapter 15.

Deborah A. Lee, DClinPsy, is a consultant clinical psychologist, head of a national treatment center for post-traumatic stress disorder (PTSD) in Berkshire, UK, and an honorary senior lecturer in clinical psychology at the University College London. Lee has worked with adult survivors of rape, interpersonal violence, and childhood abuse for more than twenty years and specializes in treating shame-based PTSD and complex trauma. She has pioneered the use of compassion-focused therapy with those suffering from shame-based PTSD and complex trauma and widely disseminated her clinical knowledge through writing and delivering clinical workshops in North America and Europe.

Sophie James is a lawyer and writer. After practicing law for over a decade, she changed her career to take up her passion for writing. She has particular interest in writing for the self-help market, and is dedicated to making clinical research and practice accessible to the general population.

Foreword writer **Paul Gilbert, PhD,** is a professor at the University of Derby in the United Kingdom, director of the mental health research unit at Derbyshire Mental Health Trust, and author of *The Compassionate Mind.*

MORE BOOKS *from*
NEW HARBINGER PUBLICATIONS

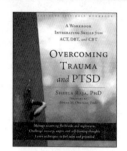

OVERCOMING TRAUMA & PTSD

A Workbook Integrating Skills from ACT, DBT & CBT

US $21.95 / ISBN: 978-1608822867

Also available as an e-book at newharbinger.com

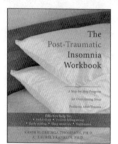

THE POST-TRAUMATIC INSOMNIA WORKBOOK

A Step-by-Step Program for Overcoming Sleep Problems After Trauma

US $21.95 / ISBN: 978-1572248939

Also available as an e-book at newharbinger.com

THE COMPASSIONATE-MIND GUIDE TO OVERCOMING ANXIETY

Using Compassion-Focused Therapy to Calm Worry, Panic & Fear

US $16.95 / ISBN: 978-1608820368

Also available as an e-book at newharbinger.com

MIND-BODY WORKBOOK FOR PTSD

A 10-Week Program for Healing After Trauma

US $21.95 / ISBN: 978-1572249233

Also available as an e-book at newharbinger.com

THE REALITY SLAP

Finding Peace & Fulfillment When Life Hurts

US $16.95 / ISBN: 978-1608822805

Also available as an e-book at newharbinger.com

A MINDFULNESS-BASED STRESS REDUCTION WORKBOOK

US $24.95 / ISBN: 978-1572247086

Also available as an e-book at newharbinger.com

newharbingerpublications, inc.
1-800-748-6273 / newharbinger.com

Like us on Facebook

Follow us on Twitter
@newharbinger.com

(VISA, MC, AMEX / prices subject to change without notice)

Don't miss out on new books in the subjects that interest you.
Sign up for our **Book Alerts** at **nhpubs.com/bookalerts**

Check out www.psychsolve.com

Psych*Solve*® offers help with diagnosis, including treatment information on mental health issues, such as depression, bipolar disorder, anxiety, phobias, stress and trauma, relationship problems, eating disorders, chronic pain, and many other disorders.